Jonathan Clements is the author of man
history, including *A Brief History of the Sa*   *...uuern Japan: All That Matters*, and biographies of Admiral Tōgō and Prince Saionji Kinmochi. His *Anime: A History* was a 2014 *CHOICE* selection as one of the year's outstanding academic titles. He wrote the 'Asia and the World' chapters of the Oxford University Press *Big Ideas* history series for schools, which won an Australian Publishing Association award for Excellence in Educational Publishing in 2012.

ALSO BY JONATHAN CLEMENTS

Modern Japan: All That Matters

Anime: A History

The Art of War: A New Translation

A Brief History of Khubilai Khan

A Brief History of the Samurai

Admiral Tōgō: Nelson of the East

Mannerheim: President, Soldier, Spy

Prince Saionji

Wellington Koo

Wu: The Chinese Empress Who Schemed, Seduced and Murdered Her Way to Become a Living God

Marco Polo

The First Emperor of China

Confucius: A Biography

Pirate King: Coxinga and the Fall of the Ming Dynasty

The Moon in the Pines (published in paperback as *Zen Haiku*)

Christ's Samurai

The true story of the
Shimabara Rebellion

....

JONATHAN CLEMENTS

ROBINSON

ROBINSON

First published in Great Britain in 2016 by Robinson

1 3 5 7 9 10 8 6 4 2

A CIP catalogue record for this book
is available from the British Library.

ISBN 978-1-47213-741-8 (trade paperback)

Typeset by Hewer Text UK Ltd, Edinburgh
Printed and bound in Great Britain by Clays Ltd, St Ives plc

Papers used by Robinson are from well-managed
forests and other responsible sources

MIX
Paper from
responsible sources
FSC   FSC® C104740
www.fsc.org

Robinson
An imprint of
Little, Brown Book Group
Carmelite House
50 Victoria Embankment
London EC4Y 0DZ

An Hachette UK Company
www.hachette.co.uk

www.littlebrown.co.uk

In Memory of

Father Andrew Dorricott

and

Father James Hannon

Contents

Maps

Acknowledgements

....

At times when wading through the immense amount of material relating to the Shimabara Rebellion, I felt, like Jerome Amakusa, that I was 'foolishly attempting to measure out the sea with a shell.' Kameshi Kenji, curator of the Christian Museum collection at its temporary home in the Hondo Municipal Museum of History and Folklore, was generous with his time, advice and help. He confirmed my suspicions about the past of the rebel ringleaders, allowed me to take several crucial photographs, and sent me packing with an armload of photocopies and local history documents.

My photographer (and wife) Kati Clements carried a hefty sack of camera equipment from Nagoya to Nagasaki and all points in between, learning as she went about the story, so that by the time we reached Amakusa it was she who found the site of the Battle of Hondo. My research assistant Tamamuro Motoko helped with sourcing of materials from her own family archives, and never quite expected her working life to be caught up with arguments over the names of flowers, Buddhist religious terminology, or the Japanese pronunciation of Latin terms. Martin Stiff drew and re-drew maps of places that no longer existed, and learned more about early Tokugawa era clan liveries than he ever really wanted to.

Satō Hiroyuki of London's Jaltour arranged an itinerary that took me right across both the Shimabara peninsula and the Amakusa archipelago, including Hara, Unzen, Ōyano and Tomioka. He had made the same pilgrimage himself in his youth, and his diligence ensured that I would not need to walk on water at any point. I should point out, however, that the reader will no longer be able to duplicate my journey precisely – the railway line south of Shimabara to Hara Castle has since been shut down and replaced by a bus.

My agent Chelsey Fox of Fox & Howard has overseen this project with all the cunning of a Hosokawa, and the tireless patience of a Matsudaira. I would also like to thank the staff of the Library of London's School of Oriental and African Studies, as well the Nagasaki Memorial Museum of the Twenty-Six Martyrs, the Nagoya Museum of Christian Relics, the Amakusa Shirō Memorial Hall in Ōyano, the Tomioka Castle Visitors' Centre, the Hondo branch of the Amakusa Tourist Board, and Nagasaki Dejima, all of which have contributed in some way with information, exhibits, hints and legends. I am grateful to Dominic Clements, Andrew Deacon, Sharon Gosling, Alex McLaren, Reiko McLaren, Adam Newell, Ellis Tinios and Stephen Turnbull for many small kindnesses from the loaning of books to the giving of lifts. In 1993, my father, Michael Clements, developed the perplexing conviction that I would one day need a 300-year-old copy of Crasset's *The History of the Church of Japan*, despite no evidence to support this. It might come in handy, he said, and he was right, eventually. There are also many others who remain nameless, chiefly Japanese locals in Kyūshū, who made researching and writing this book a joy of discovery, from the kindly bus driver who decided on his own initiative to take me to the site of Jerome's camp in Hondo, to the Shimabara waitress who decided I needed a bowl of *guzōni*.

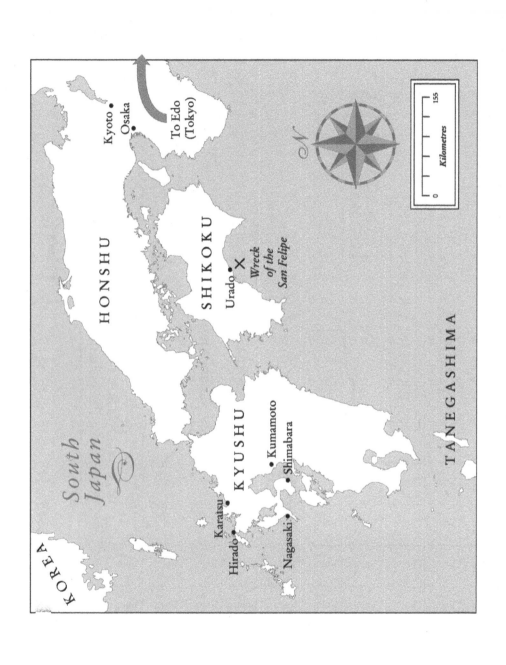

KOREA

South
Japan

HONSHU

Kyoto
Osaka

To Edo
(Tokyo)

SHIKOKU

Urado
Wreck
of the
San Felipe

KYUSHU

Kumamoto
Shimabara

Karatsu
Hirado
Nagasaki

TANEGASHIMA

N

Kilometres

0   155

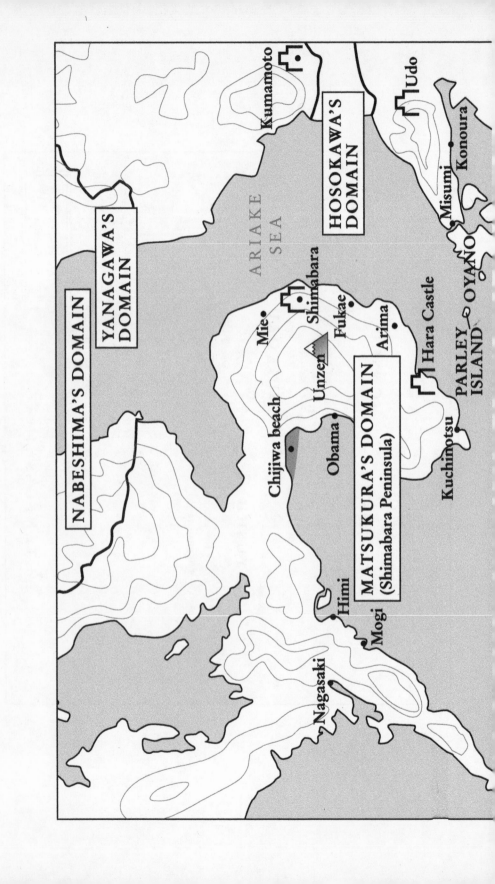

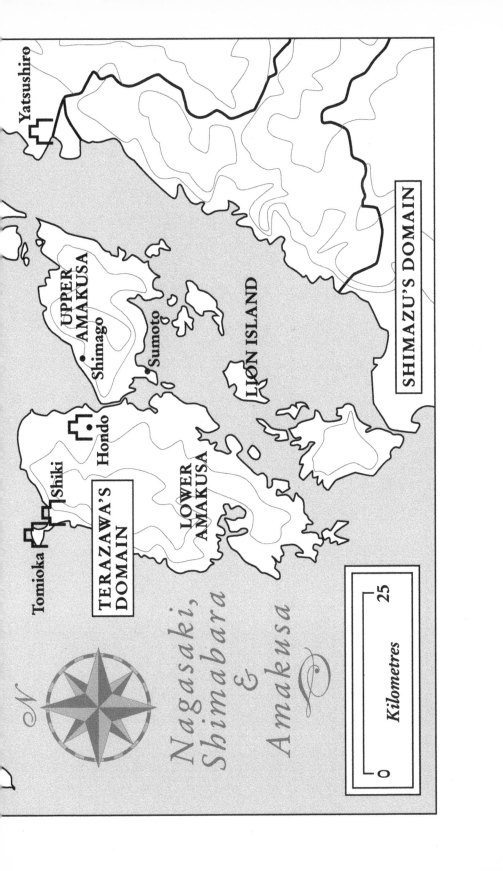

Nagasaki,
Shimabara
&
Amakusa

N

TERAZAWA'S
DOMAIN

LOWER
AMAKUSA

UPPER
AMAKUSA

SHIMAZU'S DOMAIN

Tomioka

Shiki

Hondo

Shimago

Sumoto

LION ISLAND

Yatsushiro

Kilometres

0   25

Introduction

....

In 1638, the ruler of Japan ordered a crusade against his own subjects, a holocaust upon the men, women and children of a doomsday cult in the remote south-western district of Shimabara. Introduced a century earlier by foreign missionaries, the sect was said to harbour dark designs to overthrow the government. Its teachers read and wrote a dead language, impenetrable to all but the innermost circle of believers. Its leaders preached love and kindness, but had helped local warlords acquire firearms. They encouraged believers to cast aside their earthly allegiances and swear loyalty to a foreign god-emperor. They urged their followers to seek paradise in terrible martyrdoms and, for many years, the Japanese government's torturers and executioners had obliged them.

The hated cult was in open revolt, led, it was said, by a boy sorcerer. Farmers claiming to have the blessing of an alien god had bested trained samurai in combat and proclaimed that fires in the sky would soon bring about the end of the world. The Shōgun called old soldiers out of retirement for one last battle before peace could be declared in Japan. For there to be an end to war, he said, the Christians would have to die.

For centuries, the Shimabara Rebellion was a taboo subject in Japan, its leader a bogeyman not to be spoken of, its battles and heroes conspicuously absent from plays and prints. Its supposed instigator was one Jerome Amakusa, a.k.a. Masuda Shirō, Tokisada, Francisco, Nirada. He has a legion of names, and little else that is verifiable. He may have been a charismatic youth, welcomed by the underground Christians of a poverty-stricken region as their long-awaited saviour. Or he may have been the unwitting pawn of a handful of aging war veterans, who sought to add an apocalyptic sheen to a mundane peasant uprising. In the years that followed, Jerome was a shadowy figure, a symbol of revolution itself in an age when dissent was forbidden.

In modern, tourist-friendly times, southern Japan is littered with images of him. In Ōyano, a beady-eyed, smiling cartoon version beams out from public information signs at his Memorial Hall, with a samurai hairstyle and an incongruous Elizabethan ruff. Outside in the well-tended gardens, a more reverent sculpture depicts a puffy-faced boy, his hand raised in Buddhist benediction. Further along the Amakusa island chain, another statue shows a pious Christian youth, his head bowed in prayer as he clutches a crucifix. In Hondo city, his image is that of a calm, ponytailed leader, clad in Western clothes, pointing resolutely into the distance at an unidentified objective. Notably, his *katana*, the longer of his two swords, is slung over his shoulder, as if he is too short to wear it at his side. In Oniike (Devil's Pond), he stands proudly on the shoreline, staring out to sea towards distant Shimabara, wearing Japanese clothes and the Elizabethan ruff again, one hand resting calmly on the *katana* and *wakizashi* swords on his hip that mark him out as a samurai. In Matsushima, his clothes are the same, but an admiring dove perches on his outstretched hand. An older, stouter Jerome, also wearing swords in the samurai style, is the subject of identical statues in Shimabara and Hara. But a crucifix is prominent on his chest, his eyes are closed, and his hands are clasped in solemn prayer. None of these statues is more than a few decades old; all are products of modern tourism and local pride.[1]

Fictional accounts, including modern novels, movies, comics and cartoons, emphasise his boyish credentials, depicting him as an earnest, androgynous, beautiful youth. Despite a recurring sense of the incredible, and regular lapses into apocrypha and sorcery, such stories tally surprisingly often with what is reported of him in the historical record.

At one point in the Rebellion, he was believed to be in three places at once. Authorities in Nagasaki were scouring the docksides after reports of his arrival. Meanwhile, on the Amakusa islands, a local lord was trying to lure him out of hiding with letters written under duress by captured relatives, while in Shimabara an official claimed to have seen him leading the first attack on the local castle.

One contemporary account, an eyewitness report so exacting as to even describe the embroidery on his clothes, refers to an eerie, white-robed child-messiah, crowned with a garland of leaves, a cross painted on his forehead, and wielding the paper-ribboned wand of a Shintō priest, stepping ashore at the head of an adoring army. Another alludes to a boy with a skin disease so debilitating that he was once rendered unable to move – although that may itself have been a lie told by his supporters to excuse his absence at a critical time. However he may have looked, his supporters credited him with magic powers, and his charisma helped hold an army together in the face of certain death.

The sources for the Shimabara Rebellion are vast. There are eyewitness accounts told to foreign merchants, rumours picked up in prisons and taverns, Shōgunate reports or minutes of meetings, and the testimonies of some of the rebels obtained before their inevitable executions. Meanwhile, official dispatches, particularly from the discredited officials whose malpractice may have forced the rebels into action, played up the influence of Christianity, long held to be a sinister death cult that lured true-hearted Japanese into alliances with conniving, covetous foreigners.

There is a surfeit of hard but useless facts. Jerome's many thousands of followers rose up in the Amakusa islands, briefly terrorised the government with the threat of a Christian revolution, and then retreated to an old castle on the Shimabara Peninsula, where they waited to die. By the end of spring, they had perished in a brutal massacre, regarded by some as the last battle of the samurai era, before Japan settled into two centuries of stern, oppressive peace.

The Shōgun's bureaucracy kept detailed records of troop movements and logistics. There is even an extant copy of the account books for the siege army's mess hall – kegs of *sake* ordered, bags of rice tallied, and notes on the number of cauldrons in use. Such concise trivia from the government side is counterbalanced by very little from the rebels themselves. In fact, the government troops, lacking any useful knowledge about their enemies' beliefs, disregarded essential information of religious significance. Vital documents about the rebel state of mind were ignored until after the Rebellion because they used terms in Latin, the secret cant of the Christians, unintelligible to non-believers. Biblical allusions in rebel correspondence and rhetoric sailed completely over the heads of their enemies. Jerome Amakusa held his army together through a long siege that lasted through Lent 1638, only to discover that his most trusted lieutenant was plotting to betray him on Easter Sunday. This irony escaped the notice of the government troops, who did not know what Easter Sunday was.

In the centuries since the Rebellion's bloody end, the focus has been blurred still further by a wealth of legend and exaggerations, glosses for the tourist trade, local folklore and modern movie mythmaking. Historians cannot even agree on what the Rebellion should be called. Some call it the Arima Uprising, associating it with a small cluster of hamlets in the south of the Shimabara Peninsula, but also with the lords of Arima, a family of Christian sympathisers who had formerly ruled the area. Other sources, particularly on the Amakusa islands where Jerome was probably born, prefer to call it the Amakusa Rebellion. Posterity seems to favour the 'Shimabara Rebellion', but it is not plain whether this is because the first full-scale battle was fought on the road to Shimabara Castle, or if the term was intended to refer to the Shimabara Peninsula, the site of the rebels' last stand.

Sifting through the evidence, we can see several factions among the rebels. Underground Christian believers were classified as troublemakers months before the eruption of hostilities. Plans were made for a religious protest in Amakusa days before the fighting broke out. Meanwhile in Shimabara, veterans-turned-farmers may indeed have risen up against harsh taxes and a hated ruler. Starving peasants may have joined simply to gain access to government storage barns – two of the major actions on the peninsula were fought for control of rice granaries. Still others joined the rebel banner because they feared that otherwise the rebels would kill them.

Lacking much material from the rebels themselves, we must sort through the baffled suppositions of their enemies. The sources can be contradictory – the *Shimabara-ki* (*Shimabara Chronicle*), for example, notes a turning point where the rebels decided to die in glorious battle, but does so repeatedly, as if different groups of rebels resolved at different times that their uprising was to be a suicide mission. This, too, may be true – one might argue that some of the old veterans, particularly those whose families had been murdered and defiled by government forces during anti-Christian purges, had nothing left to live for.

But if the iconography of Jerome Amakusa sounds exotic and confused, we should consider it in the context of Christianity itself, which had arrived in Japan less than a century before the Rebellion, and was cast out shortly after it. Christianity was a wholly unfamiliar religion to the Japanese, and its missionaries were mysterious curiosities from the Far West.

CHAPTER ONE

The Rending of Heaven

·················

Blink and you'll miss them.

The statue is on the landward side of Minoshima bridge, where the airport buses shift gear and accelerate on the road towards Nagasaki. This is the old castle town of Ōmura, little known in Western literature but for its mention in an opera as Omara *(sic)*, birthplace of Puccini's Madama Butterfly.

Palm trees dot the small park, which contains a cluster of concrete poles and metal trellises representing the masts of a galleon. And at the edge, on a plinth, there are four boys cast in bronze, clad in doublets and hose.

One, Mancio Itō, is in his early teens. He is pointing inexplicably towards the sky. The other three, Michael Chijiwa, Julian Nakaura and Martino Hara, huddle, unsure, at the other end of the plinth. They glance in all directions, seemingly not having yet heard Mancio's command. These are the boys of the Tenchō Embassy, who travelled all the way to distant Europe in 1582, before returning to Japan to tell of the wonders they saw. They are Ōmura's most famous sons.

Three would become Jesuit priests. They were the great young hopes of Japan's 'Christian Century', but their diverse fates reflected that era's swift collapse.[1] None would live to see old age. Mancio would die of illness in 1612. Of his companions, Martino would die in exile. Julian would be tortured and executed in the purges of the 1630s. Michael would cast aside his faith.

And then they are gone, hidden behind the Midori car park. Past the traffic lights, the bridge Road 38 merges into Highway 34, for the long, meandering journey towards Nagasaki.

Europeans first reached Japan in 1543, when Portuguese sailors blundered onto the far southern island of Tanegashima. They had with them examples of the kind of smooth-bore firearm that could be carried and used by a single soldier. These arquebuses found great favour with the Japanese, who swiftly copied them and named them *tanegashima* after the island on which they had been first 'discovered'. Within a few years, Japan's ongoing civil war had acquired an all-new and very dangerous faction – musketeers.

The samurai elite grumbled that the new weapons were unseemly. Real warriors hacked at each other with swords like civilised men, or spent years learning how to use a bow and arrow. The very idea that a mere peasant could be trained to wield a personal mini-cannon in a matter of weeks threatened to undermine a noble tradition of hand-to-hand combat that had dominated the Japanese military for centuries. Regardless, the new firearms got results, and they soon caused a turn in the tide of the Japanese civil war.

Only a few years after the Tanegashima landing, another European vessel arrived in southern Japan. This time it carried an even more potent weapon – religion, in the form of the Jesuit missionary Francis Xavier and several associates. Xavier's boat was merely the first of many transports from the Far West, bringing the word of God to the Japanese heathens.

Often towering a foot or more above the Japanese, the foreign men were daunting even to their local followers. Their enemies wasted no time in listing their fearsome attributes. They were veritable giants, it was said, with huge, saucer-like eyes, elongated, claw-like hands, and long teeth. Some had white hair, like old men, others had red hair like demons. A few had a bald spot shaved in the top of their scalp, like the *kappa* water sprites of Japanese legend. When they spoke, their voices were like the screeching of owls, and nobody could understand their fiendish language.

Their noses were impossibly long, often resembling crows' beaks. By chance or by design, many of the descriptions of the early

Europeans in Japan were couched in terms that made them sound like *tengu* – legendary bird-demons. In the hands of wily, facetious polemics against the Christians, aerial analogies crop up wherever possible. It was not enough for the anti-Christian lobby to paint their adversaries as devils; they seized on every opportunity to insinuate vile and bestial sorceries. One monk in a dark-grey habit went to speak with a Japanese warlord. His clothing was described as a chillingly blank robe, looking 'for all the world like a bat spreading its wings.'[2]

After initial misunderstandings, the foreign visitors offered a new explanation for their presence. They were messengers from another land, who had come to spread news of the one true religion, although they had a great deal of trouble making themselves understood. Francis Xavier, the first on the scene, soon began to suspect that his interpreter, Yajirō, was doing more harm than good.

Yajirō had only made the Jesuits' acquaintance in the first place after he had stowed away on a foreign ship to avoid being prosecuted for murder. Although he became an enthusiastic convert to Christianity, he was an uneducated, coarse man whose grasp of the finer points of theology was tenuous at best. Francis Xavier discovered that Yajirō had been earnestly telling Japanese congregations that the Christians were worshippers of *Dainichi*. This could mean 'god' to some, but only in the sense that Dainichi was one of many kinds of Buddha. It certainly was not the all-powerful, all-knowing God with a capital G that the Christians meant; complications soon ensued. Paramount among them was the assumption by numerous Buddhist monasteries that the Christians were fellow believers.

Yajirō persisted in referring to the missionaries by the Japanese term for Buddhist monks, leading many of the potential congregations to assume that Christianity was just one more Buddhist sect, albeit one with a bunch of strange-looking foreigners in charge. He also inadvertently insisted that the Jesuits had come from India. This was true in a sense; they had boarded their ship in Goa, the centre of

Portuguese missions in Asia, but the assertion left many Japanese with the impression that they were cultists from Buddha's Indian homeland. As a result, the misleading local term for the visitors was soon *Nambanjin* – 'southern barbarians.'

Within a decade, the Jesuits had hammered out these problems. They did so by introducing new words into the Japanese language. The God they worshipped was not one of Japan's Buddhist saints, nor was He one of Japan's thousands of animist spirits. He was not a waterfall, or a funny-shaped rock, or a flash of lightning in the sky. He was, they said, *Deus*, a proper, capitalised Latin word that meant the biggest God the Japanese could imagine, and then some. He was bigger and better than any other god they could think of, because when it came to gods, there was only one.[3]

The ministers of this Deus were not to be given the same names as Buddhist or Shintō priests. They were to be referred to as *padres*, although the Japanese had trouble with the foreign consonants, and eventually settled on the pronunciation *bateren*. If it was an attempt to put the Japanese at ease, it did not go far. The many locals who feared the new arrivals soon offered their own interpretation of the term. *Ba-te-ren*, claimed the gossips, meant Those Who Rend Heaven Through the Clouds.[4]

Other, unexpected foreign words entered the Japanese language, mainly via Portuguese, the language of many of the first missionaries. The padres were in Japan to save the souls of the Japanese faithful, and these souls were not the crude, bestial operating systems of native Japanese belief, but immortal, pure essences of true being: *animae*. They would teach their religion in a *Collegio* or a *Seminario* – two such institutions would spring up in Shimabara and Amakusa, and then another in metropolitan Nagasaki. *Miira* (myrrh) survives today as the Japanese word for an Egyptian mummy – the centre of a quack medicine fad in the seventeenth century. The Portuguese arrived at the same time as a strange drug from the lands of New Spain, which is still called *tabako*. They introduced the Japanese to *vidro* (glass), *capa* (raincoat) and *pan* (bread). On the latter, they might spread a sweet fruit jelly, or *marmelo*. A *capitan* on a ship would drink *alcool* from a *frasco* or a *copo*. In the Nagasaki region, where there was an ample supply of sugar among the Chinese traders from the South Seas, the Japanese came to enjoy Castilian spongecake, or *castella*. The Portuguese also introduced the Japanese to *tempero*, literally 'seasoning', which survives today in modern Japanese as tempura. And all the while, this cultural exchange continued to bring with it a flurry of words related to the religion of the new arrivals. *Jesu Cristo*, the son of *Deus*; nailed to the *cruz* that remains his symbol; commemorated on the *Sabato* day by the faithful, each of whom would clutch his *rosario* necklace as he prayed. These people, these exotic strangers with their strange inventions and their curious beliefs, always with alien delights to trade and display – these people were the *Kirishitan*.

Since *Kirishitan* was just a meaningless set of syllables to the Japanese, they found characters from their own language to encompass the sounds. The early Japanese word for Christian thereby came to be written with symbols including those for 'happiness and prosperity'.

The missionaries were prepared to play a long game. They soon settled on a plan that mirrored the activities of their distant predecessors in the pagan Europe of the Dark Ages, concentrating on the rich and powerful, in the hope that celebrity converts would drag many lesser members of society with them.

The chief Jesuit in the 'East Indies', which included Japan, was Alessandro Valignano (1539–1606), a towering Italian who dominated the Japanese Church for the last twenty years of the sixteenth century. He was tall even by European standards, and sentenced himself to a lifetime of bumping his head on low Japanese ceilings, and attracting the attention of gawping crowds. In fact, it is possible that Valignano's imposing height was a major influence on the Japanese stories that claimed the *bateren* were all giants.[5]

Valignano had led a chequered past, gaining a doctorate in Law at the University of Padua, before becoming a canon in an Italian parish. He had also served two years in prison for aggravated assault, after a mysterious incident in his early twenties, when he had knifed a woman in the face, causing her to require fourteen stitches. The reason for the attack is unknown, but one Italian observer said what everyone else was surely thinking, that it was *probabile un'avventura amorosa* with a woman called Franceschina Trona, and hardly a fitting situation for a young man of the cloth. Soon after he was sprung from jail through the intervention of a cardinal, Valignano was inducted into the Jesuits, where, after a decade of penance, ordination and dutiful service, he volunteered for the Far East posting that would occupy him for the rest of his life.[6]

Valignano's personal history gave him an unusual attitude towards the missionary life. He often clashed not only with other orders, but also with other Jesuits, about the best way to improve the fortunes of Christianity in Japanese society. He had what some regarded as a misplaced faith in the potential for training local priests, and his enemies accused him of bending all too readily to fit in with the Japanese way of life. Valignano called Japan the 'greatest enterprise that there is in the world today,' and enumerated a number of points that made the Japanese prime material for conversion to Christianity. The Japanese already paid great respect to priests of their own religions, and were sure to offer similar homage to Christians. The Japanese were 'white', as far as Valignano was concerned, always prepared to listen to reason, and 'the only oriental country in which the people have become Christians for the right reasons.'[7]

Valignano thought that Christian faith in Japan could eventually become self-supporting. He predicted that with just a little financial investment in the early stages, missionaries could rear a generation of native aspirants, who would be able to spread the Word in their own language.

It was not all plain sailing. Valignano was particularly irritated by the prevalence of concubinage and pederasty among the warrior class:

> The first evil we see among them is indulgence in sins of the flesh; this we always find among pagans ... The gravest of their sins is the most depraved of carnal desires, so that we may not name it. The young men and their partners, not thinking it serious, do not hide it ... Nevertheless, since Japan has been illuminated by the light of the Gospel, many people have begun to realise how black was their darkness; and the Christians, having listened to reason, avoid and detest these customs.[8]

But that was only a minor problem compared to Valignano's greatest fear, that other Europeans would regard the Japanese with the same kind of condescension that had led the Spanish to annex great tracts of other heathen lands. Valignano was keen to stress that Japan was not a kingdom like the Americas that could be easily overrun by conquistadors. Although he and his associates enjoyed high favour with many of the leaders of the southern provinces, he only enjoyed their support as a religious man. If politics ever got involved, or, God forbid, the military, Valignano predicted a terrible backlash.

Valignano realised that the missionaries were making little progress through the traditional means of showing kindness to outcasts. In fact, association with the unclean, lepers and beggars was only serving to ostracise some missionaries from higher levels of society. Instead, others were getting much better results by their contacts with the nobility. Valignano had no objection to helping the poor *per se*, but he wrote guidelines for his fellow priests that called for them to match their behaviour to the classes they were hoping to convert. It was fine, he argued, for brethren in other countries to take soup to lepers, but to the Japanese ruling class that would only taint them by association. Instead, Valignano wanted his order to treat local potentates in the manner to which they had become accustomed. Jesuits should cut a swathe through the streets of Nagasaki as if they owned the place, accompanied by massive entourages like those of the most powerful priests in the most sumptuous Buddhist sect. Only then, thought Valignano, would the lords and ladies take notice.

Valignano's Jesuits were an impressive sight. When they travelled around Nagasaki, they did so with bodyguards and attendants. When they entertained noble visitors, they did so at lavish banquets. The Jesuits befriended a local lord in the Nagasaki area, who was eventually baptised under the Christian name Bartholomew. In 1574, Lord Bartholomew of Ōmura became such an enthusiastic convert to Christianity that he ordered anyone who did not similarly want to accept baptism to leave his domain immediately. The entire region around Nagasaki, with some 60,000 inhabitants, became a nominal Christian society in a matter of weeks, while Ōmura's men raided and burned the Buddhist and Shintō temples and shrines in the surrounding villages.

In 1576, the Jesuits scored an even greater victory, when the aging ruler of the kidney-shaped Shimabara Peninsula, the area between Nagasaki and Amakusa, accepted the baptismal name of André Arima. In a whirlwind half-year romance with Christianity, 12,000 of André Arima's subjects also accepted baptism, before the old ruler died.

His infant son's regent was not so welcoming and attempted to undo the previous six months of good deeds. His lieutenants 'expelled the Padres, burned the church and forced the Christians of their region to apostatise.'9

But within a couple of years, the Jesuits had worked their magic on the young son of André Arima. A Portuguese trading vessel, which normally would have ended up in Nagasaki or Hirado, just happened to put in at Kuchinotsu on the southern tip of the youthful lord Arima's domain. Arima, who was facing trouble with local enemies, was deeply grateful for the sudden arrival of Portuguese arms and ammunition, which turned the tide of his war with an enemy lord. Just before Easter in 1580, the thirteen-year-old Lord Arima accepted the Christian faith and was baptised by Valignano himself, eventually taking the name Protasio. The Shimabara Peninsula was restored to the conditions under Protasio's father André, creating a crescent-shaped Christian enclave with Nagasaki at one end and Ōyano, the easternmost of the Amakusa islands, at the other. Valignano established a seminary on the Shimabara Peninsula, where he hoped to attract young scholars who could form a new generation of Japan-born, Japan-trained Jesuits. He also offered to teach the sons of the nobility the exotic foreign knowledge that was behind such miraculous things as the beliefs of the Christians and the workings of the *tanegashima* guns. He did so in an abandoned Buddhist monastery. Despite scandalised complaints from other Jesuits, Valignano left the decorations in the monastery as they had been under the previous occupants. As far as he was concerned, the locals expected a monastery to look a certain way, and as long as they accepted that the monastery was his, he would take the decorative path of least resistance.

Valignano knew all too well that conversions made under a threat of exile were not what the Catholic Church had in mind, and the sheer numbers of new Christians in the area were stretching his organisational skills. With fully qualified native priests still a way off, he was obliged to co-opt a number of lay assistants to handle the sheer volume of supposed Christians.

In 1580, a slightly embarrassed Valignano wrote to his superior. He had, he confessed, accidentally become the owner of Nagasaki. In an act remembered as the 'Donation of Bartholomew', the zealous Lord Ōmura had handed a huddle of fishing hamlets and the neighbouring district of Mogi over to the Jesuits. Although officially control was still in the hands of locals, the Jesuits had the power of selection and approval, and were effectively running Nagasaki from behind the scenes. They even took a substantial cut of the trade tariffs from the silk merchants' ships that were still expected to dock there. It was a move calculated to keep Portuguese trading vessels docking in Bartholomew's domain, and also to keep the territory out of play in wrangles between Bartholomew and non-Christian rivals.

In steering Portuguese ships to call on their new ally Bartholomew, the Jesuits made enemies elsewhere, and they were soon embroiled in local intrigues. Several prominent local noble families were at each other's throats, and the arrival of the Christians with their foreign merchandise, particularly dangerous weapons and lucrative silk, only aggravated the situation.

The Donation of Nagasaki 'for always' was an incredible achievement in the history of the Church in Japan, but it was fated not to last. It was an expedient born of a particular situation and a particular rivalry between local lords, and the political map of Japan was a volatile place.

The Donation would cause other problems for the Jesuits. As soon as the news made it back to Rome, the Jesuits were ordered to ensure that their ownership of such a secular property was temporary. They had, they were sternly reminded, been sent to Japan to win souls, not to dicker with Chinese smugglers over cargoes of silk. Five years after the Donation, an angry missive arrived from Rome, demanding to know why the Jesuits were still the lords of their own Japanese city. City of God or not, the Church was not supposed to be in the politics game.

Valignano's reply to his superior was polite but firm. He was not, he said, dealing with a few curious old ladies and some earnest young believers. He had suddenly inherited a region of Japan now with 150,000 alleged Christians in it. True, many of them had been *forced* to become Christians, baptised not confirmed, but Valignano was working on that – he had 200 churches across the

THE RENDING OF HEAVEN

Nagasaki-Shimabara-Amakusa region, with eighty-five priests and a hundred local acolytes. Valignano argued, with good reason, that he was the intendant of a critical generation in the history of Japanese Christianity. Maintaining his flock required an annual expense of 12,000 ducats, and right now he was getting that money from the tariffs and trade of Nagasaki. As soon as someone would come up with the cash from another source, Valignano would give up on Nagasaki, but for now it was shoring up a vast area of Christian belief. It was, said Valignano, a matter of conscience, and his was clear.

Another local ruler, this time on the eastern coast of Kyūshū, also accepted the faith. Ōtomo Sorin, or 'the good king Francisco' as he was soon known, had finally tired of his wife, to whom the Jesuits unkindly referred as Jezebel. Eventually, he absconded to a country villa with his mistress, who was baptised as Julia, and soon married him in a Christian ceremony. Ōtomo's years of marriage to the heathen Jezebel counted for nothing.

Determined to demonstrate to both the Jesuits and the Japanese how marvellous an opportunity was presented by Japan, Valignano organised a superb publicity stunt. He persuaded the lords Arima, Ōmura and Ōtomo, or Protasio, Bartholomew and Francisco, as they were now known, to send an embassy from their domains to the Holy City itself. Ōtomo sent his nephew Mancio Itō, while Arima and Ōmura sent Michael Chijiwa, a young relative. Two relatively high-ranking commoners from the Ōmura region accompanied the boys, along with a handful of Jesuit novices and servants. In an eight-year pilgrimage that spanned 1582–90, the Japanese youths made the long journey from Japan to Jesuit Goa, around Africa and eventually to Portugal. From there, they travelled through Spain to Italy. They met King Philip II of Spain and the dying Pope Gregory XIII, and attended the coronation of Pope Sixtus V, scoring incredible points for the Jesuit order. They were feted in southern Europe as visiting princes, to which Valignano took exception, but it was difficult indeed to explain the political situation in south Japan without suggesting that the local lords were more like petty kings.

Valignano himself did not accompany the mission. Instead, he stayed back in Goa, but sent them on their way with special instructions. They were, of course, to make sure that they represented Japan well abroad, but they were also to come back with a vital device for the Japanese Church. Valignano wanted a printing press.

When the boys arrived back in Goa in 1587, reporting their mission as a spectacular success, they brought with them a printing press from Lisbon. They also brought new orders for Valignano – he was to quit Goa and return with them to Japan; a likely sign of great Papal approval.

The boys who had returned to Japan also brought their own wide-eyed reports of what they had seen, told and retold by word of mouth around the seminary. Consequently, several local tales and legends in the Japanese region appear to owe at least part of their origin to the experience of the Japanese boys in Europe, where their memories of tales, historical personages and saints' relics gave certain stories far greater prominence in Japan than they might have otherwise enjoyed outside Iberia or Italy.

The Japanese, still in the late stages of a civil war that had endured for decades, were particularly keen on military escapades. One popular story with the Japanese was that of Saint James, or in Spanish, *Santiago*, the humble fisherman who had become one of Christ's apostles, and supposedly preached the message of Jesus in Roman Spain. During the Middle Ages, he had gained the name 'Moor-slayer', after soldiers reported seeing his apparition at the battle of Clavijo against the Muslims. The battle cry of the Spaniards, at first in the Iberian Peninsula, and then taken all around the world, had been *Santiago y cierra España*, 'Saint James, and strike for Spain.'

Most admired by the Japanese Christians was the tale of King Sebastian I of Portugal (1554–1578), whose adventurous life-story and tragic end was the talk of the Portuguese throughout the period of the

Japanese mission. Raised by Jesuits, the consumptive, frail Sebastian probably owed his weak condition to his genes – his parents were so closely related that he only had four *great*-grandparents. The young Sebastian grew up with a fanatic sense of religious destiny, and regarded himself as a Christian knight who would lead a crusade against the Muslims of Africa. During the brief flourishing of Christian sympathies among the lords of Japan, Sebastian became something of a poster-boy for the samurai, and was even the recipient of a sword, a gift from a Japanese Christian nobleman. However, Sebastian's path to power was not as triumphant as his supporters hoped – in his early twenties, he suffered a crushing defeat against his Muslim enemies at the battle of Alcazarquivir, and was never seen again. Although he was probably dead on the battlefield, he became the subject of an enduring myth of Arthurian proportions. Sebastian, it was said, had been captured by the Muslims, and now was merely in hiding, waiting for the day when he would return to lead the Portuguese to victory.[10]

Other stories not found in the Bible that would endure among Japanese Christians include that of Veronica, a woman said to have given water to Jesus as he was carrying his cross to the place of his execution, and whose veil became miraculously imprinted with the image of Christ's face. This particular tale is notable because it would have been passed on by people who considered themselves as witnesses to the evidence – Michael Chijiwa and the other Japanese youths whom Valignano had sent to Europe had seen the Veil of Veronica for themselves in Genoa in 1585.[11]

With Nagasaki under increasing pressure to enact anti-Christian orders from the Shōgun, the Amakusa islands and the nearby Shimabara Peninsula became a new heartland for the Christians. Shimabara and Amakusa were nicely off the beaten track, easy to reach by ship, but otherwise separated from the mainland by arduous and troublesome journeys. It was the ideal place to nurture new

Christian souls in Valignano's *seminario* and *collegio*, and to go about missionary business in the hope that the occasional fads for persecution would blow over.

Back in Japan in the summer of 1590, Valignano got to work. He installed his printing press, newly arrived from the West, at first in Katsusa, a tiny village in the south of the Shimabara Peninsula near Kuchinotsu. The following year, it was moved to the Amakusa islands, where it remained until upheavals in the civil war led to its removal back to Nagasaki in 1597.

At its height, at the beginning of the 1600s, the Jesuit press had a staff of thirty, churning out guidebooks for the faithful, and textbooks designed to help in the teaching of Latin and Japanese. Constantine Dourado, a Japanese chaperone for the ambassadors who had also studied printing during the European expedition, became one of the leading printers, and also taught Latin to a new generation of boys.[12]

None of the books seem to have been intended for the purposes of direct propaganda. The complications of setting type with Japanese script limited the early output of the press to the use of Roman letters, so that the books were no more than meaningless squiggles to anyone who had not learned how to turn Roman letters into the sounds of Japanese. Consequently, they were unintelligible to any Japanese who had not graduated from Valignano's seminary. Later, the press moved into *katakana* printing, using a phonetic Japanese script that was able to represent the sound of a word on a page. With the publication of a Japanese dictionary, the press even began to print *kanji* – Chinese characters. The most concise level of meaning in Japanese, these symbols appear to have been carved by craftsmen in Macao on wooden blocks, and then shipped over to Japan.

Today, only a handful of editions survive, scattered around the world's great libraries, although asides in letters allude to many other lost manuscripts. A copy of the Jesuits' *Extracts from the Acts of the Saints* can still be found in Oxford, and another in Venice. A copy of

Doctrina Kirishitan, believed to be the Jesuits' first attempt to set down a catechism in Japanese, is still intact in the Vatican Library.

Multiple copies, in Munich, Paris, and other places, still exist of *Guia de Pecadores*, an abridged Japanese-language edition of a 'guide for sinners' on the path to virtue, translated by Martino Hara, another of the Japanese youths who had seen Rome with his own eyes. A single *Salvator Mundi* ('Saviour of the World' – a guide to confessions), can be found in Rome's Biblioteca Casanatense. A lone copy of *On Baptism and the Preparation for Death*, the presumed title for a coverless manuscript on the Christian life, survives today in Japan's Tenri library.[13]

The output of the press was not entirely religious. In the British Library in London, there is a monster volume binding several texts together. It contains a Romanised Japanese version of *Aesop's Fables*, along with a collection of old Chinese proverbs and a simplified version of the *Heike Monogatari*, an account of Japan's medieval wars. Publications seem to have been intended to teach the students about Christianity, but also to help their Jesuit mentors develop a better understanding of Japan and the Japanese. A *Vocabulary of the Language of Japan* helped teach the teachers, while a *Rakuyōshū* compiled a series of Chinese characters – a dictionary, of what was then both Chinese and high-class Japanese.

On one occasion, Valignano found some of the boys sneaking around the seminary at midnight, surely up to no good. The boys, however, offered the highly unlikely explanation that they had been planning to peruse the press's latest work – a Latin grammar. Remarkably for a man of such wisdom and experience, Valignano seems to have completely fallen for this outrageous excuse and even mentioned it in a straight-faced letter back home, as an example of the intense passion that his charges had for learning. In the unlikely event that the boys were not lying through their teeth, it is possible that the study of Latin was already regarded as a form of initiation into an inner circle among the Jesuits. Knowing Roman letters would afford

Christians access to many texts printed by the local press, but understanding Latin would open up the world of books from beyond Japan.[14]

There is one book that many historians would like to read. According to a contemporary chronicler, the most popular title produced by the press was a *Doctrine in Ten Chapters*, now sadly lost. But similar books still surviving give us a clue as to its contents. In 1903, a scholar in a Lisbon library uncovered a book that had been printed at 'Amacusa' in 1592. Seven years later, the book had supposedly disappeared, 'eaten by rats', but it cropped up again in Madrid in 1913, and eventually made its way, via America, to the Netherlands, where it was bought by a Baron Iwasaki and returned to Japan. Its contents list offers a glimpse of something undoubtedly similar to the *Doctrine in Ten Chapters*, with the following table of contents:

An explanation of Christian Doctrine
The Sign of the Cross
The Lord's Prayer
The Hail Mary
The Salve Regina
The Apostolic Creed
The Ten Commandments
(the eighth chapter is missing)
The Precepts of the Church
The Seven Sins
The Sacraments
Other Things: including works of mercy, virtues, the gifts of
the Holy Spirit, the eight beatitudes, the confession of sins,
and prayers suitable to be said before and after meals.[15]

The book ends with an appendix of 'various matters which a Christian must know', in ten short articles.

It would be, however, the height of the Christian conversions in Japan. There was still antipathy towards the Christians, particularly in the lands north of their Kyūshū stronghold. The further information travelled from its source, the more likely it was to be twisted into misunderstandings. The bat-winged demon priest-people in the south, it was said, encouraged their followers to participate in a bizarre ceremony where they ate the body and drank the blood of their saviour. On a weekly basis, they would transform household foods into the corpse of *Jesu Cristo*, which they would then devour in a clandestine feast. In secret meetings, they would list their misdeeds in an act called *confissan*, but having sworn never to sin again, they would often do so, leading to yet more secret meetings. Detractors scoffed at the contradictory claims made by these bird-like, owl-eyed giants. According to the strange foreigners, at an indeterminate future date, the world would be consumed in fire and come to an end. The dead would then rise from the grave and be restored to life. Many confused outsiders interpreted this as a portent of some kind of zombie apocalypse, in which the Japanese would be unable to participate because they had been cremated instead of buried.[16]

Worst of all, it was eventually discovered that the foreigners were not all in agreement. Their place of origin was not a single enlightened European state, but a cluster of feuding kingdoms, which did not even agree on religion. Even among the missionaries, there were now *Italia* men of one religious order, and *Hispania* men of another. Meanwhile, Portugal and Spain were at odds with each other, until one day when they suddenly appeared to gain the same king, by accident, with the death of Sebastian and the coronation of Philip II. They were rivalled by men of the Netherlands and England (in modern Japanese, *Oranda* and *Igirisu*, from 'Hollander' and 'Inglez'), who had strongly held views about certain of these issues. Sometimes, when detractors mocked the bizarre behaviour of the *Bateren*, these men of Hollander and Inglez would agree, and reveal that the Jesuit missionaries were Catholics, a sect of the *Kirishitan* that had been rejected by their own kingdoms.

When a missionary was close at hand, it was often possible to explain these apparent contradictions, or to point out where the anti-Christian propaganda had got everything mixed up. Where no missionary was available, the Jesuits settled for the next best thing, training lay assistants in the barest essentials required for understanding the Bible and the faith, and setting them to ensuring that the subjects of the mass conversions never drifted too far off-message. However, over time, the protestations of the missionaries were drowned out by their detractors. With the wars of the samurai drawing to a close, there was a reduced need for foreign guns, and an increased emphasis on keeping the peace. After a century of changing fortune, the time approached when Japan would be united once more. The Christian missionaries hoped that final victory would fall to a warlord sympathetic to their cause. Their prayers were not answered.

CHAPTER TWO

The Mirror of the Future

....

Today, a series of majestic bridges spans every strait of the Amakusa archipelago. It once took a week to pick one's way from Kumamoto on the mainland, former seat of House Hosokawa, all the way to Tomioka, the distant spit of land that faces the East China Sea. The Shōgun's messengers of choice were called 'flying feet'. They comprised a pair of super-fit runners, one to bear the message itself, and another to jog alongside with a lantern and, if the going got tough, a sword. But even the flying feet crews ran into trouble on Japan's south-west coast. Nobody could walk on water, let alone run on it. The speed of the flying feet would sink to a shipbound crawl at the straits between each island, yoked to the mercies of wind and tide.

If the going was slow for men with a message, it was even slower for an army on the move. Although each of the islands is within sight of the next, it would be a logistical nightmare transporting samurai and horses, guns and powder, food and sake, across each of the dividing straits. Today, a modern motor vehicle can make the trip in a couple of hours.

It is a lovely day. I get off the bus in blazing sunshine, without a cloud in the sky, the moon itself also overhead and clearly visible in the morning light. I am by the side of a wide, sparsely populated coastal road, lined with rows of impossibly tall Washington palm trees. I could easily be in Santa Monica, but I am on the tiny island that was the home for Peter Masuda for many years. On the cliffs above me, one of the region's many statues of Peter's son Jerome raises his arm in blessing. From a distance, it looks like he is pointing vaguely at the sky. Along the roadside there is a line of blue sashimono banners, just like a samurai might have attached to his back, fluttering in the breeze and proclaiming that I have found the Amakusa Shirō Memorial Hall.

One gets the feeling that the Amakusa archipelago feels a little left out. Owing to the unreliability of the confessions obtained under torture from members of Jerome's family, it is not entirely clear where he was born. The Shimabara Peninsula has the two great battle sites of the uprising, but Amakusa, where the Rebellion arguably began, was deserted by the rebels, who never returned. In the wake of the Rebellion, the depopulated domain became a special protectorate of the Shōgun – by the time Christianity became a tourist boon instead of a historical embarrassment, much of the evidence had melted away.

This is perhaps why the Shimabara Peninsula has its castles, its volcano, and its relics, and why the Amakusa archipelago must recreate its heritage anew. There are four statues of Jerome on the island chain, none of them pre-dating 1966. This one is on Ōyano Island, one of several candidates for Jerome's birthplace, standing on a steep ridge that overlooks the sea. Close by, there is the teapot-shaped folly of the Amakusa Shirō Memorial Hall. It seems designed, in part, as a gateway to the Rebellion experience. If you are travelling on a bus from Kumamoto, breezing along the archipelago across its soaring 1960s bridges, it is all too easy to drive right through Ōyano. The Memorial Hall seems to have been put there for that reason, as a firm attempt to supply bus tours with a destination worth heading for – a place to stop for lunch.

Beyond the hall's unique movie, a 3D experience that retells the story of Jerome in a quarter of an hour, the holdings of the museum seem a little thin. Dioramas re-enact some crucial scenes with model soldiers, and a few dummies sport period costumes, but the Memorial Hall clearly expects its visitors to be getting their 'real' history further down the road. The Hall is merely a primer, a brief introduction that shows things as they once were, all the more to educate newcomers about the story behind the ruins they will see on the other side of the strait. At its heart is an empty space, a 'Meditation Chamber' where visitors are expected to sit on beanbags and contemplate what is to come.

The first anti-Christian edict was issued by the great samurai unifier, the regent Hideyoshi, as early as 1587, and cited the Christians' attacks on native shrines and temples as intolerable acts of hubris. Ironically, such desecrations were nothing to do with the Jesuits, but largely the work of overzealous Japanese converts like Sebastian Ōtomo, son of Francisco and 'Jezebel', who had rebelled against his Buddhist mother by refusing to enter the Buddhist priesthood, converting to Christianity and celebrating his new faith by leading a series of wrecking missions at local temples.[1]

There were other incidents – simple misunderstandings that were blown out of all proportion by the mood of the times. A Franciscan friar, lacking the linguistic ability of the rival Jesuits, had mistaken an innkeeper's welcoming smile for hospitality – well, it was, but the innkeeper still expected to be paid, and the Franciscan was accused of being a thief. As time passed, ill will towards the Christians grew, and the anti-Christian lobby tallied incident after incident of misunderstandings and bad omens about the foreign priests.

Terazawa Hirotaka, who was at the time the lord of the Nagasaki area, happened to run into a pair of Valignano's fellow priests at a port on Japan's Inland Sea. Or rather, they ran into him – in what was soon regarded by all sides as a terrible omen, Fathers Martins, Passio and Rodrigues accidentally rammed Terazawa's ship with their own. Terazawa was already in two minds about Christians, and the incident seemed to make things simpler for him – he was suspicious about Christians' motives thereafter.[2]

The last straw came in October 1596, when a galleon out of Manila, the *San Felipe*, was wrecked off the coast of the island of Shikoku. It had made an ill-starred crossing, shadowed by an ominous comet overhead,[3] and by what those aboard the ship could only describe as fiery crosses in the sky over Japan. But the *San Felipe* had more mundane problems – it was dangerously overloaded, and had sailed right into a fierce typhoon. Its rudder and mast broken, the *San Felipe* finally reached the Japanese coast, where the soaked and windswept passengers staged a minor mutiny. They did not want to limp around to Nagasaki by sea; they wanted to get off the cursed hulk as soon as possible.

Negotiations commenced with a local lord, and it was agreed that the aging vessel could be towed into a nearby port. But within sight of its destination, the *San Felipe* breathed its last. Scraping on a sand-bank, it split along its keel and sank.

The passengers and crew waded irritably to safety, while the *San Felipe*'s cargo of silk, damasks and velvet washed out into the open sea, creating a rainbow-like slick across the waters. 'Cargo floated in the sea by the port for three or four miles,' wrote one chronicler, 'as if it were displayed on matting, painting the white waves with the five colours.'[4]

The local Japanese were swift to come to the aid of the *San Felipe*. Fishing boats chased out into the patchwork sea to reel in the sodden cloth – a sight that was greeted at first with elation by the damp and bedraggled passengers. It was only as time passed that they, and more importantly, the *San Felipe*'s pilot, began to fret that the local people were not retrieving their cargo, but stealing it.

As a vessel of the Spanish crown, the *San Felipe* was technically a friend of the Portuguese-sponsored Jesuits – Spain and Portugal were now supposedly a united kingdom, although at the grass-roots level there was great rivalry, particularly between the Jesuits in Kyūshū and recently arrived Franciscans in other parts of Japan.

The situation for the survivors steadily worsened, while missionaries dashed up to Edo to plead their case, and local samurai argued instead that the new arrivals were little more than pirates or, worse, the vanguard of an invasion fleet.

What happened next is difficult to determine. According to Jesuit sources, some of the regent Hideyoshi's samurai tried to confiscate the *San Felipe*'s cargo. The pilot tried to scare them off by boasting of the immense power of the Spanish king, the uncountable troops of the Spanish imperial armies, and Spain's manifest destiny to conquer the world. This was precisely the kind of bravado that the Jesuits had tried to downplay during their long sojourn in the south. In a fatal, disastrous flourish, the pilot added that the front lines of any Spanish conquest were the missionaries who arrived first, preaching a message of peace, but all the while steering the will of the next generation to accept Christian Spain as its lord and master.

> He told them that this was done with the Help of Missioners, whom his Master sent to all Parts of the World, to preach the Gospel of Jesus Christ, for so soon as these Religious had gained a sufficient Number of Proselytes, the King followed with his Troops and joining the new Converts, made a Conquest of the Kingdoms.[5]

Ready to believe such accusations, Hideyoshi declared all the Christians in his realm to be spies. The Franciscan friars in Kyōto, feebly protesting that the whole thing was a Jesuit slander, and nothing to do with the *San Felipe* at all, were the first victims, but Hideyoshi's revenge was exacted on all Christians, regardless of their denomination.

Some sources have suggested that the Spanish are to blame – that when Japan was in the hands of the Portuguese missionaries, everything went well, but that with the unification of Portugal and Spain, a more confrontational attitude crept into the new arrivals in Japan, and incited a backlash. But not even Valignano believed that. In fact, he had noted a great degree of suspicion among the Japanese, who had many stories of their own about meddling monks, and were all too ready to believe that the Christians were up to no good.

One of Valignano's associates, Father Francisco Passio, would observe that the ruling class, including Hideyoshi himself, did not share the Christians' faith, and hence could only interpret their actions in terms of earthly gains:

> As Hideyoshi believes that there is no other life, he cannot understand that such is their desire for the salvation of souls that the Jesuits come to Japan ... He has it firmly in his head that it is not salvation that is being sought, but the desire to make many Christians who would unite like brothers and could then easily rise up against him.[6]

In 1597, twenty-six Christian believers, including six Franciscans, three Jesuits and seventeen Japanese laymen, were crucified in Nagasaki on what is now known as the Martyrs' Hill in the centre of town. It was the beginning of the end for the Christians in Japan. It was hoped by Hideyoshi

> ... that the Death of these six and Twenty Christians would strike a Terror into the rest, and oblige them to renounce the Faith. But contrary to Expectation, finding them more resolute and in a Disposition generally to suffer Martyrdom, he resolved to renew the war in Korea, under the Conduct of the Christian Princes and Lords, whom he intended to establish in those Parts; and by that Means secure to himself their vast Possessions in Japan, and so Prevent the Possibility of a Revolt ...[7]

Korea was Hideyoshi's next project – with Japan united, he needed somewhere for the thousands of warriors to divert their efforts, and a foreign conquest was the ideal excuse. It was also a cunning ruse to divert the Christian converts of the south, and Hideyoshi was sure to place many of the Christian samurai in the front line of the Korean conflict.

A man called General Augustin Konishi and the regiment he raised in Amakusa were a major part of the samurai army's early victories against the Koreans. Konishi was an apothecary's son who had risen to military prominence in the later stages of the civil war. He had been rewarded for his efforts with a small fief in the far south of Japan, stretching across the Amakusa islands and onto the mainland to Uto Castle. Both Konishi and his parents had converted to Christianity but, despite this, he had enjoyed the support of the regent Hideyoshi – at least officially. Konishi and his men had been the first ashore during the first invasion of Korea, and had won great glory for themselves in the prolonged fighting.[8]

They were less successful in the second invasion, and would eventually conclude a truce with the Koreans, when the news reached them in 1598 of Hideyoshi's death. Barely eighteen months after he had ordered the crucifixions in Nagasaki, Hideyoshi passed away, and with him, it was hoped, would also die the anti-Christian sentiments he had nurtured among his vassals. But as the crusade in Korea came to an end, and the soldiers returned to their homeland, Japan erupted in one final conflict, from which a new ruler would emerge triumphant.

With Hideyoshi gone, his lieutenants argued over who would become his successor. Initially, they agreed to act as regents to his young heir, in what the Jesuits hoped would turn out to be a long power-sharing bureaucracy with no final decisions, and hence no real dangers. The Jesuits believed that Tokugawa Ieyasu was the strongest of the regents squabbling over Hideyoshi's legacy, but hoped that he would be more liberal in his attitude towards their faith than his predecessor. Valignano himself, back in Japan for his last visit before his death, commented that the future was bright – Christianity had gained so much ground during a period of nominal persecution; how much better were its chances now that the great enemy of Christianity in Japan was dead?[9]

In 1599, the good signs continued. As members of the new regency were sworn in, two of the lords present preferred to do so in the name of Deus, and not in the names of Japanese gods. Meanwhile, requests arrived in Nagasaki for new missionaries in provinces whose faith had previously been doubtful. From the offshore island of Tsushima, a vital staging post on trips to and from Korea, the ruling Sō family requested Christian priests to administer to their local believers. House Kuroda ruled lands in Christ's name, and Gracia Hosokawa, the wife of the leader of House Hosokawa, had ensured that her two sons had been baptised; the Amakusa islands were Augustin Konishi's; the Arima clan ruled a Christian Shimabara, and now there were reports that other lords, albeit not Christian themselves, were nevertheless prepared to lift persecutions against Christians in their own domains.

However, several domains maintained a policy that regarded Christians as dangerous insurgents. Eight hundred believers were expelled from Hirado and sought sanctuary in Nagasaki before being allowed to settle in Augustin's Amakusa fief. But even at this point, many Christians were ready to believe that such incidents were the last gasp of anti-Christian behaviour. The new regime, it was hoped, would be more progressive and liberal, and bring around the conservative fiefs. In 1600, an elated Valignano wrote that Tokugawa Ieyasu himself had proclaimed freedom of religion in his domain:

> ... everyone can choose the faith that they thought best, and [Ieyasu] gave the Christians of Nagasaki permission to live freely and in peace as Christians, and with this we consider ourselves all to have been reinstated, and as such we can reveal ourselves [i.e. come out of hiding] ...[10]

Valignano spent the Lent of 1600 in Augustin Konishi's Amakusa island realm, which was now a chiefly Christian district of some 100,000 residents. They were, however, merely baptised, not confirmed – Valignano knew that confirming a Christian's belief was another matter entirely, and there were indicators that many of Augustin's 'believers' had converted under duress.

In one case, an old lady on the Amakusa islands claimed to be a Christian, but was caught worshipping a Buddhist image when she thought she was alone. The image was taken from her by a lay preacher, who demanded that she be punished for her lack of Christian faith. Despite protests from foreign priests in the area, local law enforcers decided to burn down the woman's house as an example to her fellow villagers, 'owing to which, they were all terrified and from then onwards, very obedient to the Church.'[11]

Any doubters were soon freer to express their opinions, when the entire Nagasaki-Shimabara-Amakusa region, as part of the reorganisation of feudal domains, gained a new overlord who was fervently anti-Christian. But the attitude of the Christians remained one that had faith in the balance of power. For as long as the guardianship of Japan was split between a group of rival regents, there was always leeway for rival beliefs. Even if a single lord decided to turn against Christians in his domain, there would always be another domain to run to until the storm blew over. That at least was the hope.

Unfortunately for the Christians, Japan would shortly be reunified, under a single, enduring ruler. The arguments between Hideyoshi's successors escalated into full-scale war.

The multi-sided conflict soon resolved into just two factions contending for the Shōgunate. Christian soldiers fought on both sides, although a large number of them were concentrated, through geographical and personal connections rather than religious affiliation, in the army of one Ishida Mitsunari. Other Christian lords remained neutral, and several even revealed the fair-weather nature of their beliefs, renouncing their Christian faith as part of the deal to keep the war out of their lands.

The great turning point came in the autumn of 1600, far from the centre of Christian sympathies, at Sekigahara, a valley in central Japan through which a vital crossroads ran.[12] It came to be known as the Battle that Divided the Realm, and it began with a storm that drenched the entire area on the preceding day.

The soldiers in the camps spent a dreary, sleepless night listening to the rain pelting against their tents. Still more were forced to huddle in the darkness with nothing to protect them except their straw rain-coats, giving them the appearance of small, bedraggled haystacks topped by coolie hats or helmets. Others were still marching through the night, keen to reach the fields of Sekigahara before battle was inevitably joined the following morning.

An hour after midnight, Ishida Mitsunari reached the edge of the plain, his cavalry officers soaked through, his infantrymen sloshing wearily along the muddy road. Conferring with the allies who were already there, he reached the excited realisation that friendly forces held all the high ground. All his men had to do was hold their front line, and let the forces of the hated Ieyasu dash themselves against it. They could gradually draw their enemy forward and then allow their allies in the hills to charge down from both sides, smashing Ieyasu's flanks and winning the day.

It was an old ruse familiar to any military man. The Chinese had called it 'the crane's wings' – a poetic image of a deadly, all-encompassing embrace. No tactician worth his salt should have fallen for it, but Ishida was feeling lucky. Down the valley, his scouts had reported several divisions of enemy soldiers bunked down for the night in and around the village of Sekigahara. They were awfully exposed, seemingly unaware that they were surrounded on three sides.

Ishida's soldiers were put to work. Despite a forced march and the driving rain, the men were ordered to sink trenches around Ishida's command post. As they toiled miserably in the storm, the rain slackened off, turning instead to an impenetrable mist that wreathed the battlefield. All around the valley, friend and foe held fast to their positions, unable to see more than a few feet into the gloom.

The fog was so thick that one group of Ieyasu's soldiers, moving up to the front ready for the dawn, bumped into a group of Ishida's allies. There was a brief scuffle, a clatter of gunshots from the most alert, and a flurry of clashing swords and angry shouts. Within moments, both sides retreated back into the mist – neither side was sure who might have the upper hand. Officers on both sides fretted that they had been ambushed by a wily foe, and ordered their men to disengage. Glory could wait for the dawn, when everyone would literally know where they stood.

Sunrise swiftly dispersed the fog, giving each of the armies their first real glimpse of each other. Many familiar clan crests were dotted among the flags of the Tokugawa army. The triple hollyhock leaves of House Tokugawa; the bold swastika of House Hachizuka; the black dots of House Terazawa, and the nine stars of House Hosokawa.

The army in support of Ishida had similar clan emblems, but scattered among them were some new arrivals. Augustin Konishi's banner was a stark shape like a mathematical plus sign, each of its arms terminated by a blunt crossbar – the *cruz* of the foreign deity *Jesu Cristo*. House Shimazu had a similar theme – a circle sliced into quarters by two lines that met at right angles in the middle. This alien design, the crucifix, was a symbol of the newly adopted faith in the western regions. It made its way onto many of the samurai banners, and could be found sawn into the handguards on swords, carved into the hilts, and depicted on the breastplates of many of the Christian soldiers. Some were intricate and carefully crafted, others daubed on in an apparent afterthought, as if the wearer were hoping for some sort of supernatural assistance from the exotic, alien Deus.

The Tokugawa army attacked first. Disobeying orders to hold his position, Ii Naomasa, his helmet topped by a pair of giant horns, charged headlong towards enemy lines at the head of his elite Red

Devils cavalry unit, all clad in spectacular scarlet armour. The glory of leading the charge had been promised to someone else, a general who shouted at the Red Devils to retreat as they hurtled past him, with ever decreasing levels of politeness. The Red Devils maintained the thin pretext that they were only going out to 'check' the disposition of enemy troops, and had no intention of engaging them. This, of course, was news to the enemy, who charged to meet them, initiating battle by default.

The Red Devils smashed clean through their target battalion and out the other side, wheeling to avoid a neighbouring regiment and scattering back towards safety. Before the enemy could recover, the allies whose place they had usurped had organised an attack of their own. The infantry let loose with the first salvo of musket fire. Their powder, painstakingly kept out of harm's way in the night rain, was dry and deadly. Hot on the heels of the Red Devils, other cavalry divisions rushed to join the fray.

Subtlety was not the order of the day. Several units, including those led by scions of House Kuroda and House Hosokawa, charged straight for Ishida Mitsunari's command post, intent on ending the battle with one swift, surgical strike at its leader. Enemies who had once fought side by side in Korea now slaughtered each other in a desperate scrum. Stab wounds and slices accounted for many of the casualties, but not all. If a soldier lost his footing and stumbled in the mud, he risked being trampled to death or drowned in the shallow, churning waters of the rice paddies.

Ishida could not, would not pull back. He needed to hold his line in order to lure the bulk of Ieyasu's troops further into the trap. Even as some of his closest lieutenants were wounded and killed beside him by a barrage of musketry, he ordered the line to hold. Back in the rear of Ishida's lines, five artillery pieces were called into action. The cannons were intended for siege warfare, and had little real effect against such a mass of soldiers. But they were loud, and threw up great plumes of water and mud in the distance. Some of the Tokugawa soldiers lost their resolve. The guns were entirely useless with the opposite sides packed so close together, but the sight of the cannon balls falling was enough to convince some that the tide of the battle was turning against them.

From one of the mountainsides, a waiting division got its orders to charge. Its soldiers hurtled down the slopes into the side of the Tokugawa samurai. 'Ally and foe pushed against each other,' wrote one participant. 'The musket fire and the shouts echoed from the heavens and shook the earth. The black smoke rose, making the day as night.'[13]

By ten o'clock in the morning, there were signs of trouble. Ishida sent a message over to a general from his Shimazu allies, urging him to stop waiting on the mountainside and pile in. The messenger did not even get off his horse before yelling Ishida's orders. The Shimazu general scowled at the breach of battlefield protocol, and said nothing. Eventually, Ishida himself rode over to the Shimazu lines to ask for help. Instead, he was curtly informed that each of them had their own battles to fight. The Shimazu would enter the battle when they were good and ready.

The Battle of Sekigahara was a watershed moment, and not only for the rulers of Japan. Among the fighting men were many of the Christian soldiers who had fought in the Korean wars. Many of them were in the prime of life, still in their twenties and thirties, hardened and trained by a decade of crusading. Many of them were natives of the Nagasaki-Shimabara-Amakusa area, serving in units commanded by Augustin Konishi, or, on the Tokugawa side, the Lords of Arima. One was a man called Yamada Emonsaku, a tough warrior with an incongruous artistic streak, fighting among the Arima troops beside fellow soldiers from Shimabara, and responsible for some of the Christian insignia among the samurai. Among the Konishi regiments, fighting alongside other Amakusa natives, was Peter Masuda, a devout Christian from the Amakusa islands, who was devoted to Augustin Konishi and would follow him anywhere. Most, however, are nameless to posterity. One group, whom we must call the Gang of Five for want of any better form of identification, would come to play a role in the history of the Amakusa-Shimabara region a generation later. They were company commanders, each experienced in leading hundreds of men, each having fought up to his rank the hard way, in innumerable Korean sieges, and in a string of battlefield promotions. They had left Amakusa and Shimabara as teenage boys; they hoped that Sekigahara would be their finest hour, the day that they could speak of to their grandchildren, when they backed the winning side in the greatest battle of all. But they were wrong – they were going to lose.

Up in the hills above the battle, one of the samurai lords had already decided to betray Ishida. He did so simply by not moving. Even though some of the troops behind him were loyal to Ishida, they assumed that they had not yet been ordered into battle, and waited for the order to charge. After noon, several other companies rushed into the battle. They were supposed to form the 'wings' of Ishida's trap, but when they charged, they charged against Ishida himself. The turncoat forces ruined Ishida's plans, and threw his troops into deadly confusion. Without warning, wrote one Jesuit chronicler, 'several of the General Officers, together with the Troops under their Command, marched straight over to the Regent's [i.e. Tokugawa] side, which put the rest of the Army in so general a Consternation, that instead of Fighting, they turned Tail and fled without looking behind them.' Augustin Konishi's men were overwhelmed by the onslaught of new and unexpected enemies:

> This Great Hero seeing his Men in a Rout, and no possibility
> of rallying again, threw himself into the Midst of the Enemy's
> Troops, slaying on every Side, and bearing all down before
> him, till wounded from Head to Foot, and overpowered by
> Numbers, he was forced to yield to Fate, and surrendered
> himself Prisoner . . .[14]

Augustin Konishi did not long survive his defeat. Any other samurai would have committed suicide immediately, but Konishi made things more complicated for his enemies by allowing himself to be taken alive. 'After the Battle was lost,' wrote one chronicler, 'he had a violent Temptation to kill himself, after the Fashion of the Country, and nothing but Respect to the Law of God could have held him from it.'[15] Under interrogation, he said that he was sure that his captors would kill him, but added he did not beg them for his life, but merely for the chance to have his confession heard by a priest before his execution.

Augustin was executed several days later, in a botched beheading that took three hacks to sever his neck. With his death, 'the Support of Religion in Japan, that Cause in every one's Opinion was grown perfectly desperate.'[16] A letter concealed in the lining of his clothes was supposedly retrieved by his servants and handed to his Christian wife Justa. It read, in part: 'What I earnestly recommend, and that which most concerns you, is that you serve God faithfully, and love him with your whole heart.'[17]

It was another generation before Japan's civil war was finally over, but the seeds of the Tokugawa victory were sown at Sekigahara. There were a few Christian soldiers to be seen at the concluding siege of Ōsaka castle fourteen years later, by which time the fad for the worship of Deus among the nobility had largely passed. Whereas even the Shōgun himself had once been seen sporting a rosary and a crucifix as a fashion accessory, the symbols of Christianity were no longer icons of foreign exoticism and newfangled ideas. Instead, for the victors, they were a sign of old enmities and unwelcome interference; a warning to keep one's enemies close. To the minor nobility, they were often a trivial embarrassment, a youthful silliness for aristocrats who set aside such childish things when they ascended to positions of responsibility in their fathers' domains. Crucially, with the onset of enduring, final peacetime, there would be no more last-minute reversals or sudden deaths. The battlefield promotions and changes of fortune of wartime were brought to an abrupt halt. When Tokugawa Ieyasu became Shōgun, initiating the Tokugawa era in Japanese history, he froze ranks, positions and alliances. From that moment on, nobody would change residence, or allegiance, or religion without his order.

The many soldiers who had paid lip service to Christianity drifted back to their former, government-approved beliefs of Buddhism and Shintō. Among many of the common people in the south, Christianity was a dim memory, a weird fad that they had been obliged to follow for a few years, before a new government representative had arrived and told them all to stop again. The fair-weather Christians, created by lordly fiat, disappeared from the lists as easily as they had arrived. It was only among those who had taken the new religion to heart that it endured in the years after Sekigahara. Neither the missionaries nor their congregations were entirely sure how many true believers were left.

Ieyasu won the day at Sekigahara, and soon enough, when his power was secure, he would turn his vengeance upon the districts that had opposed him. He would outlaw Christianity, and unlike many former edicts against the foreign religion, this one would stick. Sancho Ōmura, son of the beneficent Bartholomew, revoked the Jesuit control over Nagasaki in 1606, and renounced his own Christian faith. He turned back to Buddhism, and his closest retainers, knowing what was good for them, followed suit. Despite Christian sympathies, the Arima clan kept hold of Shimabara, at least for the time being. But other regions were parcelled out among cronies of the victor.

A generation after Sekigahara, Christianity had gone underground. Its books were burned, its preachers banished. Anyone suspected of believing in the Christian God, and hence owing allegiance to barbarian kingdoms beyond the shores of Japan, was called upon to prove they were not a Christian. They would need to provide written, notarised proof that they were a registered worshipper at a

Buddhist temple, and properly demonstrate their contempt for the Christian religion by walking across an image of one of its saints. If they refused, torture and death awaited.

A 'trampling image', or *fumi-e*, became a common sight in the toolbox of a Shōgunate official. Although any Christian image would do, the real professionals preferred a hard-wearing metal artefact. Some survive in modern Japanese museums, the image of Jesus or Mary or a saint all but worn away by thousands of feet, on thousands of occasions, as Japanese villagers queued up to prove that they were not infected by the *Kirishitan* virus.

In Japan, where folk do not dare to offend their own house by wearing shoes indoors, it was a terrible insult against an image to step on it. It was believed that no true Christian would dare to do so, but this was a doctrinal issue that divided the Christians themselves. For the Protestant Dutch merchants in Hirado and Nagasaki, the *fumi-e* was just a pointless metal picture. It certainly did them no harm to step on it, and in doing so, they evaded any association with the dangerous *Kirishitan*. For the Catholic Japanese, however, with their reverence for relics and holy artefacts, stepping on a saint was a sinful act of desecration. Some of the Japanese believers even welcomed the chance to refuse, seeing it as a message from Deus that the time had come for their glorious martyrdom.

The mainland portion of Augustin Konishi's old fief ended up under the control of House Hosokawa, whose previously baptised sons renounced their faith to keep in the good graces of the Shōgun. The Amakusa islands were tacked on to the domain of House Terazawa, whose lord was based in the distant town of Karatsu. The new ruler, Terazawa Hirotaka, 'began like a Fox and ended like a Lion.' At first, he showed consideration for the many thousands of Christians in his new lands. However, after a few months, he banished any Christian sympathisers from his sight, forcing any in his service to deny their faith.

To pervert the Gentry of his Court (by a Diabolical kind of Invention) he ordered all to sign a Paper, wherein was written by Way of Title on the Front of the Piece: *Here follows the Names of such as have abjured, and renounced forever, the Christian Religion.* This on pain of Forfeiture of Estates.[18]

The general attitude of many in the nobility seems to have been one of 'Don't ask; don't tell.' Nobody, the Christians were often assured, really cared what anyone believed in their heart of hearts, but it was necessary for the preservation of outward harmony that some names be signed on a piece of paper.

The Shōgun's government hoped that Japan was finally at peace. Foreign influences had been shut out, weapons stored in castle armouries. The enmities of the samurai who had fought over Japan's spoils for centuries were now, supposedly, buried. The Japanese would worship in their local Buddhist traditions, pay homage to their native gods, and offer respect to their ancestors, with no place for the Christians.

There had been many reversals of fortune for the Christians, and many edicts both for and against them. They had been handed an entire city on a plate, only to have it snatched away again. Entire islands had been 'converted' en masse, only to be switched back to Buddhism with equal disregard for their actual beliefs. Edicts had been issued banning Christianity, but often by warlords whose career paths ended in bloody defeats. Although nobody could be sure of it at the time, the victory at Sekigahara and the subsequent rise of the Tokugawa family was different, simply because it would last so long. In fact, House Tokugawa would remain in charge of Japan for the next two and half centuries, giving Ieyasu's edicts an enduring, ancestral infallibility. He was the first Tokugawa Shōgun, the founder of the ruling house, and it was unlikely that anyone would dare contradict him. If Ieyasu had come out in support of the Christians, the religion would be sure to flourish once more in peacetime Japan. However, he did not.

Ieyasu soon abdicated as Shōgun, preferring to rule behind his son Hidetada. The very continuity of rule that brought peace to Japan also ensured that there would no longer be any relaxation of the persecution of Christians, or indeed a sanctuary within Japan for them.

The arrival of an embassy from the Philippines in 1614 only made matters worse. Intended as a friendly mission to encourage trade, the procession from the Catholic Philippines got short shrift from the Shōgun, who, 'after mature Deliberation, sent back word that the Embassy came not from any crowned Head, but was all Trick and Design of the Priests.'[19] Although the foreign ambassadors had hoped to establish friendly relations once more, the claims of the pilot of the *San Felipe* still rankled after a generation. The Shōgun noted that:

> His predecessors indeed formerly admitted of them, upon the Account of Commerce, but of late it was found, they had other Designs in View, and intended to establish their wicked Religion in the country, and for this Reason he was resolved to banish every Man of them out of Japan, and not for the future, to set Foot in the Island, on what Pretence of Excuse soever.[20]

With no dissenting voices left, and no refuge for the Christians, there was no opportunity to countermand the Shōgun's order, or even to remain lax in enforcing it. He had decreed that all Catholics would be banished from Japan, and the system in place, now so much more efficient than it had been a generation earlier, ground into action.

On 1 February 1614, the Shōgun Hidetada issued an edict that would steer the attitude of the Japanese government towards Christianity for as long as House Tokugawa was in power. 'Japan,' he said, 'was the land of the gods.' The Japanese had plenty of gods of their own, just as the land was their own, and not the property of the unwelcome worshippers of Deus. Christianity, said Ieyasu, was a 'pernicious doctrine', and it was no longer welcome.[21] All Christian missionaries should leave Japan, along with half-breed children of foreign merchants and other unauthorised personnel.

> The Shōgun commanded his Officers to . . . take in the Names of all Foreigners and banish them out of Japan, Hollanders excepted, as being professed Enemies to Priests and Religion, trampling upon the Crucifix, and Saints' Pictures, so much reverenced and honoured by the Catholics.[22]

The purge against the Catholics was brutally thorough. 'The Tyrant,' continued one chronicler, 'not content with Tormenting the living, declared open War against the dead, too.' The Shōgun's men even tore down the monuments in Nagasaki's Christian graveyard, and planned on exhuming the bodies and casting the bones into the sea. However, in this last aim they were largely thwarted, as the Christians had sneaked into the cemetery themselves the previous night and stolen the bones of their deceased relatives for safekeeping.

One of the reluctant exiles was the middle-aged Martino Hara, one of the four boys who had once returned triumphant from the Japanese mission to the Pope. He would live the rest of his days in Macao, where he continued to serve the Society of Jesus. After his death, he would be buried in the local church, close to the crypt of his mentor, Alessandro Valignano.

In one of the legends that sprang up around the mass exile of the foreigners from Japan, it was said that one of the departing Jesuits left a curse, or a promise, or a prophecy. The story remained suspiciously untold for an entire generation, and only came to the attention of the authorities when it was too late. It was carried from Nagasaki by some of the veterans of Sekigahara, and, so they claimed, offered them hope in the bleak years ahead, as they put their warring ways behind them and tried to blend in with the local population.

Called variously a *Divine Revelation* or a *Mirror of the Future*, the document made a series of unlikely predictions about the year 1638.

> When five by five years have passed
> Japan will see a remarkable youth
> All-knowing without study.
> See his sign in the sky
> In East and West the clouds will burn
> Dead trees shall put forth flowers
> Men shall wear the Cross on their heads
> And white flags shall flutter on the sea
> Fires engulf fields and mountains, grass and trees
> To usher in the return of Christ.[23]

CHAPTER THREE

The Mouths of Hell

················

At first, it seems like a completely normal mountain village. The road winds through the centre of town, past a couple of shrines, a gift shop, and a plush hotel. But the fog rolls steadily and unceasingly, as if there are chimneys ejecting clouds of steam at ground level, all with the eggy tang of sulphurous gases.

Follow a path behind a main street in most parts of Japan, and you find another street, more houses, a vending machine ... but here there is a shocking sight – a desolate, rocky landscape scattered with shallow, bubbling pools. At the edges, scorched, yellow grass clings to life, edged by green slimes of algae. This is the point where the red-hot core of Mount Unzen first becomes apparent, a series of boiling lakes and blasted heaths, once regarded by the Japanese as the place where the essence of the Buddhist hells came to the surface. One pool emits a piercing hiss as the steam escapes from the ground nearby – this is the Hell of Screaming As You Fall Into the Abyss. Another, which bubbles and spatters with a noise like a flock of wheeling birds, is the Hell of Sparrows. Shortly beyond it is the Hell of Ten Thousand Torments.

Unzen has attracted visitors for centuries – some saw it as a place of simple mystery, others as an area touched by divine or demonic power. Despite the attempts of the local authorities to dress it up as a nature sanctuary and an ecological curiosity, there is still an air of deep menace about it. In the Meiji era, a heartbroken local woman supposedly threw herself into one of the pools, sentencing herself to an awful, searing death. As I walk along the wooden decking I stop by a crag and put my ear close to the warm rock. The earth itself throbs with a steady KA-THUMP . . . KA-THUMP, as if a malevolent heart is beating beneath the ground.

A messy spaghetti of water pipes issues forth from one of the volcanic pools, channelling the boiling streams out of the ground and into a nearby hotel, where tourists can bathe in the waters that were once used to scald Christians. Linger too long near one of the pools, and a hawker will try to sell you an egg, which she will then shove beneath the ground for a few minutes, boiling it to perfection using nature's own oven.

The waters of Unzen have legendary, curative properties. Rich in minerals, they were said to cure a variety of skin complaints. That is, of course, assuming they are allowed to cool down a little. At their point of exit from the ground, their temperatures can climb up to twenty degrees above boiling point. Although a place of pilgrimage and of healing, Unzen was also a place of torture.

Masuda Shirō Tokisada, later baptised with the Christian name of Jerome, was born in the early 1620s, somewhere on the Amakusa island chain, to a family of secret Christian believers. It is believed that his father, Peter, was one of the Christian samurai who survived the debacle at Sekigahara. Peter and his fellow soldiers made their way back to their home town, where they hoped to melt into the local population. They were, however, high-ranking enough to be registered on the rolls of service of Lord Arima. Before long, as the new regime sought to assert itself, the Christian samurai were ordered to relocate, assigned to new postings in what seems to have been a deliberate attempt to thin them out and keep them from contacts with their old friends. Peter Masuda, however, remained in close contact with associates in Nagasaki, Shimabara and along the Amakusa islands.

Most foreigners had been banished from Japan, but for a small coterie of traders corralled into small ghettoes in Nagasaki and

Hirado. Japanese converts, mainly in Kyūshū, were told en masse that they were no longer Christian. Many shrugged their shoulders and obeyed with much the same resignation as their parents had accepted the original conversion. They were obliged to swear that they were loyal Buddhists once more, and many did. A surprisingly large number, however, clung to their belief in the foreign Deus. Some simply lied to the local Buddhist priests, and continued their rites in secret. Others acted like the twenty-six Martyrs of Nagasaki, proclaiming their love of Deus with reckless glee and daring the Shōgun's government to deal with them.

The generation after 1614 is a litany of tortures and torments, as Shōgunate officials hunted down the last of the *Kirishitan*, and any book that might help their religion survive. The persecuted Christians also searched for a sign that their faith would be rewarded, and, according to popular legend, one was soon forthcoming.

> There's a high Mountain in the Kingdom of Chikuzen, and at the Top of it a Cross, where the Christians in Lent Time made their Pilgrimages of Devotion. Some walked thither with heavy Stones on their Shoulders, and others disciplining themselves to Blood. In the late Persecution, the Cross being pulled down and burnt: On holy Saturday [i.e. Easter Saturday] in the Year 1616, there appeared on the Top of this Mount a terrible Fire, and in it a Cross . . .[1]

Some even claimed to be able to read messages in the cruciform lava flow, a miracle confirmed by 'clouds of witnesses.' But even at that time, the sign was regarded not as one of hope, but of a promise of further persecutions to come.

If a believer would simply sign a piece of paper renouncing his faith, he was free to go. Simply walking across an image of Mary or a saint would secure a Christian's release. It was that most Japanese of gestures, a white lie to save face with the majority, and government officials were mystified if Christians refused to do it. They were also a little scared, as refusal implied that the Christians truly did recognise and serve a higher power than the Shōgun. What if, some reasoned, that same power ordered them not to die for their faith, but to fight for it?

Shōgunate officials continued to root out foreign missionaries, who had ignored the 1614 exile order and gone into hiding. Brandings and mutilations of Christians continued throughout the decade, as the cult refused to die. The stories are often horrific, many of them tragic, but just as believers took constant heart from the many martyrdoms, their persecutors became increasingly unsettled by the sheer conviction of their victims.

Sometimes, it must have seemed as if every successful arrest only hatched further conversions. In Nagasaki, an inquisitor entered a house demanding to know if there were any Christians present. A simple 'no' might have sufficed to send him on his way, but instead he was accosted by an excited eight-year-old girl, demanding that he put her at the top of the list, 'that I may die for Jesus Christ.' The girl's mother then volunteered herself as another believer, and as the aghast official left the building, she chased after him shouting apologies. Perhaps hoping that he had been the victim of a prank in terrible taste, the investigator turned, only to discover that the mother wanted to add a second child to the list. Her baby was, she explained, asleep when the investigator called, but it was surely a Christian and needed to be included.

In 1618, a judge celebrated the arrest and sentencing to death of one Leonard Kimura, a Japanese-born Jesuit priest, one of the dwindling survivors of Valignano's seminary. However, in the year that Leonard had spent in jail awaiting trial, he had successfully converted eighty-six of his fellow prisoners. When the time came for the death sentence to be carried out, the judge was then 'not a little nettled' by the discovery that the executioner was himself a Christian believer. Although happy to lop off the heads of thieves and murderers, the executioner refused to 'execute so unjust a sentence, and withal advised his Companions to do the same.' The irate judge was forced to draft in an executioner from out of town; far from removing one more Christian from his sight, he had inadvertently uncovered a nest of several others, and moreover, had to live with the disturbing knowledge that they had been quietly serving on his own staff.[2]

There were still foreign missionaries in hiding: thirty-six in 1621, the year that Jerome Amakusa was born, but the number was swiftly declining. Before long, it was suspected, Christian belief would be in the hands of none but the Japanese themselves. Jerome Amakusa's parents did not display any of the suicidally keen lust for martyrdom of many other Christians. Instead, they kept their religion quiet, and may have even been the sort of Christian to merrily stamp on the image of the Virgin Mary when asked to do so, knowing that such an act would keep them safe.

It seems that the authorities, too, suspected that the fanatics were a distraction, and hoped to eradicate the faith by other means. Playing a long game, they hoped to ensure that future generations would simply lose the chance to hear what Christianity was by targeting books along with beliefs. In June 1622, Nagasaki authorities created another fifty-five martyrs, but also burned a 'mountain' of Jesuit books.[3] Much of the surviving output of Valignano's printing press was destroyed on that day, as well as in sporadic later pyres.

Valignano's press, obtained with such effort from Portugal, had already been safely spirited out of Japan, but the last of its publications now went up in flames. Over the generation that followed, surviving Christian texts were hunted down, in an attempt to destroy the very words that seemed to program believers with such zealotry.

Meanwhile, Shōgunate officials tried to get on with other business beyond hunting down the cultists in their midst. Lord Protasio

Arima was dead in 1614, discredited and despised for his love of the Christian cult. His son Michael tried to cling to his position by renouncing his faith and turning on the Christians in Shimabara, but his superior did not trust him. He was moved to another fief, taking only a handful of his closest retainers with him. His replacement, Matsukura Shigemasa, inherited a domain notorious for its contacts with the Christian cult, riddled with suspected half-breeds and Christian sympathisers, and stricken with poverty. He had a lot of work to do.[4]

Power and wealth in Edo-era Japan was measured in rice. The standard unit was a *koku*, a quantity of dried rice equivalent to just over 180 litres, or almost 48 gallons – perhaps two or three modern wheelbarrow-loads, enough for a man to live on for a year.[5] Fifty *koku* was enough to fill the hold of a small merchant ship – almost eight tonnes of rice. A landowner was considered well off if his fields produced 500 *koku*. At that level, a samurai was considered rich enough to be obliged to supply a musketeer and three pikemen for military service when called upon by the Shōgun.

Obligations rose with each increment of rice-defined wealth. Landowners with larger domains were obliged to provide more musketeers, then more pikemen, and the occasional archer – archers taking longer to train than gunners. As wealth rose, cavalrymen became part of the equation, along with occasional auxiliaries. A unit might become so large that it was expected for a wealthy lord to provide a bannerman to help control them, and servants to help with putting up tents and digging trenches.

At 10,000 *koku*, a landowner was at the periphery of what medieval Europeans might have called the military aristocracy. A 10,000-*koku* lord had a military obligation amounting to a hundred men, half of them pikemen, with over a dozen cavalry. Such a lord might be the master of a small village, and castellan of a small fort, more likely to look to untrained eyes like a walled mansion, with stabling for his retainers and storage for some of his rice-based wealth. We might, if we were prepared to make shaky cross-cultural comparisons, call such a man a baronet.

At 100,000 *koku*, a lord would be expected to administer a force of around 750 soldiers – what we might call a battalion. Upper levels proceeded at similar increments, to the regimental level of around 1,500 soldiers, and then vast divisions of ten or twenty thousand men. Several such armies would play a part in the events of the Shimabara Rebellion – in 1638, among many miscellaneous battalions, the largest single units among government forces would be those of Houses Hosokawa, Arima, Kuroda and Nabeshima, whose leaders might be reasonably referred to as 'dukes' in the European sense, alongside lesser regiments commanded by representatives of Houses Tachibana, Terazawa, and Mizuno, and others.

After the fall of Ōsaka Castle, the Shōgun introduced a series of reforms, aimed not at preparing for further conflict, but at maintaining an enduring peace. Rules of engagement and propriety were carefully defined, in the first true flowering of the code that would endure for two centuries. Japan had a warrior tradition already, but its most famous element, the code of *bushidō*, was born from a time when the warriors were idle, and needed to be kept from turning on each other. Other reforms attempted to prevent new alliances and enmities forming. There were restrictions on marriages between various realms, which some lords cunningly circumvented by allowing their children to be 'adopted' by other clans. Meanwhile, sumptuary restrictions attempted to keep a lid on needless luxuries – wartime austerity now extended into peacetime while the farmers struggled to recover from the upheavals.

The reforms had been followed in 1616 by a military service edict that rearranged some of the obligations based on one's wealth in *koku*. At the upper levels, the expected size of army was broadly the same, but lower down the scale the requirements of service were extended into relatively small sectors. At the level of a mere 200 *koku*, a landowner was now expected to have a pikeman and a foot-soldier at his command, attended by a further six non-combatant retainers – footmen, pages and porters. Such a man, to draw a European parallel once more, would certainly not be worthy of a baronial title. Instead, we might regard him as a landed gentleman or village headman. The reforms of 1616 were no longer about putting men into a battlefield; they were about a much more focussed, localised form of control. Under the new rules, every hamlet, every winding road between farms, would have its local bigwig, tasked with keeping the peasants in line, settling local disputes, and ensuring that the Shōgun's laws were enforced at the level of the neighbourhood watch.

Government assessors established the level of taxation. Too high an obligation, and a local ruler would be a burden on his subjects; too low, and a local ruler might not have the wherewithal to maintain infrastructure, put down a local uprising, or, say, provide humanitarian aid in the wake of a natural disaster. It was thus in everyone's interest that the valuation of the *koku*-yield of any given area was fair and correct.

Unlike his predecessors, Old Matsukura could not care less if the 'farmers' in his domain were old soldiers fallen on hard times. Surprisingly for many locals, he also seemed happy to turn a blind eye to the presence of Christians in his workforce, at least for a few years. In fact, Old Matsukura had another plan. He was going to make his domain the jewel of the Shōgunate, and instead of hunting the Christians down, he intended to work them to death.

> The Emperor at the time commanded that he should not tolerate any Christians in his State, but being naturally of a meek Disposition, [Matsukura] never offered any Violence, and was free to let such as he found there of the Persuasion before his Time enjoy their Liberty, provided they made no outward Show of it.[6]

Nicholas Couckebacker, head of the Dutch merchants in Hirado, noted that under Old Matsukura the Christians lost the chance to die for their faith, and were instead simply treated like all the other peasants – badly.

> At his departure, [Michael Arima] left nearly all his retainers and nobles behind, taking only a few with him to his new post, whilst the newly appointed prince [Old Matsukura], on the contrary, came hither with nearly all his retainers. The servants of the departed prince were then deprived of their income and obliged, by poverty, to become farmers, in order to procure for their wives and children the necessities of life. Although thus becoming peasants in name, they were in reality soldiers well acquainted with the use of weapons. The newly arrived lord . . . imposed moreover upon them and upon the other farmers more taxes, and forced them to raise such a quantity of rice as it was impossible for them to do.[7]

Shimabara was not a plum posting for any government officer. The people had associations with Christian converts, with foreign traders, and with the defeated side in the civil war. The huge peak of Mount Unzen dominated the entire peninsula – in fact, to a certain extent, the peninsula *was* Unzen – such that, despite covering a large area of land, only the coastal perimeter was flat and arable. The coastline soon gave way to the sleep slopes and winding roads of the mountain itself, home to tall pines, volcanic waters and administrative delays.

Local folktales often seem to favour stories of canny farmers getting one over on the rest of the world, and even each other. One features a local trickster who shoves coins up a horse's anus, in order to convince his gullible brother that the creature can excrete money. Wily farmers trick their neighbours into getting eaten by sorcerous mice, or frame their neighbours' daughter for theft as a means of snatching a new wife.

The geography of Shimabara lent itself to some peculiar local beliefs, particularly regarding the rumbling volcano, occasional earthquakes and hot springs. Local tradition held that malicious serpents, which could transform into human form in order to tempt and trick passers-by, inhabited the boiling waters. There are hints in Shimabara stories of a savage ancient fertility cult, in which young brides were 'given' to the spirits controlling the land to prevent crops from failing. Tellingly, there is also the ghost of neglected religion – one Shimabara tale is a horror story about a Buddhist statue that comes alive at night to murder the villagers who have stopped coming to pay it homage.[8]

It was the job of the local ruler to keep such cranky locals under control; a task that must have been considerably easier in the good old days of the late sixteenth century. When the region was a Christian enclave, the non-believers hounded out of town with the Jesuits' blessing, the homesteaders were united even in hard times by their shared beliefs; Shimabara might have even been something of a paradise. But with the sudden change in the attitude of the government towards Christianity, the ruler of Shimabara, Amakusa and its environs would have his work cut out for him.

There were several places in the region that might be reasonably described as 'fortresses', but the Arima family's residence of choice had been Hara Castle, set on an imposing crag just off the south-eastern shore. A century earlier it had been Hara *island*, but the nearby river had silted up, and a thin neck of tidal marsh and sand now connected it to the mainland.

Old Matsukura didn't like it. Hara was too small for his grand ambitions – it was a fantastic defensive point, but it could only really defend *itself*. Matsukura wanted a fortress that could be continually expanded until it became the nexus of a city; he imagined walls ten miles around, with the castle sitting proud at their centre.

He didn't like the locals, either. The farmers in the region around Hara were all friendly to the Arima family. Many were Christians, and even veterans of the army of Augustin Konishi. The word for them in contemporary slang was *kinōbushi* – literally, 'warriors who have returned to the land.' Although Matsukura enjoyed the power of life and death over the surly natives, he still shied from the idea of quartering too many of his trusted retainers amid a hostile crowd.[9]

Old Matsukura thought that Hara was too old-fashioned. In the Middle Ages, with its archers and swordsmen, Hara would have been an invulnerable fortress, but times had changed. Its coastal position gave it the worst of both worlds – Matsukura wanted a harbour for his burgeoning sea enterprises, but Hara Castle did not have one. Instead, it boasted high cliffs – great for defence, but inappropriate for trading vessels. Hara was close to the sea, but its beachside aspect put it well within the range of modern cannons, yet also left it vulnerable to land-based artillery.

Instead, with the full approval of the Shōgunate, Matsukura selected a new site to the north, at Shimabara. There, he would build a castle that was state-of-the-art, with all the knowledge he had acquired in his years of warring, ready to take on the challenges of a new century – future-proof.

The site of Shimabara Castle was a soldier's dream. Its towers could see clear across to Amakusa – no ship, foreign or domestic, could hope to sail the Ariake Sea without coming to the notice of its lookouts. And yet, despite its commanding coastal view, it was far enough inland to be beyond the range of most ships' guns. When it gained outlying houses and an outer township, the township grew *up* northwards from the castle, remaining parallel to the shoreline, never straying too close within the range of an imaginary enemy's cannons.

Shimabara Castle was shaped to perfection. Its steep turrets were given slightly irregular bastions, in order to ensure that each provided cover to the other's blind spots. Even to a spy in the hinterland, Shimabara Castle gave up no secrets. Instead, it was impossible to see inside its high walls, even from a mountaintop perch.

The whole Shimabara district was riddled with volcanic springs – indeed, Buddhist pilgrims came from miles around to drink the water at the nearby shrine, which was said to have restorative properties. Instead of a paltry single water source like Hara, Shimabara Castle boasted seven wells within its grounds, with a powerful enough flow that the castellan could regulate the depth of his own moats at will. Shimabara's surrounding watercourse could be left to drain, or suddenly flooded at short notice, and there was ample drinking water for its residents in the event of a siege.

All along the Shimabara shoreline, ancient megaliths once formed silent, prehistoric sentinels. Now they were ripped out of the ground and dragged off for a new purpose, forming some of the massive slabs of Shimabara's castle walls. Demolition crews fanned out across the Shimabara region to decommission the many smaller strongholds that had once dotted the landscape. This was both in accordance with government rules (only one castle was now permitted per domain), and also simply part of the never-ending quest for building materials. Some thirty fortified locations, ranging in size from small strongholds to simple mansions, were dismantled. Many of them were used as material for the new super-castle.

The construction site, visible even from passing ships, became something of a tourist attraction, and before long the expense of the castle, and its sheer muscle, began to concern the government. A message from the Shōgun Hidetada was politely worded, but an ominous sign: 'Please use moderation in building the castle. There will be no more wars.'[10]

The Shōgun was not the only one who was worried about Matsukura's project. There are signs that, in the later months of construction, the castle ran far over budget, and initial promises of bonuses were withdrawn or otherwise avoided. It is, perhaps, no coincidence that the last section of wall to be completed also seems to have been the most shoddily built – the only section that collapsed many years later during an earthquake.[11]

There are signs of other corners cut. Shimabara folklore tells of thirty massive stones left on the beach. They had originally been intended for Ōsaka Castle, but had been left over in the construction, and shipped hundreds of miles south to Shimabara. There, the castle architect had rejected them on a manufactured pretext, in order to avoid paying the men who had brought them so far. The transporters left, empty-handed and weeping, while the stones sat, abandoned on the beach at Shimabara until the 1950s, when they were incorporated into a sea wall.[12]

Altogether, perhaps a million workers were at the site at one time or another. The population of Shimabara swelled from a tiny village to a building site of some ten thousand artisans and their families. Many stayed after the castle was complete, their tax revenue helping to offset the vast expense of the castle that they had built – or at least, that was the plan.

The residents brought new problems with them, which Matsukura tried to ignore. In a country recovering from a prolonged war, with many old soldiers now idle, a great building project was a magnet for good and bad. With such a close proximity to Nagasaki, and with foreign influences facing such heavy persecutions, Matsukura realised that his enterprise was attracting a few people with dark secrets. Christians, Chinese, half-breeds and other undesirables were sure to have been mixed in among the labour force and new residents.

Shimabara might have looked impressive, but it was constructed at a crippling cost, and Matsukura expected the people of his fiefdom to foot the bill for their 'protection'. Taxes in the region soon rose, and kept rising. All residents of Shimabara, be they Buddhist or secret Christians, were ordered to pay ever higher rates.

Even as Old Matsukura was completing his monument to Fortress Japan, his domain was a haven for foreigners. The period of the castle's construction coincided with the supposed departure of English and Portuguese traders from Hirado, and with fierce competition between Chinese merchants over the remaining trade. Christian missionaries were rumoured to have sneaked into the south of the Shimabara Peninsula, particularly in the Kuchinotsu area, where any ship would have had to drop them, lest it round the cape and become visible to lookouts at Hara or Shimabara. Shimabara legends suggest that even if Old Matsukura had not known of the Christians in his territory before, he was prepared to employ them now. Several captive Christians, it was alleged, were put to work on unspecified secret missions for Old Matsukura, and then quietly killed on completion, in order to maintain their silence.[13]

Matsukura was sure (once again, rightly) that enemies in Edo would wait for him to complete the hard work on the castle, hoping to have him fired for misconduct if Christians and foreigners were still found in the Shimabara region thereafter. His orders from the Shōgun specified that he was to suppress the Christians and construct the castle. If he failed in half of his mission, the castle would be forfeit, and he would be packed off to a new assignment like his predecessor.

The population of Shimabara had tripled to 11,000 by the time the castle was completed, affording further opportunities for undesirables to blend in. We have no record of how many of the labourers on Shimabara Castle were illegal aliens, but we may assume that the toughest labours attracted workers with nothing to lose, or perhaps something to hide. The cost of building materials led to further taxation on the local inhabitants.

If Old Matsukura's behaviour seemed harsh, we should remember that a death sentence awaited him, too, if he failed. Old Matsukura's agents took particular pleasure in hunting down tax evaders in the region. Nicholas Couckebacker wrote of one of the tortures used by Matsukura's men – nicknamed the Minō Dance, after the sedge raincoats that formed part of the spectacle.

> Those who could not pay the set tax were dressed, by his order, in a rough straw coat, made of a kind of grass, with long and broad leaves and called *minō* by the Japanese, such as is used by boatmen and other peasantry as a raincoat. These mantles were tied round the neck and body, the hands being tightly bound behind their backs with ropes, after which the straw-coats were set on fire. They not only received burns, but some were burnt to death, others killed themselves by bumping their bodies violently on the ground or by drowning themselves ... This revengeful tyrant [Matsukura], not content with his cruelty, ordered women to be suspended quite naked by the legs, and caused them to be scoffed at in various other ways.[14]

But despite Matsukura's persecutions, the endurance of forbidden beliefs in his domain had not escaped his superiors. In 1624, he journeyed to Edo to deliver a proud report that the castle was complete, only to be given a brusque reminder of his duties. Instead of praising him for his castle, the Shōgun Iemitsu (Ieyasu's grandson) observed that Matsukura had been assigned the Shimabara post in order to wipe out missionary work in the region, but that reports were still arriving of local Christian sympathies. If Old Matsukura did not show some better results, he risked being reassigned out of his new home, and losing his castle before the paint was even dry.[15]

It is in this simple series of events – the building of a fortress, the costs involved, and the continued ingress of Christians and half-breeds – that we can see the origins of the Shimabara Rebellion. Old

Matsukura returned, fuming, to his fief and initiated new efforts to stamp out Christians. In his resolve to do so, and his continued attempts to pay off the castle's massive construction fees, he would press the residents of Shimabara so hard that they would eventually push back.

Old Matsukura's torments gained a reputation for their grisly inventiveness. On the Shimabara Peninsula, he issued a proclamation calling for all Christians to come forth. Any foolish enough to follow his order were lined up and branded on cheeks and forehead with the characters *Kiri-Shi-Tan*. Two of his own pageboys turned out to be Christians, and when a samurai inquisitor threatened to cut off their fingers and toes, they cheerfully extended their arms to him. Irritated but also a trifle spooked, the official ordered them out of his sight.

Shimabara Castle, as the seat of the feudal lord, became the epicentre of the persecutions. The castellan found himself in possession of eighty local Christians, who were made to walk through a door guarded by 'four big-boned Fellows', who struck at them with enough force to kill several. Meanwhile, several families of other Christians were shipped up the coast from Kuchinotsu, tied to stakes in a public place, branded and left to the winter elements for two days. When this failed to achieve anything, they were shipped back home and subjected to similar torments. It seems that Old Matsukura hoped, by this transportation, to make such an example of the Christians that the others would give him no trouble. If that really were his intention, then he had learned nothing from the persecutions of the previous generation.

The women travelled by ship, but the menfolk were made to travel back to Kuchinotsu on horseback, in a procession that elicited a disturbing amount of roadside prayer and support from local villagers. Mutilations, brandings, burnings and crushings then ensued, which the martyrs 'endured with so much Patience that the very Executioners were tired with torturing them.'[16]

At Himi, near Nagasaki, a number of newly discovered Christians were subjected to brandings and the removal of fingers. The appalling parade was more successful in Himi than elsewhere: 'Most of the Faithful in those Parts terrified with these dismal Spectacles, surrendered at Discretion, and the Rest to the Number of 150, fled into other Countries.'

'Other countries,' here, would mean Nagasaki itself or the Amakusa islands, but as far as Old Matsukura was concerned, that was somebody else's problem. He was happy merely to purge the Christians from his own domain, and the chronicles report a tediously long list of drownings, danglings, mutilations and roastings as he sought to stamp out the faith. For the samurai, there was a similar roll-call of willing martyrs – small boys happily jumping onto hot coals when ordered to do so or lose *Jesu Cristo* from their lives, and believers who preached and sang from the cross or stake, and even thanked their persecutors for bringing them closer to Deus.

The most infamous of Old Matsukura's punishments was his novel use for the waters of Unzen itself.

Two Leagues from Nagasaki there's a High towering Mountain called Unzen, and on the Top three or four vast Lakes with boiling sulphurous Waters, heated by subterraneous Fires. These Waters break out sometimes in wide Openings and Gapings of the Earth, with whole Mountains of Flames, called by the Japanese the Mouths of Hell . . . or Infernal Waters. These wide Openings happen only once in Eighteen Years, but then it overflows like a Deluge, with whole Torrents of stinking Waters, mixed with Sulphur and Brimstone, insomuch as one can't look upon them without Horror. The Waters smoke and boil as if they stood upon a hot Fire, and make so hideous a Noise that we may properly compare them with the Lakes of Brimstone and Fire mentioned in the Apocalypse. For the rest, the Waters are so hot . . . that the least Drop penetrates to the Bone.[17]

Eighteen Christians, four of them found among Old Matsukura's own subordinates, were taken in procession up the slopes of Unzen to the boiling lakes. One, gazing upon a Mouth of Hell, brightly opined that for him it would be the Gateway into Paradise. Another shouted praises to *Jesu Cristo* and hurled himself into the lake, much to the annoyance of another Christian, Paul Uchibori, who warned the others that they were there to be martyred, not to commit the sin of suicide. Thereafter, the Christians were thrown one by one into the waters of Unzen, all except Paul, who was vengefully dipped head first several times.

It was not the last time that Old Matsukura's men would climb Unzen with a party of martyrs. One of Matsukura's own officers turned himself in at Shimabara, claiming that he had gone into hiding in Fukae, but had realised that his lord would get into trouble with the Shōgun if it was found out that he had allowed a Christian to escape. After making this incredible confession, he was duly sent up the mountain with another group of Christians, whereupon Old Matsukura's men attempted to get some better results.

Simply killing the Christians had been proven unproductive, particularly since so many of them went uncomplaining or even gratefully to their deaths. Instead, Matsukura's men tried to prolong their agony, dipping them in and out of the lakes, splashing them repeatedly with scalding water, and even slicing gashes into their flesh, to increase the pain. When none of this had any appreciable affect, they resorted to a far crueller method. They separated one John Chizaburo from the survivors, and allowed him to sit down and rest for a while. They then told the survivors that the man had been allowed to sit down because he had agreed to cast aside his Christian faith.

It was calculated to wound the believers at a spiritual level and almost worked, but for John Chizaburo unhelpfully bellowing: 'I declare before you all, that I live and die a Christian.'

Eventually, the torturers gave up, tied the survivors together and doused them in scalding water until they died. The pitiful corpses, which 'appeared as if they had been flayed alive,' were then weighted with stones and dumped in the lake, in an attempt to discourage other Christians from filching holy relics.

Meanwhile, the natural world obliged with a series of omens of its own, adding to an already impressive list of portentous phenomena, none of which escaped the notice of the apocalyptically minded farmers of Amakusa.

'Some time after the Death of these Martyrs,' wrote the chronicler Jean Crasset, 'there appeared on the Sea Lights like flaming torches, which shined with marvellous Lustre. The Christians believed that these *Phenomenoms* [sic] to be so many Arguments and Instances of the Martyrs' Glory.'[18]

The lights on the sea were not merely visible to the Christians. They spooked Matsukura's own men, who did not know what to make of them. This, perhaps, was only to be expected from samurai (and Jesuit chroniclers) who were not only strangers to the area, but also not that well read in ancient Japanese verse. In fact, Kyūshū had been known in Japanese poetic tradition as the 'isle of unknown fires' for almost a thousand years, when the weather phenomena above the region's marshland were first noted in poem by Ōtomo no Yakamochi. Jesuit chroniclers were happy to report the phenomena as the shades of Christian martyrs, while Matsukura's samurai went about their duties none the wiser, and presumably a little worried.[19]

The Christians were a great irritation to the authorities, but one that was being scrubbed from the Shimabara Peninsula one martyr at a time. Old Matsukura's men perhaps failed to see that their campaigns were only working against certain kinds of Christian – the zealous would-be martyrs, the unlucky, the urban and hence obvious, and the carelessly caught. All the while, Old Matsukura's persecutions bred a local population of toughened, underground believers, able to keep their faith secret from all but their closest family circle, able to survive without the dangerously obvious accoutrements of books and rosaries. Old Matsukura bragged that his holocaust was achieving great successes, but it only hardened the resolve of hundreds of survivors in the Shimabara region, and swelled the ranks of the faithful in nearby Amakusa.

Old Matsukura even offered to help the magistrates of Nagasaki hunt down Christians in their own region in 1629. Although his offer was accepted, and his vicious methods applied to a new target group, he also made some powerful enemies. He boasted in Nagasaki of his desire to take the battle against Catholics away from the coasts of Japan and south to the Philippines. It was, at least in theory, an excellent plan. The Shōgun was, after all, officially the 'Barbarian Suppressing Generalissimo' – it would surely be an excellent scheme to focus samurai attentions on a new foreign conquest.

The last Japanese attempt at a foreign expedition had been something of a failure – the abortive crusade in Korea that dragged on for several years. But Matsukura may have failed to realise the implications of his plans. For as long as Japan was closed off to outsiders, there was money to be made by the town authorities in Nagasaki and Hirado, the only ports that were permitted to trade with foreigners. Matsukura's aspirations, along with his newly completed castle in a sheltered harbour town, may have seemed too much like a challenge to the Nagasaki port monopoly, particularly now that he was offering the service of his own vicious inquisitors.

On the way back to his neat new castle, Old Matsukura's retinue stopped at the Obama hot springs resort on the western slopes of Mount Unzen. There, he hoped to bathe his old soldier's bones in the warm volcanic baths – not the scalding, boiling waters of Unzen itself, but at a more sedate, comfortable temperature. But Old Matsukura never left the Obama resort alive. Crasset's 1707 *The History of the Church of Japan* has an exacting and detailed account, taking considerable glee in what happened next:

This Monster of Cruelty to satiate his bloody Passion, went himself to Nagasaki, and his Design was to petition the Governor for Leave to try his cruel Inventions on some of the Religious in his Prisons. But ... he fell sick on the Journey, and though the Distemper proved only a Tertian Ague, and the Fits moderate, he immediately lost his senses, crying out like a Madman.[20]

Crasset's version of events has Old Matsukura heading to Obama after two hundred recommended cures fail to do anything but exacerbate his condition. According to Christian legend, Matsukura fled to Obama in frantic search for a release from his torment, after a series of bungled remedies 'heightened his Distemper to that Degree that he did nothing but howl and roar like a wild Beast.' In desperation, he turned to the curative baths of Obama, seemingly uncaring of the historical irony, that Obama derived its spa waters from the same volcanic source that had provided Matsukura with his most famous engine of martyrdom.

[S]pecial care was taken to temper the Waters, but this not withstanding, so soon as he stepped into the Bath, he roared out as if they had put him into the hottest Pool of all the Mountain. *Turn out of the Company* (he cry'd) *for besides the Heat of the Bath, I have a Fire within, that's sufficient to set the Room in Flames.* Then he complained (as before) of Multitudes of Heads that gnashed their Teeth and tormented him without Respite. In this Manner he died, and as there's too much Reason to fear, sunk from the scalding waters of Unzen into the glowing Furnaces of Hell, to weep and gnash his Teeth for all Eternity.[21]

Japanese sources present a less sensational account of his demise. Shōgunate documents claimed that Old Matsukura had simply suffered a cerebral haemorrhage at the Obama bathhouse. But this blunt and unadorned explanation, while dull in comparison to the rancorous Christian account, seems a little too simple for words. The Obama innkeeper, who was in the best position to know the truth, later claimed that in fact an agent of the Shōgun, or perhaps business rivals in Nagasaki, had speared Old Matsukura to death in his bathtub.[22]

CHAPTER FOUR

The Latter Days of the Law

····················

South of Nagasaki, among the farms and fishing villages, the Rebellion is the most spectacular event in local history. A manga chronicle of the region tries to play up some of the supposed achievements of prehistoric cavemen, and enthuses earnestly about south Japan's first steam train, but centuries on, if a tourist has heard of Shimabara, it's either because of the Rebellion or because of the Unzen volcano.

At the southern tip of the Shimabara Peninsula is the township of Kuchinotsu, close to where Valignano's printing press was once based. For centuries, it has been the point to catch a boat across the water to the Amakusa islands. On today's shoreline, right opposite the jetty for the Amakusa ferry, there is a garish fibreglass statue of a Dutch trader, ten feet tall, his facial features as grotesquely exaggerated as in an Edo-era print. Here, it is said, a Dutch ship once put in to trade. Here was where Old Matsukura invested all his hopes of a southern trading empire to rival Nagasaki's – ships to the Ryūkyūs, to Taiwan, to the Philippines. Some thought of trade, others, like Matsukura, thought of conquest: a colonial dominion to outlast the Shōgun's failed invasion of Korea. Sometimes there is wistful talk of the Nanban era, literally the time of contacts with the 'Southern Barbarians'. Some of the influences are obvious, such as the obsession of Nagasaki tourists with castella sponge cake. Others, particularly in the Shimabara region, seem misremembered, forgotten or actively suppressed.

Some said that there was something 'special' about Shimabara girls, alluding in as many words to the continued presence of foreign blood in the gene pool, despite the purges of all non-Japanese. Their noses, it was suggested, were often a little large, their eyes a little bit rounder than the norm. Some had a certain Chinese quality, whatever that was supposed to mean. The comments may have been a confusion based on a distant pun – up in the imperial capital, a different Shimabara would also become the name of the brothel quarter; you bet there was something 'special' about Shimabara girls.

Amakusa and Shimabara retained a certain fascination among the Japanese. It was said that the poverty-stricken girls of Amakusa, sold into slavery in the Victorian era, formed the main part of the army of fallen women found in Japanese brothels across Asia. This sense of melancholy, mystery and erotic promise was preserved in a poem written by Kitahara Hakushū, one of his Songs of Amakusa, composed in the early years of the twentieth century, and addressed to an anonymous, bewitching girl with a secret love she cannot speak of.

> Neither your mother nor father can know
> Just keep it in your heart, cherish it, treasure till you die
> Leave aside the whip of sin's oppression
> Just keep it in your heart, the sign of love of the Cross.[1]

As late as the twentieth century, it was said that there were two accents in Shimabara. You could tell if a resident's family moved to the region pre- or post-Rebellion. When I step into the noodle bar in Kuchinotsu, the words of greeting from the husband and wife who welcome me don't seem to have any accent at all. Which is part of the problem.

'Are you a teacher?' says the wife, unable to contain her curiosity. 'You must be an English teacher from one of those schools?'

'No,' I say. 'I'm an author writing a book about the Shimabara Rebellion.'

I honestly expect it will impress them; I'm expecting a chorus of excited squeals and appreciative advice – maybe even a few local folktales I can use. But instead they smile with icy politeness and scurry off to make the tea.

It's easy to forget that the Rebellion is a livelihood to those in the tourist business, and maybe a matter of local pride to those who count themselves as locals. But for many it can also be an embarrassment – a great national disaster, without which their ancestors would never have been able to take over the land of dead martyrs. If most of the rebels died in the uprising, then their places were taken by out-of-towners.

The aftermath of Old Matsukura's death reeks of a cover-up. He was replaced by his inexperienced son, Matsukura Shigetsugu (a.k.a. Katsuie), a twenty-seven-year-old upstart who had grown up at the Shimabara Castle building site, raised on his father's justifiable paranoia about enemies within and rivals in Edo.

Young Matsukura had similarly low patience with the Christian sympathisers, who he associated not only with the exiled foreigners and hated half-breeds, but also with the departed Lord Arima. Young Matsukura, when he succeeded to his father's domain, was a 60,000-*koku* lord, expected to command a company of a little over 300 men – ten platoons of pikemen, archers and musketeers, with an additional squadron of 90 cavalry. But Young Matsukura had ideas above his station. He independently reassessed the value of his domain at 120,000-*koku*, a decision that would literally double his obligations. It seems that Matsukura was not attempting to upgrade himself to the level of what we might call a count or earl, at least not deliberately. Instead, he was probably trying to find a way to grab enough wealth to help pay off the outrageous expenses incurred by the construction of Shimabara Castle, and perhaps also to commence preliminary planning for his grand scheme – thought to have been an invasion of Taiwan and the Philippines, an attempt to carve out a personal empire overseas.

Young Matsukura could not have picked a worse time. The apocalyptically bad weather showed no sign of relenting, and the local peasantry had already been taxed into starvation. On the opposite shore of the Ariake Sea in Kumamoto, the older, wiser Hosokawa Tadatoshi, head of House Hosokawa, wrote: 'districts are destitute, and because they could not farm or harvest, people have left their lands to find temporary work away from home. The fields have fallen into ruin.'[2] In the domain of House Terazawa, which included the Amakusa islands, the people were reported to have been scrabbling for roots and leaves on mountainsides after the failure of their crops.

The narrow strait between Amakusa and Shimabara was also the borderline between the Terazawa domain and that of Young Matsukura, where the peasantry was taxed doubly hard. 'Year by year,' complained one chronicle, 'the peasants grew more exhausted, and were not able to have either the children or the cattle and horses due normally. How could they sustain life under those circumstances?'[3]

The zeal of the Matsukura clan for tax collection was already legendary, climbing to an extreme where farmers were expected to give up 60 per cent of their already meagre crops. Barely able to make ends meet themselves, the peasants were obliged to pay in barley or wheat, but could never be sure that their yearly payments were all done. Some farmers moved into cash crops, growing the recently arrived tobacco plants from the New World – only to have tax collectors snatch the highest-quality leaves for themselves.[4] In one notorious incident, a scuffle broke out over a single aubergine, with the collector eventually hacking off a slice as his due.

If we believe the evidence of a salt merchant from Kumamoto, Young Matsukura did not merely exact a heavy toll from the peasantry, but did so retroactively. In the year that the peasants finally snapped, Young Matsukura decided that the time had come to collect an additional *backdated* levy, after seven lean years.

It is said that they started a riot because the Shimabara domain exacted seven years of unpaid tax. Moreover, an additional 300 *koku* was also charged to the people to cover the loss when a ship that was heading to Kyōto was wrecked. They tortured women and children. It is also said that they rose up because of Christianity.[5]

The first stirrings of what would become known as the Shimabara Rebellion occurred in the late autumn of 1637. Crasset's *History of the Church of Japan*, drawing on Jesuit reports from the time, assigns blame to local interests, not external agitators.

The same year [1637] happened an unfortunate accident, which helped to complete the ruin of Christianity in Japan. [Young Matsukura] being severe/on the Christians in his states, loading them with heavy taxes, and tormenting their wives to make them to extort money from them, these poor desperate people gathered together in a body, to the number of seven and thirty thousand . . . Soon after, the [lord] marched with an army of two hundred thousand men, and laid close siege to the place. [. . .]

The Emperor [*sic*] concluded this revolt was contrived by the Portuguese, in order to possess themselves of Japan, as also that religion was mere pretence, to debauch his subjects and bring them under the Spanish yoke; and these jealousies were improved by the heretic ministers at his court, who to engross the commerce to themselves, rendered all Portuguese, Priests and Religious, suspected of ill practices.[6]

The Portuguese, of course, were already gone. The number of foreigners in Japan was now extremely limited, and soon to fall even further. Even if foreign agitators had no part in the Shimabara Rebellion, the foreign trappings and associations of the rebels' religious beliefs were likely to confirm the Shōgun's suspicions. After all, had not the pilot of the wrecked *San Felipe* claimed that precisely such a thing would happen – that the Christians would build up local affiliations until Japanese subjects themselves would form an army, turning on the state that ruled them, ready to establish a foreign dominion on Japanese soil?

But not even the Shōgun could pretend that the rebels were led by foreigners. No foreigner is known to have marched with the rebels. Instead, they were supposedly led by a teenage Japanese boy, Jerome Amakusa.[7]

Jerome Amakusa was described by Shōgunate documents as 'having no pedigree' (*yuisho mo naki*), and his family background was one of a family fallen on hard times. A doubtful legend claims that Jerome Amakusa was the son of Michael Chijiwa, one of the four Japanese youths sent by Valignano to see Europe.[8] There is no evidence of this, but Jerome's real father had undoubtedly moved in similar circles, probably met at least one of the celebrity voyagers, and was acquainted with many graduates of Valignano's seminary. Born sometime around 1581, Masuda Yoshitsugu or Masuda Jinbei came from Ōyano, a small island at the eastern end of the Amakusa chain. A retainer of General Augustin Konishi, he had become one of the many Christian converts in Konishi's army, taking the Christian name of Peter. He left Ōyano in 1600 as one of Konishi's soldiers, surviving Sekigahara when Konishi did not. With the region under new management, Peter was moved from Ōyano to become a village headman near Uto (or Udo) Castle, Augustin Konishi's former residence.

The Battle of Sekigahara had been the end of Peter Masuda's samurai career, as it was for his fellow soldiers like Yamada Emonsaku and the Gang of Five. Even though he was supposedly in the warrior class, the Shōgunate had already made it plain that 'there would be no wars.' His life in Uto was little different from that of the farmers over whom he had nominal authority, but Peter found himself in a Christian community. Although we have Japanese names for many of his relatives, most of them also used Christian names, a sign of baptism in the good old days of Portuguese missionaries, or even of the presence of local, home-grown ministers. Peter's wife, Martha Watanabe, was of the same faith and probably his cousin, and the couple had at least five children.

The eldest, Regina, was a girl born in 1615, the year the siege of Ōsaka Castle established the Tokugawa as the undisputed masters of Japan. The youngest known, Marina, was born in the late 1620s, in the midst of the anti-Christian persecutions. Of the others, there may have been a girl called Tsuru, and Jerome is known to have survived, but his Japanese name Shirō ('boy four') implies that perhaps two other births separated his and Regina's, and that at least one died in infancy. Although some sources reported that the boy once had the Christian name of Francisco, he appears to have received an official name at a baptism in Nagasaki. Thenceforth, he was known as *Hieronimo* – Jerome.

That information is solid enough, since it was reported in the diaries of House Hosokawa, Peter's immediate superiors.

A masterless samurai formerly of Konishi's employ, [Peter] Masuda was originally from Ōyano in Amakusa, but of late he has been hiding in Uto, working as a farmer and visited his hometown Ōyano. This man is a rebel who is deeply involved with Christianity and his son [Jerome], 15 years of age, is intelligent and the leader of the rebellion. Five other *rōnin* of Konishi's [old guard] are involved. They sneaked around the Shimabara domain and swindled the common people.[9]

The statement from House Hosokawa was based on direct knowledge, citing a letter from a local informant, who had first-hand acquaintance with the family, which claimed it was an 'unmistaken truth' that Peter had made multiple trips to the Shimabara peninsula and Nagasaki to spread the word of the banned Christian sect.

Jerome grew up during the period of persecutions, and was told that he was one of a Chosen Few of clandestine believers in a true faith. His father, Peter, continued to make regular visits to Ōyano, where the locals were supposedly hiding a foreign missionary, Father Francisco Pordorino. Meanwhile, Ōyano received a demonstration of the harshness of the Shōgun's justice. Three local men, convicted of an unidentified crime, were returned to their home village in pieces. They had been executed on the mainland by *ikidameshi* ('the living experiment'), by which a samurai would test the quality of his blade by hacking at live criminals.

The mysterious Father Pordorino had sneaked into Japan himself in 1625, when Jerome was four. There, he and Peter Masuda preached Christian sermons among the fishermen and whalers. Supposedly, the whalers reported that their catch always improved if they prayed to Francis Xavier before setting off.[10]

There are two main strands of information about Jerome: tall tales about his magical life, told by his fanatic supporters to sceptical investigators, and contemptuous dismissals of his folly from government records. Sitting somewhere between the two is a mixed account from Jerome's mother Martha, obtained under interrogation during the siege that would end both their lives. This last source is equally doubtful, and shows signs of a protective mother trying to downplay her son's role in events. These contradictory and doubtful sources are the shaky foundations of any account of Jerome and his Rebellion.

His adoring followers in the 1630s told of miracles seen and wonders worked, which make Jerome out to be a messiah. The stories began with a breathless boasting common to almost all biographies of historical figures in the Far East, although some may have been designed to fit the claims made in the *Mirror of the Future*. Jerome was supposedly a child prodigy, 'all-knowing without study', possessed of a supernatural ability to absorb information, and a great love of learning. Supposedly, he was able to read by the age of four, and possessed an unearthly, hypnotic presence and charisma.

According to his mother, Martha, Jerome spent the early years of his childhood in a village on the Uto Peninsula that reached out from the mainland towards the Amakusa islands. House Hosokawa's own annals noted that Jerome had once been a pageboy to a local samurai, Susami Hannoin, and also the chronicler's belief that Jerome had been a *kozōritori*, or 'sandal bearer'. The title originally referred to a page whose job it was to trail in a lord's wake, carrying his shoes. However, at the time the chronicle was compiled, a *kozōritori* was also a euphemism for a catamite.[11]

Can we tally this with the many later accounts that paint Jerome as a beautiful, androgynous child? Pederasty was common among samurai of the period, although drifting slowly out of fashion by the seventeenth century. It was a subject of great annoyance to the missionaries, and had been cited by both Francis Xavier and Alessandro Valignano as a major problem among both monks and warriors in Japan. But according to the Jesuits, denying homosexuality was a fundamental part of one's Christian conversion – Peter Masuda cannot have possibly entertained the idea that a post of *kozōritori*, a smart career move for many other young retainers, was acceptable to his Christian son.

If there is any truth in the story, then it goes some way towards explaining what happens next. At the beginning of his teens, Jerome the angelic young pageboy was suddenly hustled off the mainland and away to the Amakusa islands. Was his father squirrelling him out of harm's way, before a lecherous lord of the manor could get his hands on him?

Sources also differ as to Jerome's precise whereabouts in the years that follow. He seems to have travelled with his father, sometimes along the Amakusa islands, sometimes in Nagasaki itself. Jerome may have even provided a handy cover for his father's wanderings, making occasional approved trips to Nagasaki for 'study', at which his father may have played the role of chaperone. In fact, Peter was preaching the Christian Gospel, or conducting underground services for the Christians who were already in hiding, everywhere from Nagasaki to Ōyano. Jerome was baptised, possibly for the second time, in Nagasaki, where he also may have spent some time learning calligraphy, or the trade of an apothecary, or both. Links are made between Jerome and the Chinese community in Nagasaki – his apothecary mentor may have been a Chinese herbalist – and with the healing waters of Unzen, by now a site of pilgrimage not only for those in search of medicinal cure, but also for undercover pilgrims searching out the location of famous martyrdoms from bygone years.

There is only one story surviving from the period when Jerome was supposedly in Nagasaki, and that is very dubious. According to a man of Chinese ancestry called Iquan, who lived in Nagasaki in the early 1630s, he was present at a party in the town's Hamamachi district where a young Jerome was working as a server. One of the Chinese guests fancied himself as something of a face-reader, and suddenly began staring very intently at Jerome, and asking him who his father was. The guest then remarked that Japan was a truly strange place, if a 'superior being' was forced to work as a mere waiter for Chinese visitors. 'He could be the leader of the country,' commented the guest, 'but his luck will expire early so his dream will not come true.'[12]

There are elements of wizardry, alchemy or, at the very least, conjuring tricks in the stories of Jerome's youth. No sympathetic account survives of the nature of the sermons preached by Peter Masuda, but parts of them would seem familiar. Peter told stories from the Bible, and hectored the crowd with admonitions about the nature of sin and the glorious afterlife that awaited true believers. Jerome would also speak, showing off his knowledge of the same stories. There are garbled reports that allude to his hypnotic presence, and also to a bizarre scene in which he would call down a bird to perch on his finger. He would fix the bird with his mesmeric stare, and the bird would lay an egg on his palm, before flitting off screeching: 'Zuisō! Zuisō! Zuisō!' ('Good omen'). To the great delight of his audience, Jerome would crack open the egg, to reveal inside a rolled up Christian 'sutra' – presumably a Bible quote. A similar trick, apparently with a different bird, involved Jerome's stare holding the attention of a sparrow, such that the bird would not fly away, even when Jerome shook its bamboo perch.

More importantly, Jerome was a young blood-and-thunder preacher, who was able to exert a similar hypnotic presence on a crowd of onlookers. We have no record of what it was that he said when he spoke about the Christian faith, but he is recorded as giving twice-weekly sermons throughout the Rebellion, to rapt audiences.

Both Jerome's mother Martha and 'uncle' Jibei, in what seem to have been separate statements obtained under interrogation, suggested that Jerome suffered from a skin disease. Jibei called it *hizenkasa* – scabies. Martha called it *kogasa* – which is a more problematic term. It literally means 'the little boils' or 'the small pox' (not smallpox), but can also mean syphilis.[13] The disease was used as an excuse for Jerome's absence from his authorised place of residence. Supposedly, he fell ill on the Amakusa archipelago while travelling with Peter, and was consequently quarantined and unable to return to his home village when he was originally supposed to. The story may have been a fabrication to keep the government off his trail – Martha may have hoped to imply that he had leprosy, which would have discouraged the authorities from approaching too close. Certainly, there is no mention of any signs of illness in the most reliable and thorough description of Jerome, from an eyewitness to his arrival at Mogine beach.

For anyone in search of portents of doom, the mid-1630s provided plenty of opportunities. In the summer of 1635, an earthquake had struck the Shōgun's home base in Edo. Barely a month later, a savage typhoon in north Kyūshū left thousands homeless and wiped out the year's crops. In January, a downpour in Edo was so severe that it washed away some stone boundary walls at the Shōgun's palace. A fiery drought then set in until August, when torrential rainfall did even further damage.

Restrictions on the presence of foreigners, already in place for a generation, reached their height in 1636 with an edict of 'maritime restriction', in which the country was closed to outlanders, on pain of death. Only limited contact was permitted to licensed traders in the ports of Nagasaki and Hirado. Otherwise, all foreigners were excluded – in Nagasaki, the local magistrate personally exiled 276 newly illegal aliens on a boat to Macao, including his own Chinese wife and child.

In January 1637, officials were so worried by a solar eclipse that the Emperor did not perform the traditional New Year sacrifices to the gods. Nor did he throw the traditional New Year's banquet for his officials, although this may have had more to do with the impecunious circumstances of the imperial family at the time. A 'fireball' flew across the sky in May, and yet more heavy rains, along with yet another earthquake, which hit Edo in July.

Understandably, the Shōgun took to his sickbed, from where he issued a series of proclamations aimed at hunting down scapegoats. *Someone*, surely, was responsible for all the bad luck the Japanese were having. He could not blame foreigners any more, and so the target turned to the dishonest, the disobedient and the just plain unlucky. While he fretted over his misdeeds, the great crater of Mount Aso in south-west Japan added to his troubles with a spectacular eruption. Mount Kōya, one of the holiest sites for Japanese Buddhists, 'caught fire' in September. Later in the month, the sky itself was aflame.

Unknown to the Japanese, their adverse weather conditions were a worldwide phenomenon. Violent storms in Central Asian deserts had thrown tonnes of dust into the atmosphere, which would cause spectacular red-orange dawns and sunsets for the remainder of the year. In some places, the particles of desert sand fell back to earth as red rain.[14] Modern historians with better access to climate data recognise the period after 1629 as a decade of severe cold and drought in

East Asia, and 1637 as the beginning of the Chongzhen Slough, the last and most drastic weather crisis in the 'Little Ice Age', recorded in Chinese annals as a time of 'cold, drought, famine, locusts, earthquakes, epidemics, sandstorms and dragons.'[15]

The red skies were a cause of mystery all over Japan, except among the Christian believers of the Shimabara region, where they were taken as a sign of approaching Armageddon. A song became popular among the Shimabara peasants, seemingly originating in an old harvest work-gang chant, adapted to contain an apocalyptic edge.

> Gather in the month of mists
> Die with the rise of spring.[16]

For old soldiers like the Gang of Five, the time was approaching for the Last Battle. They circulated their *Mirror of the Future* prophecy among their associates, supplying the story that it had been left behind by a Jesuit fleeing Japan during the purges of 1614. It is at this point that the *Mirror* enters the historical record – despite purportedly having been in existence for more than twenty years, it is not mentioned before 1637. It is not impossible that it had been lurking in the Christian communities for a whole generation, but suspicious indeed that it should only find an audience as a group of old soldiers plot a revolt.

Among a people already hard-hit by taxes and adverse conditions, some interpreted the furious elements as literal proof of the anger of Deus. With the Christian foreigners expelled from the country, their supreme deity was now thought to be visiting his wrath on Japan itself. The time was right for the peasantry to rise up in revolt, some in a protest against their treatment by officials, and others with stranger, more religious aims to do with their belief that the end of the world was nigh. The result was a two-centred rebellion in the Amakusa and Shimabara areas, incorporating multiple motivations, and reaching unexpected heights before the government forces were able to react.

The bare facts of the earliest incidents are garbled. Two villagers, Kakuzo, the younger brother of a local headman, and Sankichi, a farmer, were sometime Christian believers, who had reportedly seen some of Jerome Amakusa's miracles in person. Back home in their village, they were reported to have held a religious ceremony at a house in Arima. The 'ceremony', such as it was, involved the veneration of a banned Christian image, thought to have been a painting of a Bible character or scene.

When news reached local magistrates, the Shimabara castellan sent a boat on the short journey down the coast, where sixteen local suspects (the two men and their immediate families) were rounded up, taken back to Shimabara and executed.

The arrests, however, met with opposition from the remaining locals. One of two law enforcers was lynched, and the other only escaped by the skin of his teeth – fleeing across the mountain pass to Unzen, according to one report, or escaping by boat to Shimabara.

Extant documents from Shimabara Castle offer a slightly different nexus for the trouble, not in Arima but slightly to the south, in the village of Kuchinotsu: 'There was a man in Kuchinotsu who hung a portrait and chanted to it. When the magistrate Hayashi Heizō tore the portrait up, the men killed him on the spot.'[17]

Among the Christians, the tale soon gained a magical, miraculous element. According to the interrogation of Jerome's cousin Kozaemon:

In Hinoe [near Kuchinotsu] in Shimabara, there was an old portrait, the bottom of which was worn out. I was thinking about mounting it but left it as it was. Around 25th November, we found it in a new mount although nobody had touched it. When they heard about it, neighbours were astonished and gathered to worship it. It was a miracle. Moreover, the local man Beyato Gasaharu told a very mysterious story. So the local magistrate arrested the man. That was why the Christians rose up.[18]

Already the story is confused, a simple act of redecoration imparted with religious significance. Beyato Gasaharu is not one man but two – sloppy transcriptions of the Christian names of Kakuzo the younger brother (Piato) and Sankichi the farmer (Gaspar). The precise nature of the 'mysterious' story, probably a sermon or Bible tale, has not been recorded by an uncomprehending interrogator. Nor were the interrogators or their victim particularly interested in the precise date. Although the events about which Kozaemon is being questioned seem to have happened in September, other local records appear to refer to an altercation that took place significantly earlier in the year, when local Christians illegally flew white banners to mark Ascension Day.[19]

Other reports pointed to Christianity mixed in with more pressing local concerns. These 'old farmers', whose resistance sounded at first so risible to the government, were men in their fifties and sixties, who had fought in Korea and at the Battle of Sekigahara, settled down afterwards and turned to farming under the new peace. The tension between them and officialdom was not merely financial – they had been loyal retainers of the dispossessed Lord Arima, and remained surly and untrusting towards his replacement.

A report sent to the Shōgun from Shimabara Castle noted that residents had been openly protesting at the demands made on them to deliver their tithes of rice to their local lord. The tone of the report implies that such protests were not unusual, and that the local people were expected to calm down and formally apologise once an impartial official had arrived from the government, assessed their ability to pay and (presumably) reduced the amount of their payment.[20]

Instead, 'scattered local reports' identified a young man who spoke 'strange teachings' to the crowd. The youth was supposedly told to stop. We may infer that the magistrates attempted to arrest him, leading to the next reported event, the outbreak of a riot. The same story occurred in another village, although the report from there also makes the unsupported claim that the boy preacher was soon executed to put a stop to the unrest.

Possibly, Young Matsukura was deliberately overemphasising the role of Christianity in local unrest in order to extricate himself from other difficulties. A few grumbling peasants, associated with a banned religion and with a leader who was reportedly dead before the news could reach the Shōgun, might have presented a useful alibi – a 'closed case' not worth the effort of a proper audit. The reports, as they have survived, identify Christian troublemakers, but also suggest that the problem had been summarily dealt with in November 1637 – nothing for the Shōgun to worry about.

Young Matsukura's officers might have also played up the significance of Christianity to avoid accusations of mismanagement. A local report preferred to blame an overenthusiastic official, Tanaka Soho, determined to punish any tax defaulters before the harvest season was done. His victim was Yōzaemon, a farmer in Kuchinotsu who had failed to pay up a paltry 30 bags of rice. Although described with reason in many sources as a 'poor' farmer, Yōzaemon was actually the wealthiest landowner in the Kuchinotsu area – persecutions aimed at him would have been intended to bring the rest of the community into line. His failure to pay suggests that nobody else could either, and that the farmers were truly at rock bottom.[21]

The official refused to grant an extension, instead taking Yōzaemon's heavily pregnant daughter-in-law and locking her in a 'water jail' – a cage partly submerged in a stream. Yōzaemon begged for a man to be allowed to take her place, but Tanaka told him that the woman would only be free when the 30 bags of rice were forthcoming. The woman endured the wet, miserable, sleepless torture of the water jail for six days and nights, until she went into labour and died.[22]

The death was a step too far – for Yōzaemon, it was also the murder of his unborn grandchild. For him, it was not merely a tragedy, but the likely end of his family line – there was now no future for him. He appealed to his fellow farmers for aid, and some seventy of them, presumably also fellow veterans of military service in the Battle of Sekigahara, swore to help him.

The Yōzaemon story also draws direct connections between Kuchinotsu, the site of the initial problems, and Amakusa, where a second revolt broke out. The father of the pregnant woman whose death triggered the incident was a resident in Amakusa across the water. He, too, had just lost a grandchild, and was ready to drag his own Amakusa neighbours into a similar mission of vengeance. A similar story appears to survive in this French account, derived from a contemporary missionary chronicle:

> One final act of savagery would ignite the gunpowder. In order to escape the pursuit of the bailiffs, one village head-man took refuge in the mountains: immediately, his daughter was arrested and exposed nude in public, and her body was burned with hot brands. The father, informed of this barbar-ous treatment, ran to his village, hastily assembled his friends, and attacked the residence of the tax collector, killing all that came into his hands.[23]

The meagre harvest was over; there were a lot of people at a loose end. The bereaved grandfathers might have been set on a suicide mission, and, it is implied, some of their old army comrades might have been ready for similarly drastic consequences themselves. A force ten times greater than the original number, now estimated at some 700 attackers, descended on the house of Tanaka Soho late in November. They may have intended to make his death look like an accident – the house was set alight, but Tanaka evaded his pursuers and sought refuge in nearby Shimabara Castle.[24]

In the early stages, the attacks seemed spontaneous. But before long, officials of the Matsukura regime were attacked in almost every village in the Shimabara Peninsula. Young Matsukura was away in

Edo, and had left Shimabara under the charge of his subordinate Okamoto Shinbei, who took his time responding.

Duarte Correa, a Portuguese missionary, had been apprehended as an illegal alien and was awaiting execution in Ōmura. In a letter to a fellow Jesuit in Macao, he reported seeing the rebels on the road to Shimabara, and heard reports of the violence outside from both his captors and passers-by. All in Correa's circle seemed convinced that the unrest had been caused by tax collectors, and that 'the rebellion could not be due to the rebels being Christians, since in times when there were many such, including famous captains, they had never rebelled.'[25] Correa's account cited several other incidents of cruelty, including a pregnant woman 'thrown into a frozen pond', perhaps another reference to Yōzaemon's daughter-in-law. But Correa cited yet another catalyst, when the 'only daughter of a village headman was stripped naked and branded with a rod of red-hot iron. The father could not stand the atrocity dealt out to his daughter and jumped at the official. Other farmers came to his aid, and the official was slain.'[26]

In Hirado, the Dutch merchant Nicholas Couckebacker agreed that Young Matsukura was the real problem. At the time of the outbreak of the Rebellion, Couckebacker noted that the villagers of the Shimbara Peninsula had literally nothing left to lose:

The people endured the ill treatment of [Old Matsukura] as long as he was present amongst them, but as his son, [Young Matsukura] . . . feels also inclined to follow in the footsteps of his father, and forces the farmers to pay far more taxes than they are able to do, in such a manner that they languish from hunger, taking only some roots and vegetables for nourishment, the people resolved not to bear any longer the vexations, and to die one single death instead of the many slow deaths to which they were subjected. Some of the principal amongst them have killed with their own hands their wives and children, in order not to view any longer the disdain and infamy to which their relatives were subjected.[27]

But it is unfair to dismiss accusations of Christian sympathies out of hand. According to one of the few survivors of the rebellion, the Gang of Five had been plotting revolution for several months. Taxation and persecution, it was hoped, would unite the people of the Shimabara region. According to the enemies of the Christians, at least, the atrocities were not a catalyst but a timely excuse.[28]

At some point, the villagers and farmers of the Shimabara and Amakusa communities agreed to pool their resources for revolt. By the time the armed peasants had reached Shimabara Castle, local reports identified Jerome, a boy from the neighbouring domain, as the ringleader, a messenger 'sent down from Heaven' as a last-chance herald to remind former Christians of the true faith they had renounced. The report mixed Buddhist terminology with secular facts, claiming that the Sacred Land was angry with apostate Christians, using the word *Tenjiku* – literally the 'sacred land' of Buddha, i.e. India. This appears to be a distorted reference to the Indian base of the Jesuits in Goa, but it is impossible to tell whether this confusion was that of the government observers, or of the fanatics they were observing. Certainly, Jerome's followers were described as the members of an apocalyptic cult:

> Then fire was seen on the sea and a cross appeared, and all paid homage to it along the shore. This uprising was plotted from last year, and they said they would not cultivate wheat and everyone would die soon. Therefore, when they attacked the castle, they just wanted to die and attacked without sparing their lives.[29]

A surviving note from the rebels themselves, calling sympathisers in the region to arms, shows that the government accounts were not wrong:

Attention. The heavenly man has descended to Earth, and Deus will subject heathens to a judgement in flame. In the meantime, any Christians must come here at once. Village headmen and leaders, please come here at once. Please circulate this document all along the islands. Even a heathen monk will be forgiven if he converts to Christianity. The man called Amakusa Shirō [Jerome] is a man of Heaven. He is the Chosen One, sent to be our leader. Anyone in Japan who refuses to become a Christian will be kicked down into hell by the left foot of Deus. Be aware.

P.S. Please come at once. Such is our request. That is all.[30]

With what appears to have been at least five separate interest groups among the rebels – vengeful veterans, angry farmers, oppressed Christians, apostates intimidated into rejoining the faith, and unlucky outsiders dragged along – the ringleaders seemed unable to decide upon an overall leader. Jerome himself, the closest thing to a local celebrity, may have been chosen as a compromise solution, partly because of his magical reputation, partly because the ringleaders may have hoped to control him, and possibly because those raised on Portuguese legends hoped to recreate a myth from the far west – that of the legendary boy-king Sebastian.

Something was going on at Parley Island, a small, sparsely inhabited rock midway across the ten-mile strait between Shimabara and Amakusa. Later legends would claim that Jerome had walked there himself across the choppy winter waters.[31] Instead, it is more likely that he was present at a secret meeting of Christians and veterans. The spectacular story of the uprising has obscured what might have been lesser deceptions in the days before it. Perhaps Parley Island was not originally a place of conspiracy, but a handily remote spot where fishermen could hold Christian services from a vantage point that permitted a 360-degree view of all approaches.

Notably, popular myths between Shimabara and Amakusa disagree over the identity of the ringleaders. People on both sides regarded the chief instigators as a Gang of Five, all veterans of the old wars who once served under the defeated general Augustin Konishi. The number is misleadingly exact – there could equally have been a Gang of Six, or Seven or more. There were certainly a number of old Sekigahara veterans among the farmers, and the precise number has never been determined. Suffice to say, something like half a dozen former company commanders were regarded as the main instigators of the Rebellion, at least until the day at Parley Island that they all agreed that they would swear allegiance to a higher, heavenly appointed power, Jerome Amakusa.

On the Amakusa side of the strait, the five men said to have been present at Parley Island, and to have agreed on Jerome as a compromise candidate for their leader, were: Oye Matsuemon, Chizuka Zanzaemon, Oye Genemon, Mori Soiken and Yama Zenzaimon. The names, however, have an element of the fairy tale about them. While many Japanese names are prosaic in nature, it is suspicious that this important group should have names whose meanings amount to So-and-so from the Great River, So-and-so from the Forest, and So-and-so from the Mountains, almost as if a narrative pattern is being imposed on them.[32]

Meanwhile, on the Shimabara Peninsula itself, ethnographers in the twentieth century observed a curious phrase that would close every local folktale:

Tsukaru of Koruba, Churen of Amiba, Hikoren of Enoura, Tokichi of Chijiwa and Naokichi of Ono Island.[33]

When asked to explain the sentence, locals replied that it listed the five village headmen of the prominent locations along Chijiwa beach, who had assembled in the Obama hot springs, *not* Parley Island, to plot their revolt. Reciting the phrase had entered Shimabara lore as a means of announcing that, essentially, 'all are now present and the end is nigh.' But no historian has been able to identify any of the named headmen from contemporary records, or even determine some of the places mentioned. Ono Island, for example, does not show up on any maps of the area, nor could any of the researchers' interviewees point them at it. It was believed that even if the five names had once been genuine, centuries of word-of-mouth and nursery-rhyme repetition had altered them beyond recognition.

There was, however, one person among the old soldiers who *can* be identified. His name was Yamada Emonsaku, and at the time of the Rebellion he was in his late fifties or early sixties. Born, like Peter Masuda, sometime around 1580, Yamada had been an impressionable child when the four triumphant Japanese youths returned from Valignano's European mission, brimming with stories of riches, legend and magic, the boy-king Sebastian and the magical Veil of Veronica. Yamada was one of the next generation of young boys inducted into Valignano's seminary on the Shimabara peninsula. He may even have been one of the naughty students Valignano caught in the unlikely midnight grammar session. He learned how to read Roman letters, in order to access Valignano's Japanese books printed with foreign type, but Yamada also appears to have gone further, learning Latin as well. Although he never became a full-fledged priest, he reached a high enough level of education, both general and religious, to become one of the lay preachers drafted in to help the Jesuits deal with the generation of instant Christians brought about by the mass conversions in the Nagasaki region.

But if Yamada had a true vocation, it would be elsewhere. Although he appears to have been too young to fight in the Korean campaigns, he was fit to wield a sword at the battle of Sekigahara, and also at the final siege of Ōsaka Castle. In the aftermath, with the execution of Augustin Konishi and the dispersal of the old Christian soldiers, Yamada had returned to the Shimabara Peninsula, and taken up a new trade, as a sign painter in Kuchinotsu.[34]

Yamada's involvement in the Rebellion, and indeed the life that brought him there in the first place, only became known in the years after the Rebellion's end. He had a rare talent for drawing in the style of the 'Southern Barbarians', and may have been responsible for much of the locally produced Christian iconography. Considering his artistic abilities and his place of residence, he may even have been at the very centre of the controversy over the Christian icon that led to the first skirmishes of the uprising. Famously, he is often supposed to have been the designer and artist of Jerome Amakusa's battle flag.

On 9 December, a secret conference was held on Parley Island. The Amakusa Christian conspirators agreed that they would begin their Rebellion in earnest. Representatives would gather in each town on the archipelago and proclaim their faith openly. They would set fire to Buddhist temples and Shintō shrines at dawn, creating a series of bonfires to demonstrate to their allies in Shimabara that the Rebellion was under way. In a nod to a famous moment in the Bible, it was agreed that the first signal would come from the eastern end of the Amakusa islands. On the morning of 12 December 1637, a certain temple in Ōyano would be set on fire 'when the cock has crowed three times.'[35]

CHAPTER FIVE

The Farmers' Affray

···············

Modern buildings obscure the magnificence of Shimabara Castle. As the train approaches, I only catch glimpses of its towers between the anonymous boxes of karaoke bars and supermarkets. Instead, Shimabara remains dominated by the mountains that sit behind it. Unzen is barely visible, largely hidden in the mists, but there are other peaks closer at hand.

Look east from Shimabara, and there is the Ariake Sea, stretching out towards Kumamoto. Look west, and there are three ridges on the road up to Unzen itself, each higher than the other, giving the impression of a profile like an Easter Island statue. The beak-like nose is Tengu Mountain, named for the crow-demons of old. The peak that looks to me like a prominent brow has a name that shows the people of Jerome's time agreed – Eyebrow Mountain. Above them both is Seven Faces Peak, forming the hairline.

There is a short walk to Shimabara Castle from the modern railway station, not because the shoreline has been expanded outwards, but because the castle was designed by architects wary of naval bombardment. But the castle's prime location strikes the visitor even before he has left the station concourse. Two steps outside the exit and you stumble upon a course of clear, cool water. It rushes down from the castle ground. Even as you walk through the streets, you can hear the streams gushing beneath your feet. Modern drains cover it up, but it is still there, a network of fresh water that cascades from the hills and the castle down towards the sea. To this day, it is teeming with large, lazy carp. Shimabara Castle was not a place that expected to run low on water supplies in times of trouble.

Shimabara Castle was restored to a semblance of its former glory in the 1960s.[1] The towers sit proudly above the moat, while a decorative motif along the arrow and musket slits alternates between circle, square and triangle shapes, but this modern fort is barely half the size of the original. Today, Shimabara Castle has a deep moat, steep walls, and two inner enclosures, more than enough for any castle, but in the time of Jerome it had a further, outer enclosure within which most of the townsfolk made their homes. In the seventeenth century, Shimabara Castle *was* Shimabara town. The outermost citadel might have been barely possible to defend, its walls more of a statement than a truly defensible point, but it would have struck a proud aspect in its day. The myriad fields of the hinterland would suddenly give way to the strict, regular lines of the castle, for those born and raised on the peninsula probably the largest building they would ever see.

Today, with Tomioka, Hondo and Hara in ruins, it remains the most impressive fortress in the region, rivalled only by Kumamoto on the other side of the strait. From the top of the restored tower, there is a commanding view of the whole region this side of Unzen. The Amakusa islands are clearly visible across the bay, and the watchman of Shimabara Castle would have enjoyed a bird's-eye view of much of the farmland to the south. On a good day, he would have been able to look down on his domain, almost all the way to Hara and Kuchinotsu, and known that all was well.

On a bad day in 1637, he saw threatening bonfires burning all the way down the coast, and the distant sparks of similar fires on far Amakusa. He heard gunshots ringing out from among the trees, and heard the shouts of his fellow samurai, impossibly, inconceivably retreating, towards the castle.

The first that Okamoto Shinbei knew of it, a magistrate had been murdered in the south. Hayashi Heizō, he heard, had torn down a

Christian image, or attempted to stop a Christian meeting – the news wasn't all that clear. Whatever he had done, Hayashi had paid for it with his life. But Hayashi had been done in not by an individual, but by a raging mob. Nobody knew where: Arima, said some, while others said Kuchinotsu. Wherever Hayashi had died, the people that had killed him were making for the village of Fukae.

It was late in the day on 11 December, and Okamoto was prepared to treat the news seriously. He ordered a lockdown in Shimabara itself – a rabble of farmers posed no real threat to the castle, but Okamoto knew there were other ways to bring a castle down. His men dragged what supplies they could inside before they locked the inner and outer doors. Cunningly, they also rounded up as many Shimabara locals as they could, reasoning that they were sure to be relatives of the rebels, and were bound to prove useful as hostages.

Okamoto sent out a riot squad that seemed more than adequate to deal with awkward peasants: a cohort of 300 foot soldiers, accompanied by fifteen mounted samurai (perhaps 20% of the castle's full cavalry complement), and eighty musketeers. Okamoto planned on an element of surprise – his soldiers left the castle while it was still dark, marching for several hours to reach Fukae, the rebels' expected campsite, in time for an attack at dawn. As the sun rose behind the Amakusa islands on the other side of the bay, the samurai from Shimabara took their position at a defensible point on the coastal road.

The horsemen had direct orders – they were to kill every conspirator they could find. What with Christians, veterans and surly farmers in the peninsula, none of them were any good for the grand plan of the Matsukura clan, and they were all better off dead.

'This is an affray with farmers and will not amount to much,' commented one lieutenant. 'Just break through at once, and kill all without exception.'[2]

The unrest at Fukae had taken Okamoto by surprise, but his men were not the only group on the move in the small hours. Villagers from communities south of Fukae had also arrived with the dawn, and joined the original rebels.

Before the samurai were properly in their chosen positions they were surprised by a war cry that had not been heard for some years. It was, to the Japanese, a single word, that some might have remembered from altercations with the Spanish in years gone by. It was 'Santiago', the name of Saint James, patron saint of the Spanish Reconquest. It was also very, very loud – they were not facing a small group of farmers, but a thousand charging enemies. The rebels were dressed strangely, wearing the white clothes of Christian baptism, many with crosses shaved into their heads.[3]

The Matsukura musketeers took aim as best they could and fired a volley straight into the charging peasants. When the smoke cleared, some twenty villagers were dead or dying. The rest had dived for cover.

Had the rebels stayed on the beach and coastal road, they might have soon been cut down. But now they laid low in the undergrowth or sneaked slowly up on the Matsukura samurai through the trees by the roadside. The musketeers hastily reloaded, while the horsemen yelled encouragement to the foot soldiers, urging them to give chase.

But the 'farmers' were not running. Nor were they armed with humble pitchforks and shovels. Some of the veterans had retained muskets from their army days. Still more used muskets for hunting. Whereas the Matsukura samurai were relatively young men, without much military experience to speak of, this was not the first time that many of the rebels had fought an armed foe.

If Shimabara were a hotbed of forbidden beliefs, a location for smugglers and foreign preachers and a refuge for forbidden half-breeds, we might not be surprised that its people had disobeyed other laws. The Shōgunate had strongly encouraged the Japanese to give up their guns in the aftermath of the civil war. Foreign gun technology had been excluded along with foreigners themselves, and many of the weapons still in use were family heirlooms. For the Matsukura musketeers, they were carefully maintained tools, kept in the castle armoury and rarely used. For the rebels, they were weapons that they or their fathers had wielded at Sekigahara.

Several miles to the east, across the Ariake Sea in the quiet castle town of Kumamoto, an official from House Hosokawa thought he heard thunder in the distance. He looked up at the December sky, but there were no rain clouds. With mounting alarm, he realised that someone was firing guns in Shimabara.[4]

The fatalities on the rebel side mainly came during the initial attack, when the musketeers were able to discharge their weapons into an onrushing mass of farmers. We need not be surprised by the fact that there were casualties; the numbers presented imply that only one in four of the Matsukura musketeers were able to hit their mark. They would not get an opportunity to reload.

The rebels dropped out of sight, and took aim. From behind trees, rocks on the beach or simply hidden in the long grasses, the rebel sharpshooters chose their targets and let loose. The horsemen were the most obvious targets – five or six of them were shot from their mounts.

The soldiers tried to hold their position, but were sitting ducks in the face of the rebel onslaught. A hundred infantrymen were picked off before the soldiers began a hasty retreat, falling back along the Shimabara road, back towards the castle. As they ran, they had no time to look behind them or across the strait at the coasts of Amakusa. In the distant haze, beneath the eerily red morning sky, first one, then another, then another bonfire sprang to life. The temples of Amakusa were burning.

It was not the result that castellan Okamoto had been expecting. The fire and smoke from Amakusa was clearly visible from Shimabara Castle, as were similar signals across the south of the Shimabara Peninsula. By three o'clock in the afternoon, Okamoto could hear the sounds of gunfire and battle, impossibly getting ever louder, coming towards his castle. Before long, his soldiers appeared, lacking most of their cavalry accomplices, the infantry running as best they could, while the surviving musketeers tried to cover their retreat.

Okamoto still did not believe that his men could have been bested by such a small force. He initially ordered his remaining troops to make a stand *outside* the castle gate. It was only as wave after wave of new rebels arrived that he began to appreciate that his retreating men had not lied. Despite the deaths in the initial exchange at Fukae, the rebel forces now numbered some 1,500 – with, presumably, their numbers augmented by latecomers from the south, and by new rebels picked up along the road to Shimabara.[5]

The fighting at the castle gate was fierce, but the tables had turned once more in favour of the government – the musketeers were able to take more careful aim from the battlements and reload under cover, while the castle's surviving complement of sixty mounted horsemen presented a more formidable resistance.

Although some 200 rebels fell at the Shimabara Castle gate, Okamoto was forced to admit defeat. He ordered his men inside, and had the gate slammed shut. He took advantage of the chaos to send a messenger through the melee, hoping to get word to a neighbouring governor that Shimabara Castle was under siege.

With the defenders now locked inside the castle and, it is implied, out of ammunition, the rebels turned on the town of Shimabara itself. Top on their list of targets were two local Buddhist temples, which were ransacked and set aflame. The rebels also burned nearby houses, and terrorised the local population.

In the meantime the evil conspirators roamed at large and killed without reasons those who did not belong to their party; they plundered houses and usurped power over the surrounding country. As many had no love for the Christian sect, in order to escape death they joined it reluctantly, the number soon increasing to eight thousand men.[6]

Already the rebellion was assuming inner and outer circles – true believers at the head, while the lower ranks were more reluctant, forced to switch their allegiance from one set of bullies (the Matsukura samurai) to another (the rebels). Similar antagonisms were breaking out within the castle itself. As Okamoto frantically tried to maintain order, it became apparent that many of his lower-ranking infantry-men were relatives or even sympathisers with the rebels outside. Far from being motivated to stand their ground at the castle, many were attempting to sneak out of the castle, and taking prized muskets, armour and other treasures with them.

The rampage around Shimabara continued for several days, while the surviving soldiers looked on glumly from the castle. The rebels had actually managed to break through the outermost gate, but were still relatively poorly armed. They had no heavy weapons or siege engines, and did not even have armour – the lack of which had been cited in contemporary reports as accounting for most of their casualties in the initial skirmishes.

Meanwhile, over on the Amakusa islands, rebels were achiev-ing similar successes. Jerome's cousin Watanabe Kozaemon arrived before the Ōyano magistrate at the head of fifty fellow farmers. He boldly announced that they were returning to their former Christian ways, and that, consequently, they would like the magistrate to hand over the documents of renunciation they had been forced to sign against their will. But the Amakusa rebels seem to have had more difficulty massing into a full-fledged mob. Whereas the rebels on the Shimabara Peninsula could easily congregate and charge the local castle, the multiple straits of the Amakusa islands slowed the rebel advance. In some places, this left the rebels more vulnerable. A man arrived in Sumoto, seem-ingly alone, and told the villagers that the time of Deus had come. Armageddon was nigh, and all those who knew what was good for them should cast aside the false faith of Buddhism and allow Christ into their hearts. He kept up his rant until his one-man revolt was put to a swift end when the Sumoto magistrate drew his sword and killed him.[7]

The conspirators do not seem to have been able to decide on their next course of action. One of the Gang of Five, sure that reinforcements would soon arrive for a counter-attack, counselled going down in a blaze of glory:

The ... lords of this castle are now in Edo, and there is exceeding small force in it. And more, those who were driven back from Fukae, being possessed by the spirit of cowardice, can make no defence. Come, let us capture this castle and make it ours, and spend a few days in it in tranquillity. And since there are many of our sect in the West, we will not want help. Having committed ourselves to the cause thus, there is no way of escape left. Since, do what we may, our lives are forfeited, let us fight outright; let us make a pillow of this castle.[8]

In another meeting on Parley Island, Jerome was advised to flee by some locals, and urged by others to come to Shimabara as the leader of the rebels.[9] When consulted at that time, Jerome – more likely his council of 'advisers' – favoured a march on Nagasaki at the head of an army that had now swelled to some 12,000 men, and seizing the strategic Himi and Mogi passes. This would have been little help against a long-term counter-attack, but it would serve to cut off Nagasaki from any land-based reinforcements. Nagasaki was indefensible from the land side, and control of the passes would have been a major bargaining tool in securing the town's surrender, and, perhaps, access to the foreigners and foreign shipping in the harbour.[10]

However, the people on the passes to Nagasaki were notoriously fair-weather friends to Christianity, liable to be swayed by whoever had the greatest physical presence. The official responsible for administration of the villages in the passes, Sano Sozaemon, had been in Shimabara at the time of the first rebel attack, and had wasted no time in fleeing back to his own jurisdiction.

Sano is credited with stopping the northward advance of the Rebellion – despite what must have been intense pressure to join the rebels, he kept a cool head and demonstrated incredible leadership skills. Posterity favours the underdog and the excitement of Jerome's revolt, but Sano's opposition to the rebels is no less dramatic. The area around Mogi, like Shimabara itself, had once been an area of Christian sympathisers. Regardless of actual sympathies in the area, village headmen might be forced to think pragmatically – who was going to reach them first, Matsukura samurai or rebel fanatics? Sano discovered that one local village headman had already decided which way the wind was blowing, dispatching a messenger south to pay his respects to Jerome and to ask him for a holy icon.

It was just as Sano had feared – despite their earlier claims of apostasy, there were plenty of people in the area around the passes who would switch to the rebel cause at a moment's notice. It did not matter to Sano if it was out of heartfelt belief, like Jerome's immediate circle, or fear for their lives, like the residents near Shimabara Castle – the result would be the same unless he moved fast.[11]

The Mogi headman had sent his own son to meet with Jerome. Unable to bring this up without risking getting lynched himself, Sano simply pretended not to know. He called a meeting with the headman, informed him of the troubles in Shimabara, and let him know that the people of the passes would be sending some supplies to the men besieged in Shimabara Castle. Sano was sure, he said, that this would all blow over soon enough. He knew that if he had been able to make it back to Mogi alive himself, then messengers were also already heading back east to inform the government of the troubles. Reinforcements would soon be on their way, and Christian sympathisers were sure to be killed.

Sano's confidence won the locals over. No mention was made of their earlier decision to support the rebels. Instead, they agreed to send a messenger to Shimabara to advise the besieged samurai that help was on its way. But Sano's troubles were not done. His enthusiasm and influence had a half-life that diminished with every step his messenger took towards the uprising. Ten miles out of Mogi, the messenger began to doubt Sano's plan. At Chijiwa beach, the messenger ran into another village headman, who proclaimed that his own people were already declaring their support for the rebels, and if the people of Mogi knew what was good for them, they would too. Whether through conviction or fear, the messenger was persuaded to turn back.

Sano knew that something was up when the messenger returned far too soon. Instead, the messenger bore a letter from the headman at Chijiwa, informing him it was not too late for him to join the uprising. Sano wisely decided to keep the letter secret from his underlings, but must have already felt decidedly outnumbered in his own domain.

By this point, news of the revolt had reached the next village. Five Matsukura men arrived at Himi, just down the coast from Mogi, hoping to get a boat to transport them to Shimabara. No boats were available – a likely sign that many of the Himi villagers had already sailed for Shimabara to join the rebels. Sano agreed to get a boat for them, but when he returned from finding one, he found Mogi all but deserted.

The only man he could find was the Shintō priest at the local temple, an old friend, who informed him that all the villagers, including the headman whose loyalty Sano had been right to doubt, had packed up their belongings and fled for a mountain refuge. The headman's son had returned with the much-discussed holy object, some sort of Christian image blessed by Jerome himself, and the villagers were now 'chanting and patting their chests,' and plotting to kill Sano.[12]

Even this news did not deter Sano, who lay in wait near the supposedly abandoned house of the Mogi headman. Sure enough, he did not have to lurk long before the boss arrived with his son to grab some forgotten possession – the villagers were hiding in the mountains to avoid trouble, but were still within fetching distance of their homes. Sano made his move, confronted the untrustworthy villager, and snatched his son.

In one of the forgotten adventures of the Shimabara uprising, Sano took his hostage and the five Matsukura men, and sailed for the peninsula. He somehow made it across the Unzen passes to Shimabara itself, now a smoking ruin, with the troops in the castle still glumly waiting for help to arrive. Sano fought his way in with his improbable cargo, and then, quite incredibly, sent a messenger out again. A couple of days later, the messenger reached Mogi, and informed the recalcitrant headman that he was to send 200 *koku* of rice to Shimabara castle immediately, or his son would be executed. He presumably did so bearing some token that proved not only that Sano was inside the castle, but also that the castle was still standing, and that if he knew what was good for him, he would remember who was supposed to be in charge. The Mogi headman obliged, and his enforced compliance ensured that the villagers of mountain passes to Nagasaki remained at least nominally Matsukura supporters. When the rice arrived, it was both a vital boost in morale to the men in Shimabara, and a warning sign to the rebels that more help was on its way. It would be a contributing factor to the rebels' later decision to withdraw to Hara Castle, and hence one of the crucial turning points in the defeat of the uprising.[13]

Although some reports were retroactively dated to refer to Jerome earlier, the first time he was mentioned in government despatches was 14 December. An account written in Shimabara Castle on that day makes no mention of persecutions, bad harvests or atrocities, and instead paints the Rebellion as a doomsday cult:

According to a 16- or 17-year old man called [Jerome] who has descended from Heaven, the souls of the dead have been restless because so many Christians have converted recently [to Buddhism]. In its wrath, the Sacred Land visits misfortunes upon the world. However, its messenger has come to the world to rescue the Christians, although unbelievers shall not be saved.[14]

The fate awaiting those who did not join the rebels had also been made clear to the samurai besieged in Shimabara Castle. 'The current situation is not possible by human power alone,' they were told by the rebels, 'and Japan has not seen its like before. Soon, fire will fall from the sky and burn everything down.'[15]

Meanwhile, supplies in Shimabara Castle were running low. Although the castle was not necessarily in a state of siege, its occupants appear to have been deeply reluctant to head outside the walls through a land infested with enemies. However, by mid-December, dwindling food supplies left them with little option. Castellan Okamoto knew that an auxiliary storehouse for the castle lay tantalisingly close at hand, just a mile up the coast at the village of Mie.[16]

On 17 December, he dispatched a raiding party to cross the short distance to Mie and retrieve some sacks of rice. Clearly expecting trouble, he sent fifteen horsemen, a hundred musketeers, and some 300 infantry – perhaps half the castle's remaining complement of soldiers. But Mie village was fully sympathetic to the rebels. The villagers had occupied the storehouse, and fired repeated musket barrages at the approaching Matsukura soldiers. With many killed and wounded, and facing superior numbers of muskets, the soldiers retreated back to Shimabara empty-handed.[17]

Across the strait in Amakusa, the conspirators seized upon the news of the insurrection. Jerome's sermon on the matter, at least as reported, demonstrates much the same careful manipulation of the facts as his enemy Young Matsukura. Jerome made no mention of any previous training that the farmers may have had, and carefully avoided any discussion of the rebels' superior numbers against a skeleton crew of samurai in Shimabara. Most notably, Jerome emphasises the sheer unlikelihood of victory. If the Christians have the upper hand, he said, then surely it must be the will of God?

> The Christians of Shimabara have united together and thrown away their lives for this doctrine. They await the attack of the forces of the Shōgun in order to gain their wishes after death. The taking up of arms against the government is . . . as if a child should try to measure out the great sea with a shell; or as if a beetle should lift up its foot to fight against a cartwheel. Still, when the soldiers of Matsukura . . . attacked them, contrary to expectation, the soldiers were beaten by the insurgents. For farmers to fight with soldiers and gain the victory is a thing unheard of in the past, and will be rare in the future. Now . . . this is not at all owing to the courage of the farmers, but altogether to the aid of Deus. If we do not go to their aid, it will be hard to escape the judgement of Heaven. And if we should altogether fail of victory, is it not yet the great desire of our sect to see Heaven after death?[18]

Notably, Jerome suggests that Young Matsukura has already been defeated, whereas the absent lord was actually at the head of the very same Shōgunal army that was racing towards Amakusa to avenge the early losses. Despite the inherent contradictions in the argument – no chance of victory whatsoever, certain death guaranteed – the prospect of Paradise was enough to sway the congregation.

The news of the uprising had spread fast. As early as 15 December, at Misumi, where the mainland met the Amakusa archipelago, watchmen reported scores of refugees fleeing the island chain. The watchmen's first thought was to notify Amakusa authorities that the peasantry were making unauthorised trips beyond the borders of their assigned districts, but as further boatloads arrived, hour by hour, it became clear that the refugees were genuinely in fear for their lives. They had weighed up the risks of breaking Shōgunate rules against the chances of dying at the hands of the rebels, and taken their chances with the government.

These farmers, all Buddhist or Shintō believers, gave first-hand accounts of the attacks by the Christian rebels, leading one retainer to write urgently to House Hosokawa in Kumamoto.

> Regarding the Christian uprising in Amakusa on Ōyano Island in which all the shrines and temples have been burnt. Such insolence towards the State should not be left unpunished. If your response is delayed, the rioters' power will grow daily. It is important that we flatten them immediately. If you could spare us just a hundred guns, Matazaemon Shima's unit [based in Misumi] could subjugate them, I believe. Please pardon my impertinence, but please let us help. I am telling you this, as Miyake Tobee [in Tomioka] ... could be in danger.[19]

It was a noble sentiment, but House Hosokawa's hands were tied. Misumi was not merely at the edge of the archipelago; it was also the edge of Hosokawa's domain. Although the peasants had shown remarkable bravery crossing the boundary – a sure sign of the genuine danger presented by the Rebellion – the samurai in Kumamoto were not prepared to take the same risk. No local lord could leave his domain without authorisation from the Shōgun himself. To do otherwise would be, effectively, to declare war on a neighbouring baron. House Hosokawa could not possibly take the word of a few peasants, or even a few hundred. The samurai were obliged to sit and wait for orders, while noting the increasingly frantic news from just across the border.

On that same day, 15 December, a priceless piece of intelligence landed right in House Hosokawa's lap. Not all the boats arriving from the archipelago contained refugees. One of them carried

Jerome's cousin Kozaemon, on a mission to retrieve his relatives from their mainland home before the authorities realised who they were.

As Kozaemon sneaked ashore at the small village of Konoura, coastguards apprehended him. Samurai also found the rest of Jerome's family hiding out in their home village. Jerome's mother Martha, sisters Regina and Marina, and other relatives all fell into government hands.[20]

The people on the mainland spent an uneasy night. Although they had captured several of Jerome's closest family members, they rightly suspected that their new acquisitions were valuable enough to provoke a rescue mission. Kozaemon had rowed ashore from a larger boat, which fled back to Ōyano when he failed to return.

Refugees continued to arrive on the mainland on the day of 16 December, among them several who dutifully reported that the Christians on Ōyano were stocking boats ready for a strike against Konoura before Jerome's relatives could be taken to Kumamoto.

In Konoura village, locals pressured the headman Hikōzaemon to flee, but he insisted on holding his ground. Refusing to believe the panicked reports from the refugees, he ordered his fellow villagers to prepare to resist an attack. Hikōzaemon was confident that he could hold off the Christians until such time as reinforcements arrived from Kumamoto – House Hosokawa would have no trouble sending samurai to back him up, as Konoura was within the Hosokawa domain. It would, however, take twenty-four hours for the message to get to Kumamoto and for the samurai to march or ride back. Hikōzaemon had a day to prepare to resist an attack from the sea, and a nervous night of waiting for a rebel assault.

The people of Konoura got to work. Assistance from the watchmen down the coast at Misumi amounted to just a couple of samurai, including a lieutenant who took nominal control of the defence. But it was Hikōzaemon, working with little more than a handful of musketeers and peasants, who marshalled the defenders to give the impression that far more troops were in position. It was an old trick, and one that the Christians were sure to be expecting, but every bonfire the Christians saw on the shoreline was another moment they might hesitate to put ashore. With Kumamoto reinforcements getting closer by the hour, every moment of delay was worth the trouble.

Hikōzaemon requisitioned every flammable object in the village, ordering men, women and children to stack bonfires every 150 metres along the clifftops. Down on the shoreline, they laid ropes and strips torn from discarded rice sacks, all soaked in saltpetre, ready to set off with similar fire-signs. Hikōzaemon's wife demonstrated a heretofore unknown knack for managing a smithy, casting 500 musket balls, and whisking the womenfolk into a frenzy of cooking. Vats of gruel were carried out to the workers on the cliffs and beach, and by evening, the work was done.

That night, fourteen rebel boats set sail from Ōyano, making straight for Konoura. It was their plan to put ashore without incident, and to scare Hikōzaemon with their superior numbers. Hoping to obtain his cooperation, willing or otherwise, they then planned a raid on the nearest town, both to liberate Jerome's relatives and to fan the flames of the Rebellion on the mainland.

But Hikōzaemon's bonfires were already burning on the cliffs in a line several miles long. The ships loitered off shore as the commanders debated whether it was a ruse or not. Unsure of troop movements on the mainland, they drifted closer to the coast for a better look. In response, Hikōzaemon's people began discharging muskets into the air. The majority of the gunners were untrained, and had no chance of hitting anything. But that was less important than the impression it gave – salvo after salvo, the sparks of gunfire all along the cliffs, with seemingly little concern given to wasting ammunition.

It was enough to unnerve the rescue party. The boats turned back to Ōyano, and the eastward expansion of the rebellion was halted at the edge of the archipelago, just as it had been halted to the north at the passes to Nagasaki.[21]

For the next few days, Hikōzaemon maintained his clifftop vigil, but the boats did not return. Soon enough, the fake watch fires were replaced by the genuine article, as House Hosokawa samurai assembled at the edge of their domain. Now they waited, for the day when the word would come from the Shōgun that a counter-attack was approved.

CHAPTER SIX

White Flags on the Sea

....

Of all the battlefield sites of the Shimabara Rebellion, Hondo has changed the most. Once there were broad, low mudflats stretching out for a mile, a place to dig for shellfish at low tide. Now, half a mile or so of reclaimed land forms the basis for much of modern Hondo city. The harbour is all new, the sea walls similarly so. The relics of the uprising in the Hondo Municipal Museum of History and Folklore are themselves sited on a place that has been wrested back from the sea.

At first, it is difficult for me to get my bearings. I know Hondo well from maps that are centuries old, but this is the first time I have been here. It takes me a while to mentally strip a kilometre of new ground away from the view, before I can work out where I actually am. Two stops past Mogine beach, a kindly bus driver lets me off at what was once Arrow Point, a bluff overlooking the town. Now it is one more anonymous Japanese suburb.

As I approach a modern bridge, a concrete span across sea walls that slice through where the mudflats used to be, I find a small white cross, emblazoned with a notice in Japanese. Here, right next to a beauty parlour, by the traffic lights, I am suddenly standing on the site of Jerome Amakusa's camp. Three hundred and seventy years ago, I would have been on the coastline. From here, it is barely twenty minutes' walk to the site of the Yasaka Shrine, where the rebels scored one of their most famous victories.

Like Shimabara, like Hara, like so many other places in Japan, the modern town is largely built on land that did not exist in Jerome's day. But a big hill dominates the skyline of

Hondo, as it did in 1637. Parts of it have been hacked and terraced to make space for Buddhist graveyards, but parts are still lush and green. This was where Hondo Castle once looked down upon the town.

Now the castle is a well-tended ruin, site of a museum and a park in memory of fallen martyrs. It is difficult to reach, only approachable by steep, hairpin turns on a small mountain road. It would seem that, back in 1637, when the local lord Miyake Tobee looked out of his mansion and saw the rebel campfires down below on the beach, he was worried that they would take one look at his steep approach roads and give his castle a miss.

Instead, hungry for glory and refusing to believe that a bunch of farmers could present a threat to disciplined, organised troops, Miyake and his retainers suited up, mounted their horses, and rode out to meet them. The trail up to the castle and the road out to the beach were one and the same. A third path led south, where those of Jerome's forces from the upper island who did not have boats would have to walk around the bay. The three groups converged on each other and met, inevitably, in the centre of town, at what was then the sole bridging point over the Machiyamaguchi river – literally 'the river where the town meets the mountain.'

Back then, the centre of town was the Yasaka Shrine, a poky little place at the crossroads. Today, the shrine is squeezed still further into a tiny gap between two houses, reached only by steep steps. It was once also home to the Tree of the Southern Barbarians, a towering hackberry said to offer divine protection from unwelcome foreign influences. The steps of the shrine lead straight to the Gion Bridge, an elegant stone span constructed in 1832 on the site of the former crossing – a wooden bridge smashed apart during what came to be known as the Battle of Hondo.[1]

Thanks to the pattern of response engendered by sending 'flying feet' messages to Edo and back, those barons closest to the uprising knew of it first, but received their marching orders last. Many, like House Hosokawa, made the best of the situation, reviewing their troops, preparing for action, and sending concerned letters to their fellow officials.

Tardy correspondence limped into Nagasaki, offering warnings that trouble might be afoot. Several days after it was sent on 26 December, a letter from concerned officials in Kumamoto reached the Nagasaki magistrate Suetsugu Heizō.

A man called [Peter] and his son [Jerome], who were living in Ebe village in Uto in our country, went to Amakusa in the middle of last month and apparently became Christians [*sic*]. We arranged to get them back but according to a report from Ōyano, they fled to Nagasaki. If they arrive in your domain, please apprehend them. We are sending two men who know their faces. Please understand the situation and if they visit your land, please arrest them at once. This is because [Peter's] relatives are living in the town of Nagasaki, we are sending you further details about them. We have sent two men who know [Peter's] face to Mogi, too. If [our agents] are held and questioned, please let your men know that they should be treated kindly.[2]

The warning, little more than a Wanted poster for two undesirables, seems almost comically unaware that thousands of Christian rebels were already laying siege to Shimabara Castle and just about to march on Hondo. We might even suspect that House Hosokawa was taking advantage of the situation to cover itself or discredit rivals in Nagasaki. However, House Hosokawa had genuine concerns – its officials were warning Nagasaki not of two criminals on the run, but of two rebel leaders who might try to take Nagasaki in the same way they had taken Shimabara.

House Hosokawa still had spies and supporters on the Amakusa islands, and was actually rather well informed about the movements of Peter and Jerome – a trail that was only a couple of days old. Peter and Jerome had indeed left Ōyano with every intention of travelling to Nagasaki and inciting a further revolt in support of the uprising. However, by 27 December, they had stopped in their tracks and returned by way of Parley Island to Amakusa. Possibly, they had been warned that Nagasaki was completely locked down, and that law enforcement officials had not only been instructed to look out for them, but had also been supplied with agents who would recognise them on sight. If so, House Hosokawa's panicked communiqué, although it seems frivolous and futile in hindsight, may have been as important as Sano Sozaemon's heroic ride in shutting down the rebellion before it spread.

A second missive from House Hosokawa was sent by sea, in a swift boat that skirted the Amakusa islands, and headed straight for Tomioka Castle. However, choppy seas forced it to put in to shore as soon as Lower Amakusa Island was in sight. The two messengers, presumably the usual 'flying feet' of a runner and a lantern-bearer, left their boat and proceeded on foot towards Tomioka, but had their path blocked by a group of fifty armed locals, who were in the process of erecting a massive crucifix by the roadside.

One of the messengers realised that he knew one of the villagers, and asked politely to be allowed through, as he was carrying an important letter for Miyake Tobee, the castellan of Tomioka. Miyake's name alone should have been enough to clear a path, for he was a 3,000-*koku* samurai, who had been an administrator on the island for almost a decade. But instead of acquiescing, the rebellious locals commented that Miyake's time was over, and that now it was 'the time of Deus':

We cannot let you pass. Have you not heard of the troubles in Shimabara? We will spare your lives, but you must go back immediately. If your boat remains [on the beach], we will come at you from all sides, and will kill you.[3]

The House Hosokawa messengers did as they were told and their warning never reached its destination.

Through an accident of boundary lines, the only clan authorised to intercede in the Amakusa islands without direct government approval was House Terazawa. Amakusa was technically part of the Terazawa domain, and Lord Terazawa, a man with a rank roughly equivalent to that of a European count, easily outranked the more baronial authority of the likes of Miyake in Tomioka, or Young Matsukura in Shimabara. House Terazawa was entirely within its right to send troops to help its subordinates on the archipelago. However, House Terazawa's troops were quartered in Karatsu, a sea port two days' sail past Hirado, ludicrously far from the source of the unrest. They set out anyway, in a flotilla of thirty-seven troop barges and cargo boats, and were seen passing Hirado on Christmas Day. Stormy weather made the journey difficult, but the Karatsu reinforcements limped steadily around the coastline, past Nagasaki and down towards Tomioka.

None of this, however, was known in Tomioka, where Miyake Tobee gave up waiting and decided to march out across Lower Amakusa Island to the small hill fortress of Hondo. Hondo Castle, such as it was, was a mansion atop a nearby hill, reached by a long, winding road that reached Hondo town and crossed the river at the little Yasaka Shrine. It lacked the size and defensive capabilities of other forts in the region, which may have persuaded its occupants to fight Jerome's forces before they reached the foothills and cut the defenders off from resupply.

Miyake's march across the island had another, subtler aim – it clearly demonstrated to the peasants in the surrounding villages, such as those who had just threatened the House Hosokawa messengers, that the government was in control of the situation, that steps were being taken to deal with the uprising, and that loyal citizens should not be tempted to join the rebel cause.

Soon after Miyake marched out, 1,500 men arrived at Tomioka in the flotilla sent by House Terazawa from Karatsu. It was decided to send a swift boat across the strait to Kumamoto, to tell House Hosokawa that security on Lower Amakusa Island was well covered. Miyake Tobee's forces were fresh and ready for a fight, and also kitted out for proper combat, whereas the farmers on Amakusa, it was said, were little more than a crowd of angry villagers with picks and hoes.

The message was premature. As the boat sliced through the rough waters of the Ariake Sea on the night of 28 December, its sailors noted they were not alone on the water, but crossing in the wakes of a veritable fleet of fishing boats, all making the short crossing from Shimabara to Upper Amakusa. The sailors counted between fifty and a hundred boats, each with a crucifix mounted at its prow, each loaded to the gunwales with men and weapons.

On Jerome's order, many of the rebels from Shimabara were abandoning the fruitless siege of Shimabara Castle, and instead rushing to the place where they could do the most good, fighting the next battle against Miyake's men. Many of the sharpshooters and veteran swordsmen who had wreaked such havoc in Shimabara were ferried in their own impromptu fleet to swell the ranks and augment the firepower of rebels on Amakusa. Contemporary chronicles estimated the number of redeployed rebels at between two and six thousand.[4]

This was, surely, information that would have been appreciated by Miyake and his men, but the crew of the messenger-boat doggedly clung to their original mission, and kept a steady course for Kumamoto. On arrival, the crew merrily informed House Hosokawa that everything was under control. Back in Hondo, Miyake had no clue how misplaced his confidence was.

On 29 December, Miyake sent a division of his men across to Upper Amakusa, hoping to crush the rebels in their camp at Shimago. He sent a group of cavalry and infantry numbering in the low hundreds, many of them young warriors from Karatsu, keen to test their swords on farmers. They rode out at dawn, and soon Miyake was satisfied to hear the sounds of gunfire. In the hills towards Shimago, he saw billows of smoke, and reasoned that his soldiers had found the rebel camp, and were busy demolishing it with extreme prejudice.

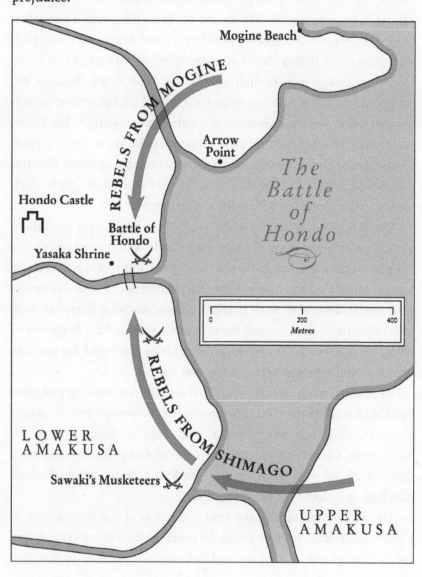

By ten in the morning, he realised his mistake. The small company of soldiers had been all but wiped out when it stumbled into literally thousands of rebels. The Christian forces waved a sea of white banners made of linen and paper, and hundreds of the rebels created an unearthly, keening wail in the air by blowing into seashells they had picked up on the beach. However, not even this haunting approach was enough to put off the young Karatsu samurai, who still believed they were dealing with little more than superstitious, misguided peasants. The Karatsu samurai drew their swords and charged headlong towards the churning, writhing mass of white banners.[5]

The Karatsu samurai seem to have been too proud, or too stupid, to run when the overwhelming odds became obvious. A pitiful handful of survivors made it back, many gravely wounded.

Instead of triumphant subordinates returning, Miyake saw the rebel fleet, carrying boatload after boatload of warriors across the shallow waters, and landing them at Mogine, on the Hondo side of the river. Soon, they were swarming down the shore to Arrow Point. But there were nowhere near enough boats to carry all the rebels.

Before long, a second group approached from the south-east. The rest of Jerome's forces were taking the long way around the bay by foot, marching slowly but surely across the narrow strait linking Upper Amakusa to Lower. At first, there was the eerie trumpeting of hundreds of seashells. Then, Miyake heard a single loud explosion – the simultaneous discharge of twenty samurai guns.

A group of fifty government troops, including twenty musketeers, had refused to believe the panicked reports of the retreating samurai. Their leader, Sawaki Hachirobei, took a stand on the Lower Amakusa side of the strait, with his men hiding in the bushes and trees. Sawaki had been ordered to fall back to the bridge at the Machiyamaguchi River, but had disobeyed orders in a typically Japanese way, by volunteering to hold the line and refusing to hear his commanding officer's countermand. Sawaki believed that Miyake had been unduly spooked, and that a disciplined stand would be sure to halt the rebel advance. He may have also hoped to use an element of stealth – with his men hidden in the scrub, the advancing rebels would have no idea how many guns were trained upon them.

'Let them be even so many as ten thousand,' scoffed Sawaki. 'Being mere farmers, they are not to be feared.'

Sawaki's bravado lasted for a single volley. His musketeers dropped a dozen of the foremost rebels, but were overwhelmed before they could reload. Some twenty of Sawaki's men, presumably the musketeers, were lost in the skirmish, and the rest fled, suddenly remembering that Miyake had told them to fall back.[6]

With rebels approaching both from Arrow Point and Upper Amakusa, Miyake realised that both groups would converge at the Machiyamaguchi River's sole bridging point – the wooden span in front of the Yasaka Shrine.

Miyake and his men picked their way down the long, winding hill road into town. By the time they reached the bridge, the rebels on foot had already got there. The river was perhaps some twenty metres wide at this point, flanked on either side by waist-high stone walls that provided infuriatingly sufficient cover for rebel musketeers. For Miyake, it was his first close-quarter sight of his enemy. There were more than a hundred gunners, largely comprising the veteran marksmen who had crossed over from Shimabara, as well as newcomers using weapons snatched from dead Karatsu samurai. But of the thousands of other rebels in Hondo, outnumbering the defenders ten-to-one, the majority still wielded garden implements and farm tools – rakes and pickaxes. A few had poles to which the swords of fallen samurai had been attached to make primitive spears – adding insult to injury. Behind them, stretching as far as Miyake could see, was the boiling mass of white banners and always, always, the howling of the seashells.

Miyake had hoped to hold the bridge himself. Now his only chance of defending the area was to charge across it and beat back the rebels before the force already at Arrow Point could link up with them. The rebels knew this too, and had already sabotaged the bridge, smashing out the planking on the south side to create a three- or four-metre gap between the bridge and the shore. Several of Miyake's bolder horsemen tried to jump the gap anyway, running a storm of musketry and arrows, only to plummet into the waters below, which soon turned into a murky, churning mix of silt and scarlet.

With the bridge uncrossable, Miyake and his men were reduced to taking potshots at the rebels, until the fateful moment when rebel reinforcements arrived on Miyake's side of the river from Arrow Point. The ensuing fight was bloody and hand-to-hand. Miyake's men had come out to do battle in their best fighting finery, and now retreated in haste, their banner poles broken and their armour dirty.

Strangely, many of Miyake's men fled *towards* Mogine beach, and seemingly not because it was a long walk around the top of the island and back to Tomioka, but because they hoped to escape by sea. This implies that the Karatsu troops had not marched across the island to Hondo, but sailed round the top from Tomioka, and that an unmentioned but equally important encounter must have taken place at Mogine, between the ferrymen of the rebels and the ferrymen of the samurai. The heavily wounded Namikawa Kyūbei, one of the few survivors of the débâcle at Shimago, made it out of the rout to a boat at Mogine with a wounded samurai from the battle at the bridge, but later died from his injuries. Miyake Tobee himself, his horse dead at the bridge, tried to make it to Mogine on foot, but was overtaken by rebels and killed. Of the rest of the government troops in Hondo, the survivors fled back across the island, running for Tomioka with dire warnings of the approaching enemy. A handful rowed out of harm's way. Of the three dozen ships that had passed Hirado on Christmas Day on the way out, just one returned a week later.[7]

One samurai wrote of the incident: 'The Karatsu troops suffered a disastrous defeat at Hondo and four or five important men were killed. They were all armoured warriors, while the rebels on the whole, wore white.' This comment seems at first to be a *non sequitur*; it may simply mean, as many authorities have assumed, that the rebels all wore white clothes, but may have been intended to mean that they were unarmoured. The 'important men' were of the officer class, but the report still downplays the damage. Other accounts of the Battle of Hondo number the dead gentry or landowners (samurai whose wealth required them to maintain and equip their own platoon) at over a dozen. No similar number exists for the rank and file, although it is likely to have been in the hundreds.

Ironically, a battalion of some 300 heavily armed samurai were tantalisingly close to the Battle of Hondo. They had been sent by the Shimazu domain, and had approached as close as was legally possible, staying just within their own borders, stationed on the nearby Lion Island. Six Shimazu men, however, did risk their luck by sneaking across onto Lower Amakusa Island, and rushed back with eyewitness accounts. Their leader noted:

> For our army to have such a defeat is truly infuriating. Most of the rebels were farmers and some seemed to be convicts. Even though they were five thousand or three thousand, they should have lacked a figure to play the role of general, so I would not have expected them to behave competently. It is thought that a small number would be sufficient [to suppress the uprising] but probably young men from the Karatsu troops were ambushed and thrown into disorder and the whole army collapsed.[8]

So now the young were getting the blame, for displaying precisely the same foolhardy hunger for glory that characterised so many other samurai skirmishes.

Jerome himself does not seem to have been at the battle, since his arrival at Hondo is not reported until 30 December. Other leaders, presumably the Gang of Five, marshalled the victorious forces at the Battle of Hondo, while their child-messiah stayed safely in the rear. In what seems to have been a carefully stage-managed arrival, eagerly awaited by the victorious rebels, and orchestrated in full view of many witnesses, Jerome was ferried ashore at Mogine beach. A local merchant reported seeing him up close. He wore a plain kimono and baggy breeches (*tattsuke-bakama*) under an embroidered white robe. A cross was painted on his forehead, and he wore a crown of Chinese ramie grass (*Boehmeria nivea*), a silvery nettle with heart-shaped leaves. In his hand he held a wand adorned with hemp and paper streamers like those used by Shintō clerics, which he used to command the forces around him. The overall effect was a bizarre combination of priest and general – Jerome dressed the part.[9]

On 2 January 1638, some ten thousand rebels advanced on Shiki, a small village with a minor fort of its own within sight of Tomioka Castle. The long spit of land that separated Tomioka from the coast made it difficult for the soldiers to accurately gauge the numbers of the new arrivals. At Jerome's order, the rebels flew scores of white banners, a daunting sight designed to frighten the soldiers with images of numerical superiority. The rebels fell on Shiki without mercy, finding it largely deserted and setting fire to several of its buildings. Shiki's 'castle', like that in Hondo, was little more than a glorified mansion. Another building set aflame was a shrine to Hachiman, the Japanese god of war, although Jerome soon changed his mind, and elected to set up his headquarters in the grounds of the smouldering building.

Similar fires broke out on the spit of land that led to Tomioka Castle, as the defenders demolished merchants' houses close to the castle walls. The intent was to create a killing ground between Tomioka village and the castle that was supposed to protect it – there would be no chance for the rebels to use nearby buildings as cover.

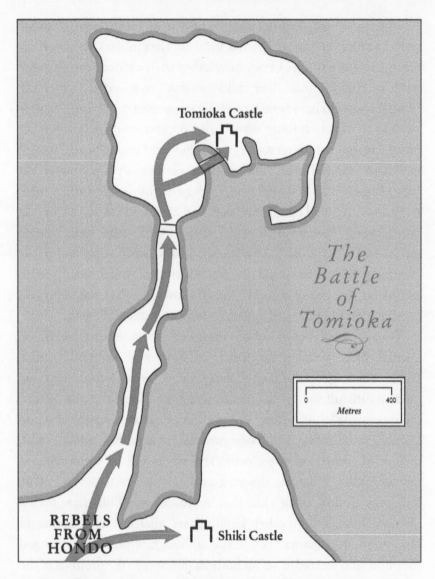

Tomioka Castle

The
Battle
of
Tomioka

0   400
Metres

REBELS
FROM
HONDO

Shiki Castle

Tomioka Castle was not big enough to offer sanctuary to all the townsfolk who lived along the cape. Many of them were abandoned to the rebels, and forced to live among them as the army advanced. Just to make it clear who was in charge, Jerome ordered for the high-ranking heads taken at Hondo to be mounted outside Tomioka prison, along with a sign that read: 'These five people, including Miyake Tobee, have been punished for being hostile towards Christians.'

Within the castle, the soldiers carefully prepared a greeting of their own, loading up Tomioka's single cannon, and taking their best guess as to the highest concentration of enemy troops. It is likely that at least part of Jerome's display of banners was designed to mislead artillery-men as to the likely places where troops might be concentrated.

Jerome need not have worried. The first shot of the Tomioka cannon blew the breech out the back of the old gun, rendering it entirely useless. Even if the rebels had not recognised the nature of the explosion, the fact that there were no further cannonballs told them all they needed to know. Tomioka Castle had lost its primary means of defence.[10]

Before sunrise on 3 January, the rebels made a daring assault on the castle. One group climbed up to the high ground behind the castle, launching arrows and firing their muskets at the castle's main turret. As the soldiers within returned fire, a second group of rebels charged the main gate. The cleared ground in front of it served its purpose well, and the alert samurai had their muskets primed and ready all along the wall. A number of rebels took refuge in a house inside the gate, belonging to a merchant known to the castle deni-zens. But personal associations were forgotten in the heat of battle, and two castle archers loosed a string of fire arrows into the wood and paper building. It erupted in flames and the rebels were forced to retreat, with losses estimated at 200. The day ended in stalemate, with the rebels having breached the castle gate, only to be repulsed. While rebel losses were heavier, the defenders of Tomioka had lost four of their officers, and an unrecorded number of soldiers.

Despite their setback, the rebels launched into a triumphant song, its lyrics all but incomprehensible to the soldiers:

> The precious reign is coming
> Respect the seven sacraments
> Zezōsu, Zesōsu, Zezōsu.[11]

The cryptic last line could have been the defenders' mishearing of 'Jesus! Jesus! Jesus!', or possibly the repeated chanting of 'Zuisō' ('Good Omen'), a term already associated with Jerome's leadership.

On the morning of 4 January, a group of a dozen Tomioka towns-folk appeared at the inner gate of the castle, begging to be let in. They claimed to be seeking asylum from the rebels, but were found to have fire-making tools on their persons. Suspected of being Christian arsonists, they were turned away.

The defenders started a fire of their own, burning a rice store-house inside the inner gate, clearly suspecting that the day's battle would find the rebels using it for cover. But much to their surprise, nothing happened. It is unlikely that Jerome suddenly decided to have a Christmas truce after fighting throughout the holy festival. Instead, the rebels seem to have spent 4 and 5 January constructing makeshift shields to protect themselves from musket balls and arrows. Wooden doors in Tomioka town were ripped off their hinges, and sliding screens dismounted and augmented with bamboo.

A final attack, the most savage of all, came around 8 a.m. on 6 January, with the rebels advancing behind these new shields. Since the sun was already up, there was little attempt at deception. Instead, the wall of shields advanced slowly on the castle, while the rebels announced their intentions to the defenders, in what appears to have been a war-chant.

> If we die we will ascend to Heaven
> If we live, we will live in prosperity
> And be masters of the castle of Tomioka.[12]

The castle's occupants were also busy jury-rigging defences, losing an officer who had been setting bamboo fencing of his own to block a breach in the second inner wall. Within the castle, the leader's rhet-oric focussed on an altogether different angle – if Tomioka fell to mere farmers, the dishonour and shame of the soldiers would be remembered forever. Jerome himself, at least as far as the defenders could tell, was prominent among the rebels. 'The leader,' wrote one, 'waving a white flag, directed the soldiers, who shouted their song of victory, beat drums and pressed forward to their attack till the second wall was taken and only the inner wall remained.'[13]

There is no further description of Jerome's flag given at Tomioka, although, miraculously, his personal standard was one of the few artefacts that survived the Rebellion. It has lasted to this day, its original colours yellowed with age, and pockmarked with arrow holes. It shows two European-featured angels, their hands clasped in prayer, flanking a giant chalice. Above the chalice is a communion wafer marked with a crucifix, and above that a motto in Portuguese-accented Latin: 'LOVVADº SEIAO SĀCTISSIMº SACRAMENTO' – *Praised be the most holy sacrament*. The banner had been made somewhere in Shimabara or the Amakusa archipelago, by an individual who knew Christian iconography. From the very short list of potential suspects, it is likely that the banner was the work of Yamada Emonsaku, the sign painter of Kuchinotsu.[14]

Despite Jerome's flag-waving efforts, fire would prove to be the saviour of the defenders in Tomioka. They had kept several hundred fire-arrows in reserve, and the mass of combustible shields presented an ideal opportunity. For a moment, the Tomioka samurai forgot their muskets, instead unleashing a storm of fire-arrows on the advancing shield wall. As it erupted in flames, the rebels dropped their shields, leaving themselves open to a volley of musket balls. Since the rebels had been allowed to advance much closer, more of the muskets hit their mark than before.

Something about this assault caused the rebels to give up on Tomioka. Jerome and his associates were fully aware that reinforcements would be arriving soon. They might have been hoping to take Tomioka for themselves, but with the castle still holding out, and Shimabara still in the hands of government troops, both options and time were running out.

Ironically, Jerome's actions in Tomioka had convinced enemy spies that he was enjoying better success than he really was. Scouts from Kumamoto had sneaked onto the island to observe troop movements on 3 January, but stopped when they saw the columns of smoke rising in the vicinity of Tomioka. They reasoned that a battle was clearly in progress, considered that to be all the scouting it was safe to do, and turned back to their home base, leaving the defenders of Tomioka Castle to their fate.

Meanwhile, the same smoke was prominent enough on the horizon to be visible from the outlying hills of Nagasaki. A panicked rumour soon spread that Tomioka Castle had already fallen to the rebels, and that Jerome's next target would be Nagasaki itself. The local magistrate, Suetsugu Heizō, immediately sent an urgent message to Ōsaka to that effect, inciting further panic among government officials.

Without Tomioka or Shimabara to serve as a defensible position, the rebels chose the next best thing. In a conference with his generals, Jerome offered the following assessment:

> It is known that recently, in consequence of our uprising, the Imperial Commissioner has arrived, and consulted with the princes of the west and will attack us with great force. It is easily seen that, in our present condition, the soldiers will speedily overthrow us. Let us then fortify ourselves in a castle, and wage war as long as we can. We number more than ten thousand men, accustomed to use firearms. More than this, as we have resolved to sacrifice our lives for the sake of our religion it is not to be supposed that we will easily be overthrown.[15]

The direct quote is usually assigned shortly after the setbacks at Tomioka, as if Jerome or his handlers had suddenly decided to go on the defensive. However, it seems much more likely that the desire to take a local castle and hold it against punitive forces was the rebels' primary objective from mid-December onwards. An initial push towards Shimabara Castle, presumably with the airy intention of advancing on Nagasaki itself, failed with the strong defence of Shimabara, and with the unsung victory scored by Sano Sozaemon.

The frontline of the Shimabara Rebellion had not been warfare, but rumour. News and gossip about the events had flown much faster than the troops, but had been neatly shut down at the Mogi Pass by Sano. Thanks to Sano's death-defying ride to Mogi and back, his seizure of the headman's son as hostage, and his subtle call for resupply, Nagasaki stayed loyal to the government. The former City of God remained cowed and obedient to the Shōgunate, and did not offer any further support to the Christians in the hinterland. If there were supporters of Jerome in Nagasaki, they were rendered powerless by curfews and clampdowns, and the Rebellion was contained within the Shimabara Peninsula and the Amakusa island chain. The armies marching south to deal with the rebels would then have crushed any further potential support.

A new frontline of rumour, this time from the government side, was sweeping down towards the south. Jerome was but a child, but his experienced military associates would have known the logistics of getting a message to and from the Shōgun in Edo. As a rule of thumb, the news of the unrest in Shimabara would have taken some ten days to reach the government in Edo. The government's reply, sure to be swift, would take some ten days to make it back. At that point, it was reasonable for the rebels to assume that local lords in neighbouring domains would be authorised to cross their borders and come to the aid of the samurai in Shimabara Castle. The Karatsu samurai, who did not require authorisation, got their sailing orders on 20 December, just two weeks after the initial uprising. Although the Karatsu samurai had been defeated, it was reasonable for the rebels to assume that there were several more armies en route, each one of them setting out the moment that the 'flying feet' messengers reached their town with the Shōgun's authorisation. Some would be more organised than others, which might buy a couple of days' leeway. Some would be planning on sailing – an idea that might be delayed by bad winter weather, buying a little more time for the rebels. The soldiers that set out first would be closest to Edo, so would take longer to arrive, but even so, the Shōgun's vengeance was closing on the rebels with great speed.

For as long as the Rebellion had been a wave spreading ever outwards, it had the momentum it required. The moment that wave was halted at Nagasaki and Konoura, the rebels had to rethink their objectives. From mid-December, whether they realised it or not, Jerome's forces were fighting to gain a fortified position, in a paltry three-week window before the Shōgunate struck back. With no castle of their own, the rebels would have to steal one from their enemies. Shimabara Castle was still holding out. The rebels knew that they now stood no chance of taking it, and that reinforcements were sure to arrive in a matter of days. It would seem that the plan to take Tomioka began in the last days of December, when Peter and Jerome cancelled their planned mission to Nagasaki.[16] However, Tomioka had put up a similarly strong resistance, and rebel options were steadily dwindling.

In hindsight, we know that a second wave of seaborne reinforcements was already en route from Karatsu, and would arrive on 15 January.[17] We may presume that, either through interrogating prisoners of war or even the open boasts of their enemies, the rebels would have known that they would soon be facing another fleet of attackers, heading straight for Tomioka. Only the fortuitously poor weather stood a chance of keeping reinforcements away for more than a week.

The rebels could even guess at the route. Reinforcements were sure to come in a pincer movement: one army along the Amakusa islands, and another down through the Shimabara Peninsula. Tomioka was the furthest point from both advances, but might also get reinforcements by sea at any moment. No castle is impregnable, but the rebels simply did not have time to starve their enemies out. With both sides reasonably predicting that Shimabara and Tomioka could hold out for another month, the rebels needed to cut their losses.

While the baffled denizens of Tomioka looked on, the rebels took to their boats, abandoning the siege in a vast fleet of fishing vessels, each with a crucifix sitting proudly at its prow. There was one more place they could go; one final refuge they might hope to make their last stand.

CHAPTER SEVEN

The Speed of Thunder

··················

The tiny, unmanned provincial railway station is still called 'Hara Castle', but there is no castle here any more. Three hundred and seventy years ago, the land where the station now stands was the site of a massive Shōgunate gun battery. In the time of Jerome, anyone standing in this spot would have soon been deafened by the firing. Today there is only the sound of cicadas chirping.

Signposts through the maze of nearby streets are uncharacteristically vague, although the place where the castle once stood is obvious to anyone. Above the hills and houses, a massive slab of tree-covered rock dominates the horizon, looking out across the water towards the faint hills of Amakusa.

The ruins of the central keep of Hara Castle have been preserved, to a certain extent. At its uppermost extremity, where the waves of Shimabara Bay crash against the base of the cliffs, the castle has been left untouched. But the 'castle' in Jerome's day stretched all the way from this high point, north across the entire promontory. The total circumference of the various citadels was some seven miles. Today it is a mix of rocky outcrops and farmers' fields. When we read of the rebels taking refuge in 'Hara Castle', they did so in a walled enclosure large enough to have its own well, two large ponds, a secluded beach, and fields growing crops. There was enough space here for some 40,000 men, women and children to live for months.

The top of the castle mound is bare. A small Buddhist statuette once gazed out to sea, but now has its view obscured by what appears to be an electrical junction box. A metal crucifix, once pristine white, but already showing signs of age and rust, stands at the highest point. It seems to have been intended to look out across the bay, visible from both land and sea, but a pair of trees on either side of it have been allowed to grow far enough up and out to almost completely obscure it. Here, too, there is a modern statue of Jerome, a clone of the one that stands in the grounds of Shimabara Castle. And a few paces away, Jerome's memorial gravestone.

Someone has recently left some flowers here, and a couple of modest offerings. Ashen scraps of incense blow away from the mossy stone whose simple inscription of name and date has already largely disappeared.[1]

Hara Castle today lacks the restored grandeur of Shimabara, but that is not unexpected. The site was also a ruin when Jerome himself arrived, 'decommissioned' to make way for Shimabara in the north, its buildings dismantled, its walls unadorned. But most importantly for the rebels, it was deserted.

The news of the Rebellion was greeted with bemusement back at the Shōgun's headquarters. On 1 January 1638 the Shōgun requested that an imperial prince perform seven days of prayers. A diarist fretted: 'Incantations and prayers were performed at court. Is it because the morning sky is red? Is it because of the Christian revolt?'[2] The uprising was clearly the talk of the town, and a matter of much speculation among the noblemen, many of whom expressed sincere doubts that it was the Christians who were really at fault.

When talking at Edo Castle about the cause of the riot, the chief retainer of the Ōmura clan, Hikōemon, was asked whether Christians habitually had such uprisings. Hikōemon said that he doubted the insurrection was because of Christians. 'During the civil war era,' [he said,] 'there were many Christian lords, but they never started riots. To tell the truth, I am now seventy years old, but I was once a Christian soldier myself.'[3]

The Shōgun's chief adviser was heard to utter that the uprising was a great benefit to the government. Although there were minor problems with logistics, particularly the alibi the uprising presented for governors who wanted to delay their own tax payments, it was still an excellent opportunity to destroy the Christian heartland once and for all. The Rebellion should be put down in the strongest, most cataclysmic fashion imaginable, if Christianity was ever to be weeded out from south-west Japan.[4]

Meanwhile in Kumamoto, the men of House Hosokawa waited impatiently for their marching orders, and continued to wage war in the only way they legally could, through interrogation and deception. Much of what we know about Jerome and the rebels' intentions comes from the documents obtained from Jerome's captured family members. Statements obtained about Jerome's early life, his father's whereabouts, and the intentions of the rebels were all dragged from the men, women and children that the rescue raid had failed to reach. Armed with this new intelligence, House Hosokawa put it to use by forcing several of the relatives to write letters to Jerome and his father, in an attempt to lure them into a trap. One, clearly written under duress by Kozaemon, to his relatives in Ōyano, read:

I heard that Peter and Jerome went to Nagasaki. Obviously, that is a possibility. Because Peter and Jerome have not returned, we have sent letters to Peter that many people including Jibee of Ebe village and his relatives, Heishiro of Uto and Peter's family members are in grave trouble. However, because there is no reply, we will not send the same request. It is hard to understand. We are living well. I believe my parents and children are worrying about me, so please tell them so.[5]

A second, more urgent letter also survives, this time from a family friend to Kozaemon's father:

> Where are Peter and Jerome? As I said before, among Peter's relatives, from farmers on the land to Heishiro of Uto, entire families of peasants are troubled by the [actions of] father and son. As I said before, many innocent people must have lost their lives. I think if Peter and his son come back, abandon their religion and help the farmers, it would be a great thing, so please advise them to do so. If you could do that and offer your support, I will do the best I can to help you in future. I am telling this because it is difficult for me to ignore, as we are close in distance and have been friends for several years. I am uneasy at the news that Karatsu is sending an army to your land and that is why I am writing to you. Looking forward to your reply.[6]

Despite the touching urgency of the letters, which somehow manage to combine professional *politesse* with a sense of impending doom, there is no evidence that any of them reached their targets. Peter and Jerome were unlikely to be swayed by a communication that had successfully run the gauntlet of guard posts and checkpoints along the archipelago, and already assumed that their relatives were in enemy hands. Some of the letters addressed to village headmen may have hit the mark, but even if they did, there is no evidence that any of the local leaders had any power to talk the Christians out of their revolt. By the time House Hosokawa was drafting its sneaky missives, the rebels were already fighting at Hondo and Tomioka.

Finally, the samurai of House Hosokawa received their permission to cross over onto the Amakusa islands from Misumi. At first, they proceeded with understandable caution, sending small platoons of outriders and boat-borne observers up ahead. When these reported no sighting of rebel forces, the army followed, but still cautious, half expecting to stumble into thousands of armed rebels waiting in ambush. Instead, they found nothing but ghost towns – the people of Amakusa had fled to Hara Castle.

Stories drifted in of those left behind. Not every sympathiser on the Amakusa archipelago had followed the rebels. Not everyone had yet left their village. As the government forces advanced along the islands, they found village after village entirely empty. Reasoning that only a Christian rebel village would be in such a state, they put every empty building to the torch. Across the bay at Hara Castle, the rebels would have been easily able to track the approach of their enemies by marking the columns of smoke on the horizon.

There are hundreds of untold stories about the advance of the Shōgunate forces. Terse, single-line reports in government documents belie the human tragedy as the massive samurai army marched along the archipelago. Scouts apprehended isolated stragglers, while behind them, their masters argued about who should get in the boat first.

Stormy weather dogged all shipping in the second week of January, leading some Kumamoto scribes to record 'inauspicious days' for sailing. A communiqué arrived from Nagasaki on 21 January, betraying the government's desire for a vengeful cleansing of the region. Magistrates from Nagasaki were now sure that the rebel advance had been rolled back to the south of the Shimabara Peninsula. It was now their concern that the rebels would return to Amakusa at the first opportunity, and melt back into the countryside, ready to deny any Christian sympathies, and, it was feared, fight another day. With this in mind, they pleaded with the Kumamoto division to make it down the archipelago as swiftly as possible, all the better to box the rebels in and cut them down. The clampdown was intended to be so severe that no Japanese resident would ever dare oppose the Shōgun again.[7]

Right through January 1638, the records of the government troops display a fighting force expecting trouble, and repeatedly surprised to find silent towns and deserted houses. On 22 January, Kumamoto forces in Ōyano demolished the local fort. They had found the town abandoned, but seem to have been worried that it might be otherwise used by their enemies as a defensive site.

The trail grew warmer on Upper Amakusa. Advance parties from the government army ran into a hundred rebels preparing to sail across the bay to Hara, and captured many of them alive. There were fugitives in the hills, and further arrests. It seems that although many sources talk of a massive rebel fleet, sailing as one to Hara in mid-January, the people of Amakusa and Shimabara actually fled their homes in several waves. Most likely, there were not enough boats to go around, requiring several trips.

By the last week in January, the march was done. The soldiers from Kumamoto had traversed the whole length of the Amakusa islands, and linked up with the survivors of the siege of Tomioka. Amakusa was back under military control, in the sense that its population now almost solely comprised government soldiers and a petty handful of prisoners.

The rebels were not the only ones observing the approaching smoke columns with dread. Young Matsukura arrived back at Shimabara Castle on 8 January, although the simple fact of his return suggests other things. If Matsukura had returned to his seat, he did so with an army of retainers – the 'siege' of Shimabara, such as it was, would have been over, with any remaining rebels fleeing ahead of the news of the approaching army. Matsukura's forces arrived to see the castle sitting proud and untouched, although its outermost citadel was a black ruin. Without delay, the new arrivals pressed on south, their numbers swollen by the troops they had rescued at Shimabara.

Several regiments marched south from the liberated Shimabara, arriving at Hara at the same time as the rebel flotilla. They had started out in December, from domains close by, and included divisions led by the lords Nabeshima, Arima and Tachibana.[8] Bringing up the rear was the deeply embarrassed Young Matsukura, forced to play second fiddle in his own fief, while higher-ranking government officials arrived to clear up his mess. The nominal leader of the new arrivals was Itakura Shigemasa, a fifty-year-old bureaucrat who had been in the inner circle of the current Shōgun's grandfather, Tokugawa Ieyasu. Extant pictures of him manage to make him look both pinch-faced and portly, with a thin, wispy sliver of a moustache. He was not a well man, and had only recently recovered from an illness.

Although Shigemasa had been present at the Siege of Ōsaka as a youth, he had not had an opportunity to win glory. Hara Castle was his big chance. The borders were closed to foreigners, and there would be no more campaigns abroad. Shigemasa knew, perhaps with greater surety than any of the other generals, who may not have enjoyed the Shōgun's confidence, that this was intended to be the last battle ever fought in Japan. This belief left him determined to take the castle before further reinforcements arrived. And as he looked across the bay at the islands of Amakusa, he could see the telltale smoke of his rivals approaching closer by the day.

In Jerome's time, Hara did not even show up on government maps as a castle any more, but it remained a natural fortress. With Tomioka still holding out and reinforcements known to be on their way, Hara Castle was the rebels' best chance of standing their ground. Hara was supposedly decommissioned, but several thousand pairs of hands can make light work of restoration. When the rebels arrived, holes in the walls were swiftly plugged. Swathes of local bamboo were hacked down to make new watchtowers and roofs. Just below the remains of the central keep, the leaders built their new home, a bolt-hole between two cliffs, roofed over and supported with bamboo struts, then covered over with a layer of turf. From a distance, it would look like empty ground, but it was the new bunker and command centre for the rebels.[9]

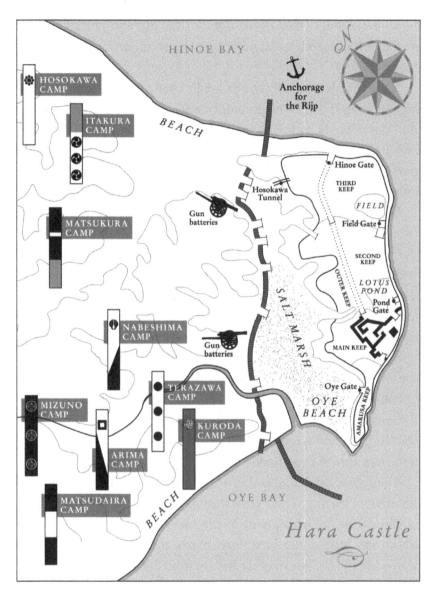

HINOE BAY

Anchorage
for
the Rijp

HOSOKAWA
CAMP

ITAKURA
CAMP

BEACH

Hinoe Gate

THIRD
KEEP

Hosokawa
Tunnel

FIELD

Gun
batteries

Field Gate

MATSUKURA
CAMP

SECOND
KEEP

LOTUS
POND

Pond
Gate

SALT MARSH

OUTER KEEP

NABESHIMA
CAMP

Gun
batteries

MAIN KEEP

TERAZAWA
CAMP

Oye Gate

MIZUNO
CAMP

OYE
BEACH

AMAKUSA KEEP

KURODA
CAMP

ARIMA
CAMP

MATSUDAIRA
CAMP

BEACH

OYE BAY

Hara Castle

Today, Hara Castle is connected securely to the rest of the shoreline. Some maps from Jerome's time even showed the same, but that
is misleading. In fact, it was an island in all but name, a great rock
jutting from the water across an isthmus of mud and sand. 'On the
east,' said one contemporary account, 'there was the raging sea, on

the west a marsh swilled by the tides, so that there was no ground for even one horse hoof to stand on; on the south and north towered craggy cliffs.'[10]

If the marsh area truly was as tidally changeable as some sources suggest, even if the waters remained only ankle-deep, it would be all but impossible to approach the castle except during predictable and obvious moments when the sea had ebbed away. Defenders would know precisely when an attacker was liable to approach, and be guaranteed long and uninterrupted periods of rest during high tide.[11]

When government forces arrived, they were forced to pitch their camps almost a kilometre away, on the first patch of firm ground. Horses were next to useless: any approach to the castle needed to be made on foot. Unless a soldier were in one of the lucky divisions, the Hosokawa on the north beach or the Kuroda on the south, the approach was sure to be a squelching, laborious trudge across uneven ground. Contemporary illustrations show the marshes criss-crossed by wooden palisades, supposedly to provide cover for approaching samurai, and to demarcate which division was in charge of which section of unsure ground. But one cannot help but speculate if some of the cross-hatching on old maps instead refers to duckboards, or wooden piers laid across the ground. Otherwise, the approach to the castle was sure to be a mudbath.

The rebels arrived ahead of their pursuers, and plainly had no intention of leaving. Their great fleet of fishing boats was broken up as part of the refurbishment of the castle, the boats were hauled ashore and turned into huts, their masts and prows refashioned as beams and pillars. The many crucifixes from the prows were mounted along the castle walls.

Shigemasa knew the Shōgunate's official policy on Hara, which was to simply starve the rebels into capitulation. As the day wore on and the samurai army took no direct action, the rebels found the prospect immensely amusing, and made sure that their enemies knew it. They saw a particular standard standing out among the others in the siege works, and recognised it as that of a local celebrity. Young Matsukura himself was close to the walls. Unable to resist, one of the rebels yelled out a challenge.

'You, who put us in the water jail,' he shouted. 'Who denounced us and persecuted us for the delivery of tax. Why don't you come after us like you did back then? We will show you what we can do. You are a coward for not attacking us now.'[12]

Eventually, the besieging soldiers lost their patience. On 2 February, samurai from the Tachibana and Arima groups approached the walls and began firing their muskets up at the castle. The rebels within soon answered in kind, in a brief exchange of fire that got Shigemasa's attention.

Unwilling to chastise samurai of a similar rank, particularly when their men outnumbered his, Shigemasa rethought his policy on waiting for the rebels to surrender. His about-face was presented, like all the best managerial upheavals, as something he had been planning all along. Shigemasa said:

> When we consider the spirit of the assailants, we see that it is useless to spend the time in besieging the place. And more, if this place is not quickly taken, there is no doubt that the villagers in the adjacent [counties] will rebel; and should the news that the work is not progressing reach the Shōgun, he will be displeased. Tonight then, let a shout be raised on all sides, and observe how it affects those within the castle, and then let the place be stormed.[13]

This was precisely the opposite of what Shigemasa had been saying since he arrived on 22 January. Although the reasoning is superficially sound, it shows signs of his inexperience in military matters. Left in charge of tens of thousands of samurai eager for a fight, facing pressure from above to resolve the situation without undue trouble, fretting about the immense quantities of provisions he would require for an extended siege, Shigemasa lost his nerve. Instead of playing a safe waiting game, he would give his men what they wanted – a charge headlong into a fight.

Shigemasa scheduled an attack for the following day. The Nabeshima division was given the deceptively simple task of launching a feint against the western, landward wall of the castle, in order to attract the attention of the rebel defenders. Once the rebels presumably rushed to the western wall to fight back against Nabeshima's men, the Tachibana regiment was ordered to launch a sneak attack on the Hinoe gate on the north beach.

The plan seemed strange from the outset. Why not launch a feinting attack on the *south* beach, as far from the north side as possible? The only conceivable explanation is that the tide was in, and the south side was unapproachable. We might presume an implied third phase – an attack to be mounted several hours later on the south side, as the tide ebbed once more.

At the appointed time, the 13,000-strong Nabeshima division sloshed across the marsh and threw themselves at the centre of the western wall, which sat atop a steep, forbidding slope of precarious pine trees, with a path so narrow that only a handful of men could approach at a time. The noise they made was loud enough to be noticed clear across the water in Kumamoto. 'The roar of guns was heard early in the morning,' wrote one chronicler, 'but it had all gone quiet by about 8 a.m., and flames were seen [on the horizon].'[14]

The distant audience did not know what had happened at Hara, but the relatively quick end to the noise did not suggest that things had gone well for the attackers. In fact, rebel marksmen turned the day into a turkey shoot, dropping some 200 attackers within minutes.

Among them were four or five hundred bowsmen able to hit even the eye of a needle, and some eight hundred musketeers that would not miss a boar or a hare on the run, nor even a bird in flight. On earthen parapets they set up catapults to hurl stones at the approaching enemy. Even the women had their tasks apportioned to them: they were to prepare glowing hot sand and with great ladles cast it upon the attackers, and also to boil water seething hot and pour it upon them.[15]

At a longer range, the archers picked off some of the Nabeshima soldiers who were simply waiting to get on the path. Before long, with several officers down, the Nabeshima attack turned into a rout. The soldiers turned back with such speed that they trampled on some of their comrades in their haste to get back down the path and undercover. However, the musket salvos from the rebel defenders continued all the time.

Meanwhile, 5,000 men of the Tachibana regiment had sneaked into position in complete silence, with a front line of shield-bearers ready to ward off any arrows. But Lord Tachibana's sneak attack lasted for only a few seconds, before a great number of his soldiers, hearing the roaring attack of the Nabeshima group, could not resist yelling back a battle-cry of their own. If the rebels had not already seen the Tachibana regiment sneaking through the dawn light, they were well and truly aware of it by the time it reached the walls, and repelled it with similar success. The battle lasted a couple of hours, before the samurai disengaged, leaving behind more than 400 of their own dead.

Tachibana's losses were not as great as Nabeshima's, but still immensely discomforting. In the shambles that ensued, the government casualties were in the high three figures, while the rebels do not appear to have suffered at all. 'The assailants,' commented one chronicler without irony, 'now appeared to be discouraged by their failure, and for some time continued to observe the castle from a distance.'[16]

The commanders were seething, particularly Tachibana, who had been seen at the front of his troops, screaming at them to get a move on while instead they scuttled past him in an ignominious retreat.

Meanwhile, the rebels maintained a constant vigil against further attacks. 'At night,' recorded the *Kirishitan Monogatari*, 'those in the castle lit many torches and bonfires, so that they could even discover an ant creeping low on the ground. And therefore those who tried to approach the castle merely invited injury upon themselves, by day or by night.'[17]

For three days, the samurai sulked in their tents, until the rebels added insult to injury by offering to surrender. The communication came in the form of a *yabumi* – an 'arrow-letter' – which was shot out of Hara Castle into the government camp on 6 February. It was addressed specifically to Shigemasa:

We men, having a common nature and origin ... are not senseless like trees or stones. Yet we are regarded by you as worthy of reprobation. Though thus regarded, we boldly ... address this letter to you. We act thus only because our religion is one for which it is difficult to thank Heaven sufficiently. In consequence of the frequent and unrelenting persecutions, and for the sake of the Lord of Heaven, innumerable persons have sacrificed their lives, and left their bodies on the plains and mountains. Their wives and children have done so also, leaving only their names to posterity. There are no words to describe the conditions of persons in our body, half dead and half alive, exposed to shame and punishment, whether innocent or guilty; and we are not soldiers, and have no desire for fame ... [T]hough we desire to plead our cause before the Shōgun, we cannot do so ... We have assembled in this castle merely to sacrifice our lives for our religion here, and then depart to the future world ... But while we are assembled together and idle in the castle, the aspect of hell is before our eyes. The fierce leaders and soldiers of nine [counties] array their spear-points against us, threatening to punish [us like] wailing criminals. Already in the castle water is exhausted, and food and fuel are consumed. Troubles increase, and famine is before us. In the present world we must meet the punishment of the sword, but in future, we will, without any doubt, be raised up on high. Our petition is that our ruler [the Shōgun] would restrain his anger, entertain a heart of mercy, and forgive the offences of the wives and children of those who have offended you. And if you should give to some ten thousand of them a piece of land then we, though we have cause to resent your conduct, will let you cut off our heads in the castle, and leave our names to posterity. To escape from our present evils and be transformed is our only desire while living or in death. In our distress, we desire to make our request known by this letter.[18]

The conciliatory tone of the letter was mind-boggling, and certainly confusing enough for the besiegers to refuse to take it seriously. Some of the samurai had their own theory, discussed around the campfires and later documented by Lord Nabeshima. He wrote that some of his men believed that the 'Christian' nature of the rebels was merely a handy ruse, and that the true intention of the uprising was to attract the attention of a government inspector. In effect, the rebels were going over Young Matsukura's head, to lodge a protest with the Shōgun about their unfair tax assessment, and doing so in the only way that they could, by rising in revolt. Although few believed this assessment, it is possible that at least some of the rebels had joined the uprising believing that they were lodging a protest, and that with the arrival of a high-ranking envoy, they would be forgiven for defaulting on such an impossible tax demand. Although it sounds far-fetched to a modern audience, and was deeply unwelcome under the Shōgun's new policy of strict control, such an uprising was a common form of protest during the civil war era.[19]

On the surface, however, the offer to surrender suggested that the ringleaders and menfolk of the rebels were prepared to hand themselves over to the government (and, as everyone acknowledged, certain death), if only the women and children were to be allowed to resettle. The claims of the letter were shown by hindsight to mix true and false – the rebels most certainly were prepared to die for their faith, but far from running low on supplies, they had enough at Hara to last another two months. Instead, it seems that the arrow-letter might have come from a faction within the castle already keen to disassociate itself from the ringleaders – perhaps some of the people in the castle had arrived with false or unrealistic expectations, and possibly were not even Christians at all, but had now discovered too late that they had doomed themselves to sit within the Hara precincts to await death.

Shigemasa paid no attention to the letter. Instead, the only extant government records for the next week are prosaic accounts for the dispatch and arrival of quantities of bamboo – Shigemasa had put some of the soldiers in Amakusa to work sourcing material for palisades and shields, which were shipped over to Hara in the days that followed. One of the most successful managers turned out to be Hikōzaemon, that same village headman who had so successfully masterminded the defence of Konoura from the rebel rescue party in December. Hikōzaemon was commended for his achievement in somehow procuring a thousand bamboo poles and a thousand rush mats in record time.[20] Along with such deliveries came a letter from Shigemasa's cousin, warning him that the Shōgunate was sending more troops, led by Matsudaira Nobutsuna, a general who was sure to outrank and overrule him.

'If you have an itch to scratch,' warned the letter, 'scratch it before Matsudaira arrives.'[21]

Shigemasa had only a few days, and he may have been spurred into even swifter action by the realisation that his replacement, already en route from Edo, was the son of an old rival. Shigemasa was not going to take orders from a younger man. Although there is no record of any direct enmity between him and Matsudaira, he seemed determined to take the castle before his replacement arrived. Shigemasa set a date for a new assault – dawn on 14 February 1638.

By the lunar calendar in use on both sides, it was New Year's Day, first light of the Year of the Tiger. Shigemasa rose early, and washed in solemn preparation. With the help of his pages, he strapped himself into his stylish black armour. Taking matters very seriously, he called for an ink-stone and brush, and composed a death poem – part of him already believed that he would not make it off the battle-field alive.

> On New Year's Day, last year, in Edo
> I tied on a hat to go to the court.
> Today I tie on a helmet and go out to battle.
> When the name only remains of the flower
> That bloomed at the dawn of the New Year
> Remember him as the leader of the charge.[22]

Some historians doubt the poem's authenticity, but its mixed meta-phors and morose self-pity do seem to reflect the bungling Shigemasa of the chronicles. In it, we can see Shigemasa's frustration with his post – he welcomed his mission when it seemed like a simple task, but now regretted his removal from the safe, bureaucratic life of Edo. He had gone out to Shimabara hoping for easy glory; now he could not face the embarrassment of being relieved by a younger officer. Shigemasa would soon be a laughing stock back at the Shōgun's court, remembered as the man who could not even bring a bunch of farmers to heel. His one chance was to end the siege on New Year's Day, or die trying.

But while Shigemasa sat brooding in his tent, his men had other ideas. The Arima division, eager for glory of its own, ran out to attack the castle at five in the morning, three hours before Shigemasa's chosen time. Instead of rushing in to help, the rest of the divisions held back. Gunshots rang out, and there were the sounds of screams from the north gate, as the Arima division's attack was beaten back, as ever, by musket-fire and rocks dropped on their heads. Those soldiers in the camp who were not already awake were woken by the noise, and peered bleary-eyed from their tents at the flashes and bangs from the wall. But the Arima division was left to disobey orders on its own.

Shigemasa took his time, arriving punctually at the originally allotted hour. By then, the Arima assault had ended in another retreat. Shigemasa approached with a great white banner, wearing a distinctive helmet with a great, shaggy mane. He was accompanied by the other divisions. As the rebels within the castle looked on in disbelief, Shigemasa attacked the same gate as the Arima division. There was no feint, no pincer movement; either because of a high tide or simple incompetence, the other gate was not attacked. Instead, all the rebels, well and truly ready after the Arima division's ill-advised wake-up call, assembled back at the walls, firing their guns and dropping their rocks upon a second futile attack.

Despite heavy losses, Shigemasa's charge made it to the castle wall. As his men turned and fled the heavy rebel resistance, Shigemasa harangued them for their lack of courage. 'Is it for you to come so near and then retreat?' he bellowed. 'Vile fellows, think what kind of an enemy is before you. Is it becoming soldiers to retreat from a small castle defended by a set of farmers, though the place is strong and strongly defended? Return and storm the place.'

Deserted by his army, Shigemasa pressed on, charging the walls with a tiny handful of retainers. His standard-bearer was shot down, but another of the dwindling attackers snatched up the flag. In the scuffle, Shigemasa's spear was broken, and he fought on with his sword. The standard was snatched from its bearer, the flagpole snapped in two. From somewhere among the rebels, the order went up: all muskets to target the man in the black armour, and to fire at will. Shigemasa was hit in the left side of his chest, and the bullet passed right through him, causing him to drop, dying in the midst of his charge.

Shigemasa's own gravestone, erected by his descendants, has a detailed description of his demise:

> On the first day of the first month . . . Shigemasa, in his zeal and courage, rushed impetuously into the middle of the enemy, where his helmet being crushed, and his lance being broken, he in the end perished, being fifty years old. How deplorable! How sad! Shigenori [his son] had followed him, and harassing his soul, had valiantly put forth his strength, but, alas! Victory and defeat are according to fate . . . It must be said that this man lost his life doing worthy deeds . . . And does not every one turn up his sleeve to wipe the tears on his account?[23]

With the exception of a few of his own lieutenants, and Shigemasa's grieving son, who saw his father shot by the rebels and fought in vain to reach his body, the death of the general was not deemed a particularly great loss by the soldiers under his command. The Nabeshima, Tachibana and Arima groups had already demonstrated their contempt for his orders by ignoring them. Even Shigemasa's own descendants, who waited 154 years to put up a memorial, saw fit to carve an ambiguous coda in Chinese, supposedly a karmic warning that the rebels were sure to pay for their crimes, but equally applicable to Shigemasa himself: 'One's punishment comes upon him as quick as thunder.'

CHAPTER EIGHT

The Waiting Game

....

Its name, *Dejima*, means the 'jutting island', or the 'isle of escape'. In the time of the Shimabara Rebellion, it was a fan-shaped scrap of land in Nagasaki harbour, cut off from the shore by a small channel. At first, this channel was traversed by a wooden gangplank. In later years, it gained a stone bridge.

Dejima was designed to keep foreign influences out of Japan. It was originally built as a quarantine for unwelcome Portuguese visitors, but when the Catholics were ousted, it soon found another purpose. In the aftermath of the Shimabara Rebellion, Dejima became the sole permissible residence for the Dutch. This tiny patch of land, just large enough for a couple of dozen warehouses and residences, with a modest town square in its midst and space for a small walled garden, would be the only place where Europeans were permitted for several centuries.

Land reclamation in the twentieth century soon obscured the original island. Dejima is now a mere city block in modern-day Nagasaki. Over the years, painstaking negotiations by the local council have slowly restored the original land area to government control, allowing the tourist office to recreate Dejima. The fan-shaped area has been marked out once more, and filled with reconstructions of Edo-era buildings. The warehouses are now filled with exhibitions and samples of life for the Dutch traders who once lived there. Only a few fragments of the original Dejima survive – such as a broken cannon dredged from the harbour, still bearing the logo of the Dutch East India Company. The same insignia can be seen on a stone arch that is all that survives of one of Dejima's original walls.

It takes an hour to walk around and explore Dejima, which on a hot summer's day feels like much longer. For the disinterested visitor, Dejima feels like a large village, but it is easy to forget that, for most of its residents, it was the only safe haven for a thousand miles, and the bleak terminus of the trade route that stretched all the way back to the Netherlands. For the inmates who were forced to spend year after year within boundaries that could be encompassed within a stone's throw, it was a place of crushing boredom.

As a stronghold of foreign influence during Japan's long period of isolation, Dejima has become a mandatory inclusion on the tourist trail. The site today is teeming with listless Japanese teenagers on school excursions, all dutifully wearing their uniforms for ease of identification, all sullenly mooching around the worthy displays of trade and cultural exchange. They face their mission with downtrodden resignation; their minds already on the larks that can be had in the Peace Park, or the tatty trinkets they can pick up in Chinatown at lunchtime.

In the aftermath of the Shimabara Rebellion, Dejima would become a home and something of a prison for the 'Dutch', the sole dock where foreign ships were permitted to unload. As ever, the Japanese would tell tall tales about the alien merchants on the forbidden island: popular myth held that they were grotesquely ugly, with unsightly, ruddy complexions, hair that deviated far from Japan's default raven black, and haunting eyes that were the colour of the sea. Dutch technology was regarded with wary awe, and local prostitutes, permitted on the island for brief rentals, did their bit for the foreigners' image with outrageous tales of sexual perversions, that soon made their way into underground erotica.

Not all the residents were from the Netherlands, but all sailed under the flag of the Dutch East India Company

– Frenchmen, Englishmen, and a smattering of other Europeans and Eurasians. But as far as the Japanese were concerned, the residents of Dejima were exclusively Dutchmen. Foreign languages and knowledge were called *Rangaku* – 'Dutch Studies'.

Although the conditions on Dejima were not ideal, they were hard-won by the men of the Netherlands. For more than two centuries, Dutch East India Company men were the only Europeans permitted on Japanese soil. They were known to be Christian; they were known to be perfidious creatures from treacherous Europe. But they were tolerated, in part, because at the time of the Shimabara Rebellion, the Dutch had come to the aid of the Shōgun. Eventually.

Soon after Shigemasa's awkward demise, four further divisions swamped the besiegers' camp – led by the lords Toda, Terazawa, Kuroda and Matsudaira. The new arrivals crammed themselves onto the already crowded ground, and filled in their comrades on their largely uneventful marches from Edo and round through the north, or down the Amakusa archipelago from the east. There was, understandably, a degree of tension between the soldiers who had already been at Hara for weeks, and the enthusiastic latecomers. The men who had served under Shigemasa were veterans of several fruitless assaults on the castle; some of them had even been through the original skirmishes around Shimabara and Tomioka. This left them mildly resentful at the easy time of it enjoyed by the new arrivals: a series of military assaults against deserted villages along the Amakusa archipelago, and scouting patrols that uncovered nothing but a few rabbits. Meanwhile, the new divisions had yet to engage the rebels in combat, and still believed the official line about the enemy being nothing more than a bunch of farmers.

Not all the newcomers were fooled. Tachibana Muneshige, an octogenarian veteran of countless battles in Japan's civil war, arrived

on 19 February in the Tachibana camp. In an exchange of pleasant-
ries with the Hosokawa samurai, he was invited to tour their
fortifications – a rare gesture of co-operation among the competitive
samurai. After walking around the castle walls, the venerable
Tachibana gave an appraisal that dismayed the younger soldiers.

'This castle will be difficult to take in a single assault,' he said. 'If
you press an attack, you will incur many casualties and that will be
against the Shōgun's will. The best plan is to stop their supplies. Even
if you wish to attack, you should wait.'[1]

Toda Saemon, a high-ranking new arrival, was keen for glory and
action, and commented that an early attack would be better.

The young, replied Tachibana, could not be expected to
understand – they thought they were immortal. Although relatively
innocuous, his words were taken as a deep insult by the eager Toda.

Playing his new role of ignorant underling for all it was worth,
Toda asked the old soldier why some of the samurai were wearing
strange scarves.

'Those are *kesa*,' replied Tachibana, identifying them as Buddhist
prayer-stoles, which the Higa brigade of his troops had taken to wearing as a form of insignia.

'Oh,' said Toda, 'I thought they were *nikesa*,' using a word that
might be taken to mean 'cowardice.'

Unruffled, the old soldier replied as if he were still discussing
military fashions.

'A *nikesa*,' he said, 'is something you wear on your nose.' His
answer invoked the grisly means by which a defeated enemy corpse
might be tallied by battlefield inspectors. If Toda wanted to blunder
into battle, he was welcome to try it, but if he came back dead he
would only have himself to blame.[2]

In the disputes over accommodation, other old hands made sure
they put the latecomers in their place. Reading between the lines of
decisions over whose tents were pitched where, it would seem that
the old guard remained convinced that the Hinoe gate on the north

side would be the easiest to take. Accordingly, they allowed the newcomer Kuroda and Terazawa regiments to pitch up on the south side of the promontory, where the south gate only appeared to be easy pickings, but was often cut off by the tide.

Among the new arrivals was the new leader, Matsudaira Nobutsuna, the man whose approach had so terrified Shigemasa that he had been prepared to lead a suicidal attack. Matsudaira was a man in his early forties whose family had already given years of loyal service to the Shōgunate. Born as a member of the Ōkouchi clan, he was only three years old when he, his father and his brother had been adopted into the Matsudaira clan by order of the Shōgun, in order to provide heirs for a noble house whose sons had died on the battlefields of the civil war. From a young age, he had been instilled with the idea that it was his job to adopt the causes of others, to offer homage and prayers to the spirits of someone else's ancestors, all the better to keep the Shōgun's system working smoothly.

Matsudaira was a man whose very name belonged to someone else, and was a sign of his fealty and obedience; he tended to see his duties as diplomatic. Ironically, he had even less real fighting experience than Shigemasa. At the time of Sekigahara, he had still been only four years old; at the fall of Ōsaka castle, he was sixteen, and liable to have been kept far from the battle, lest his luckless adopted clan lose its latest scion. He was more of an operational soldier than a tactician or strategist, a fact he made clear to his men when he arrived. Matsudaira had a very different attitude to the foolhardy Shigemasa, and he made sure that everybody knew it.

I have been educated in a peaceful time and have acquired no
military renown; still I have come hither, commissioned by
the Shōgun, though my plans may differ from yours, and may
appear to you extremely foolish, yet in the matter of taking the
castle, follow my instructions. Our recent failure to take the

castle was merely because the conspirators stake their lives on its defence . . . This is not an ordinary conflict. In this there is no difference between soldiers and farmers, because firearms are used. In my judgement, since this castle was fitted up in haste, there is no great store of provisions in it. Food will give out in not more than one or two months. From present appearances, when food is exhausted they will try to escape from the castle with eagerness. Should we attempt to take the place by storm, there is no doubt that many lives will be lost. Therefore, merely fortify the camp with pickets, and build towers from which to discharge your guns, and when the time to attack comes, I will give the word of command.[3]

Matsudaira's words, although he framed them as his own, were in direct accordance with the wishes of the Shōgun, who did not think that a 'rebellious rabble' was worthy of direct combat with samurai, and saw no need to risk the lives and reputations of government soldiers. Just in case he was not clear enough, several further 'flying feet' messenger teams arrived over the next few weeks, every one of them delivering the same communiqué from Edo: 'The troops are not to be exposed to injury Surround, do not attack.'[4]

Matsudaira also had the power to authorise troop movements between domains. One of his first acts upon arrival was to pack off an entire legion of soldiers from Kagoshima, sending them away for 'guard duty' on the Amakusa islands. Since Matsudaira had every intention of playing a waiting game, he saw no need to keep several thousand spare soldiers hanging around the castle, particularly when the camping ground was already so covered in tents that several companies were obliged to wait offshore on troop transports. Matsudaira also seems to have believed that the rebel resolve would crack at some future point, and that mop-up operations would be required to ensure that former insurgents could not simply melt away back to their farms.

The siege works were well underway, and formed an incredible, jury-rigged suburb of bamboo and earthworks right across the neck of land before Hara Castle. Palisades and duckboards criss-crossed the beach and swamp directly before the castle, walling off the attacking samurai not only from the castle, but from each other – the approaches to the castle had been carefully divided into sectors. One approach was only fair game to the Hosokawa division; another only permissible for the Tachibana regiment, and so on. Covered walkways served to conceal troop movements, guardhouses and guard-towers offered protection from the wind and rain, and a long covered pier now extended out into the water, preventing the rebels from sneaking too far around Oye beach without being noticed. Off shore, several Japanese vessels rode at anchor, almost unrecognisable behind heavy armour that gave them a squat, box-like appearance. 'Indeed,' scoffed one chronicler, 'none of the besieged could now escape, unless he were a bird.'[5]

Realising that the siege was under new management, the rebels inside the castle attempted to communicate with Matsudaira. If we are to believe the rhetoric of some survivors, Matsudaira was the man they were waiting for, a higher authority to whom the rebels could protest about their treatment at Young Matsukura's hands. A new arrow letter, signed by Jerome himself, outlined the rebels' grievances using very similar metaphors and arguments to that of 6 February.

The reason for our current confinement is certainly not a grudge against the Shōgun or anyone else. But in recent years the tax demands of the Lord of Nagato [Young Matsukura] have become absurd. He exacted high tax over four to five years, soon payable in kind, in cows and horses, wives and children. We came to resent others, we resented ourselves, but still we obeyed his orders, with tears wetting our sleeves. Despite that, we have now handed over everything we had, and have become walking corpses, unable even to flee else-where. At the very least, we wish to explain our grievances against the Lord of Nagato. Abandoning houses that have sheltered many generations, separated from our wives and children, since the beginning of the tenth [lunar] month we have endured the cold, the snow, the frost, wearing layer after layer of clothes on our heads, and warming our hands on our burning fields. We do not have any intention of coming out of the castle. Moreover, we are outmatched, like horseflies and mosquitoes swarming against a clap of thunder, or a mantis attempting to halt the wheels of the imperial carriage. This is what was said in bygone days. When the lord's cherry trees are in full bloom, the petals scatter to the sky and the ground like mist. My life will fade like morning dew in your hands, so I seek no comfort in this world. Life passes, transient, like a dream. Even fifty years of flowering fortunes are short-lived, like a Rose of Sharon. I do not have a slice of doubt that we shall all stamp on the book of the King of Hell in the next world, dance along the road of Ashura and reach Heaven with ease. We are ready to be dismissed from this life.[6]

It is easy to see how the confusion over the rebels' motives has endured over the centuries, when the primary evidence contains such contradictions. Jerome's letter, signed, on this occasion 'Amano Shirō', and not Ōyano, Amakusa, or Masuda as in the case of some others, is rich in religious allusions, and with its reminiscences on fifty years of 'flowering fortunes', could be argued to be the work of a much older man. It first openly accuses Young Matsukura of pushing his farmers too far. But then it ends with an appeal to the afterlife, strangely expressed in Buddhist terms. Although it may well have been intended as a gesture of humility, in the wake of the battles at Hondo and Tomioka, it might also be seen as a boast that the rebels intended to fight to the death.

A new and unexpected form of assistance reached Matsudaira soon after he arrived at Hara Castle. A breathless man with the odd name of Lemon (liable to be a European transcription error for Iemon) arrived on horseback to inform him that the artillery was on its way. In answer to a forgotten request from the late Shigemasa, the Dutch were sending a warship, which would arrive imminently.

In fact, it was not as simple as that. The Dutch did not have a 'warship' in Japan. Nor were they particularly happy about assisting the Japanese in a military matter. However, they had known about the uprising for two months, and had observed the jittery behaviour of government officials in Nagasaki and Hirado, which had been enough to convince them that the Shōgunate was dangerously worried about alleged 'foreign' or 'Christian' residents in Japan.

In Nagasaki, the lockdown was complete. Muskets were confiscated from local people, and any individuals suspected of Christian sympathies were arrested and held on remand. Although the official line was still that the peasants were rising up through simple disobedience, there were indications of other motives. Rice granaries were closed to civilians, and the populace instructed to live on whatever they had to hand. At the docks, the handful of Dutch traders worried that the Japanese government would lump all Christians together, and fail to see that there was a difference between the Catholics (influenced by the exiled priests and friars), and the Protestants, such as the Dutch themselves.[7] They had done their best to assure the Japanese that there was a definite difference – the *Nambanjin* from Spain and Portugal all had black hair, whereas the Dutch were *komōjin*, 'Red Hairs'. They fixated on this physical difference, and hoped that the Japanese would translate it into a palpable difference in allegiances.[8]

Unfortunately for the Dutch, the Japanese presented them with a perfect opportunity to prove their loyalties. A letter from Shigemasa had arrived on 13 January, politely requesting that Nicholas Couckebacker, the leader of the Dutch community in Hirado, should hand over his supplies of gunpowder.

Couckebacker chanced his luck, ignoring the letter and instead sending a series of florid, obsequious welcomes, fawning over Shigemasa's return from Edo, along with gifts of wine and candies four days later. He sent them by a circuitous route, perhaps hoping that the transit time would buy him a few days. With Shigemasa already on his way to Hara Castle, Couckebacker's letter seems to have been deliberately intended to languish unopened until the trouble was over. Displaying a great mastery of empty promises and false intentions, Couckebacker even wrote: 'If you require anything which it is in our power to do, please inform us of the same; we are always willing to serve faithfully.'[9]

In further letters and menacing house calls from local potentates, it was made clear to Couckebacker that he really needed to cooperate with the original request. He did so as slowly as possible, dating each of his replies to imply that he was earnestly cooperating long before each increasingly stern reminder reached him. A week later, he sent a paltry six barrels of gunpowder to Shigemasa, and offered a cynical apology, claiming that 'the request came a little too late, as our large ship had just departed; and as the two smallest of them, which remained here, had no more powder to spare than we send you herewith, we are unable to provide you with a larger quantity.'[10]

The Japanese were having none of it. The governor of Nagasaki, Suetsugu Heizō, profited greatly from his dealings with the Dutch, but was peculiarly jumpy about the turn of events. Suetsugu's own father had been a Christian convert, but swiftly apostatised when the trends swung back towards local beliefs. He counted himself as a 'friend' of the Dutch, but was careful not to be associated with them by his fellow Japanese. Worried that events in Shimabara would reflect badly on the few remaining foreigners permitted in Japan, and no doubt catching hell for the delays from his own superiors, Suetsugu sent a further curt missive to Couckebacker, haranguing him for his failure to comply, and pointedly demanding an answer as to why Couckebacker's lieutenant, Francois Caron, had not put in an appearance at Nagasaki as had been expected. In fact, Couckebacker was desperately trying to keep Caron out of Nagasaki, fearing that any Dutch vessels there might be commandeered by the Japanese for use in putting down the Rebellion.

Caron reached Nagasaki on 4 February 1638, at around the same time that the local officials heard of Shigemasa's disastrous Big Push. Caron immediately called on Suetsugu to pay his respects. Instead, Suetsugu made his displeasure very clear. The Japanese were not satisfied with tardy letters of vague intent; they had rather expected that the Dutch leaders would have sailed directly to Nagasaki and been there in person, waiting for Shigemasa's arrival, there to discuss the best course of action in real time, and not over the course of several weeks of correspondence.

One cannot help feeling sorry for Couckebacker, whose behaviour in all matters had been a textbook example of executive obfuscation, and showed a true mastery of Japanese negotiation tactics. His sole failing was underestimating the pressure that Suetsugu had been under, particularly in the aftermath of Shigemasa's second assault, when some observers noted that the attack might have gone very differently with some artillery support. Reading between the lines, someone in the government forces had raised the question of the foreigners' potential allegiance to 'fellow Christians', and by not being overeager to cooperate, the Dutch had merely aroused further suspicions.

Suetsugu announced that he never had any intention of calling on the Dutch for assistance, but that in order to save face all round, it would have been much more useful if the Dutch had made a direct offer of help, which he could have then politely refused. Suetsugu believed that a heartfelt offer, delivered in person before Shigemasa set out, would have been 'far more advantageous for the Company than all the presents . . . given during its stay in Japan.' Instead, both Suetsugu and the Dutch were faced with serious damage control.

Faced with Suetsugu's suggestion that the Dutch should immediately sail to Nagasaki to make amends, Caron pleaded that it was impossible. His vessel had a tiny window of opportunity to sail back to Batavia before it would miss the trade winds.

Suetsugu blew his top, revealing that his superiors had often commented that the Dutch seemed ungrateful for all the money they earned from the permissions granted to them by the Japanese government, and that they would comment on it a lot more if Suetsugu were not always careful to tone down what he regarded as some of the outrageously self-interested and disrespectful replies that he heard from the Dutch. He said:

> Indeed, you talk always of your profits, of your gain, and I don't know what else, as if everybody owed these to you. Consider that nobody may earn, if he has not sown and worked for it. One ought to do some service for the profits he enjoys.[11]

To his own bosses in Batavia, Couckebacker confessed that he had no reason to doubt Suetsugu's sincerity. He provided a detailed account of the stand-off, in order to show the Dutch East India Company the kind of situation he often had to deal with, and to excuse his decision to collaborate with the Japanese.

Couckebacker already suspected that he had contravened some sort of unwritten rule – on Suetsugu's suggestion, he had agreed to the dismounting of five cannons from the 20-gun Dutch vessel *Rijp* ('Hoarfrost'), which were already en route by land down to Nagasaki. Couckebacker had hoped that the cannons would be enough of a demonstration of willing cooperation, but now feared that the Japanese would call on Dutch gunners to man them once they reached Hara.

In an attempt to make the situation seem better than it actually was, he brightly informed Batavia that 'the difficulties and revolt on the island of Amakusa have [already] been wholly suppressed' – a polite spin on the truth, which was that Amakusa had been abandoned by the rebels, who were now all concentrated at Hara. Couckebacker also emphasised the supposedly bloodless nature of the government's strategy, claiming that Matsudaira was diligently adhering to Shōgunal commands to starve the rebels out, and that any losses so far had been made by belligerent young samurai disobeying the order to wait it out. In saying so, he reflected the exasperation of the authorities at Shigemasa's fall in battle on Valentine's Day.

Despite his own cunning, Couckebacker does not appear to have put the evidence together that was already in front of him. Monies owed by Edo to Batavia had been delayed, deliberately or otherwise, during the crisis, causing Caron's ship, the *Petten*, to continue to lie idle in Hirado harbour. Couckebacker wrote to a fellow captain in Taiwan that he was holding out for delivery of the cash owed to the *Petten*, and then 'we intend to go at once to Nagasaki and cautiously ask [Suetsugu] whether he thinks it is still necessary to send our ship, requesting at the same time to be excused if possible.'[12] But Suetsugu had handed over maps of the southern Shimabara Peninsula and the Amakusa islands – he had already decided that the Dutch would be putting in an appearance.

The order did not come from Suetsugu himself, who stayed out of the way. Instead, Couckebacker was ordered by the governor of Hirado to bring all his remaining ships directly to the waters off Hara Castle. Panicking, Couckebacker dashed off a message to Caron, ordering the *Petten* to set sail immediately, to any destination it could, no matter where – anywhere would do, as long as he could get his ship out of the sight of the Japanese authorities.[13]

That still left the *Rijp* in Hirado, and there was no way Couckebacker could feign miscommunications with his own ship. Instead, his only choice was to do as Suetsugu asked, and to sail for Hara. Unwilling to let anyone else take responsibility for the highly sensitive mission – military service in the employ of the Japanese Shōgun against 'fellow Christians' – Couckebacker went along himself.

Even then, Couckebacker dawdled, sailing only in daylight hours and putting in to offshore islands each night. Although the weather was fine, there were periodic claps of what first seemed to be thunder. The bangs grew louder as the *Rijp* drew nearer to the Shimabara Peninsula – the besiegers were firing cannon at irregular intervals, eking out their gunpowder supplies, but forcing the castle denizens to keep a constant vigil against bombardment.

At the end of its three-day cruise, the *Rijp* sailed past Hara Castle's jutting promontory on 24 February. 'All around the parapet,' wrote Couckebacker, 'there could be seen a multitude of small flags with red crosses on the same. There were also many small and several large wooden crosses to be seen.'[14] Regular cannon-fire boomed out from the camp of the besiegers, and went largely unanswered from the rebels. Many cannonballs overshot the castle by a considerable distance, sending up plumes of water in the bay. Unwilling to be an accidental victim of the bombardment, Couckebacker kept sailing. The *Rijp*, its Dutch colours flying, its distinctive foreign lines cutting eerily through the grey waters, sailed a mile or so to the north-east of Hara Castle and dropped its anchors off the coast in eight fathoms of water.[15]

From within the castle, there was the sound of drums, and the rebels' voices raised up in song. Even if Couckebacker could have made out the words, he would not have understood them, although two Japanese listeners did write the lyrics down:

> Onward, onward, attackers onward
> To the limit of their ammunition
> Boom, boom, the enemy's great cannon.
> But see us here, with just our small arms.
> Praise be, for the assistance of our padre,
> We smash the jaw of our persecutors.[16]

Thanks to the peculiar geography of the region, it was actually far quicker to ride to Shimabara from Nagasaki than to sail there.

Couckebacker had dropped his interpreter, Iemon, off at the tip of the Nagasaki Peninsula two days earlier. Iemon raced ahead of the ship, and arrived at Hara in time to announce his master's imminent arrival. Matsudaira, running operations after the demise of Shigemasa, was very pleased by this. Couckebacker, however, was less pleased with Iemon, whose riding skills were a considerable improvement on his translation abilities.[17]

Couckebacker rowed ashore on 25 February, believing that Matsudaira had requested that he do so. In fact, Matsudaira had told Iemon the exact opposite – it was he who intended to row out to the *Rijp*. But perhaps Iemon need not take all the blame for the misunderstanding – the Japanese were deeply curious about the workings of the Dutch ship, and clearly hoped for a look around the *Rijp* before they reciprocated with a tour of the fortifications on land.

As Couckebacker was shown around, the arrow-borne siege correspondence continued. In answer to an offer for negotiations, one communiqué from Matsudaira refused to compromise. 'Ideally for the Shōgun or Lord Matsudaira,' it read, 'only the ceremony of denomination will do.' In other words, the samurai would be happy to lift the siege, but only if the rebels would agree to stamp on an image of Christ and re-state their allegiance to a Buddhist temple.

The besiegers certainly did not expect that the rebels would agree to such terms. Instead, they welcomed Couckebacker ashore with one of his lieutenants, and allowed him to tour the fortifications and artillery battery, which used the five Dutch guns shipped across the peninsula from Nagasaki. 'When we met their lordships,' wrote Couckebacker,

They addressed us in a courteous manner, and they requested for us to inspect the fortifications and lines of approach, to look for the best point where to place the five guns sent hither from Hirado, and to report whether the straw huts and the houses of the insurgents could be set on fire by shooting

some fireworks from the said fortress . . . I saw at once . . .
that we could scarcely do anything important with our guns,
as the houses are merely made of straw and matting, the parapets of the lower works of defence being cast with clay and the
uppermost fortress being surrounded by a good high wall,
built with heavy stones. Their Lordships said they were much
pleased with the firing of our guns on land and at sea, but it
was clear that little or nothing could be done by firing guns
from the batteries of the Imperial Army, or from our own
batteries.[18]

Couckebacker's fellow Dutchmen were all in agreement: only an
idiot would waste gunpowder and shot on such a difficult target.
However, there was method in the Japanese madness. Matsudaira
wanted artillery cover for his men as they continued the slow process
of building trenches, wooden or bamboo palisades, and sandbag
walls ever closer to the walls of Hara Castle, and the Dutch were
ideally suited to provide it. For as long as the Dutch were throwing
cannonballs over the walls, the Christian rebels would have to stay
ducked and covered, and that would prevent them shooting at the
soldiers building the siege works. Matsudaira was excited to have
foreign assistants among his staff, and wrote back to the Shōgun
boasting about the high-tech gadgets he had borrowed from the new
arrivals. 'Looking through a *telescope*,' he bragged, 'I could see the
people in the castle digging their huts and stacking sandbags.'[19]

After agreeing a plan with Matsudaira, Couckebacker slept on the
Rijp that night, and ordered his gunners to open fire on the castle the
following morning. For this decision, history has not been kind to
him. While he was at Hara, if not before, he came to believe that his
gunners were firing not merely at rebellious peasants, but at a group
of true believers under persecution, quite possibly including priests.
'This war was not caused by farmers alone,' he wrote. 'Several
banished noblemen and officers, as also clergymen or priests, it was

said, had joined the farmers.' Couckebacker did not specify if he believed the priests were of foreign origin, and perhaps he would not have cared if they were – the Protestant Dutch having no love for the Catholic Portuguese. Even so, one later chronicler compared Couckebacker to Pontius Pilate himself, washing his hands of an awful responsibility, and following the lead of the enemies of Christ.[20]

On the first day, the *Rijp*'s cannons fired a total of fourteen rounds, although the swell of the sea and the height of the castle walls did not help with accuracy. Couckebacker might have managed more if he had not been summoned back on shore for what he regarded as another pointless meeting with the samurai commanders. 'They seem to take much delight in this proceeding,' he wrote, 'Since our arrival here we have been daily summoned on shore in presence of their lordships, and we fear that this may continue for some time to come.'

Frustrated by the futility of aiming shipboard cannons at an impossibly high clifftop target, Couckebacker also had to endure night-time visits from the Japanese, who found a series of excuses to send over emissaries.

> At night we receive watchmen on board . . . We do not know
> what is the reason of this, but it annoys and incommodes us
> much. Last night we had to clear our own cabin and to sleep
> in the constable's room. With such peevish fellows as we had
> last night, our discomfort will not diminish, but we have to be
> patient and will bear these annoyances if the interests of the
> company are furthered thereby.[21]

As if that were not already enough of a distraction, Couckebacker had to deal with a small flotilla of curious observers, who would row out to the ship to get a look at the foreigners at work. Eventually, he complained to Matsudaira that his constant round of visitors was making it impossible to fire the guns, and Matsudaira ordered that nobody was to go aboard the Dutch vessel without his written permission. This only served to keep the visitors off Couckebacker's ship, but not out of his hair. 'The people contented themselves afterward,' he complained, 'with rowing in a multitude of boats all around our ship. We had wished often, for the sake of the reputation of the Dutch nation, that our vessel had been a larger and more warlike yacht, although it would not have been of more use in this case.'

The following day, the *Rijp* managed a barrage of twenty-seven rounds, some of which found their mark within the castle. On the last day of February, *Rijp*'s gunners only fired some nine rounds, but the shore batteries were finally up and running, and pounded the castle with another twenty shots. An arrow fired in answer out of the castle bore a message that made its way into the diaries of one of the samurai. 'We do not desire to build a state,' it pleaded, 'nor to disobey our ruler. All we want is the return of our religion.'[22]

The Dutch bombardment continued, 'the mortars and grenades having caused,' wrote Couckebacker, 'great damage, the magazines in the principal fortress being destroyed and all the straw huts being burnt to ashes, which caused us to receive great honour.'[23]

On 1 March, *Rijp* scored a direct hit, although unfortunately against its own side, when one of its five-pound cannonballs landed in the besiegers' camp. Matsudaira sent an earnest memo that he would appreciate it if the Dutch took better aim. But in spite of the stray shots, the Dutch barrage was taking a toll on the rebels in the castle. Arrow communications shot to and fro over the castle walls, but the content was largely kept quiet from the troops. Although almost nothing was noted in Japanese sources, Couckebacker himself recorded the sarcastic contents of one such message.

The insurgents had on 1 March flung with an arrow a letter amongst the troops, in which letter they ask the reason why the Netherlanders had been called to give assistance, there being so many courageous and faithful soldiers in Japan.[24]

157

Couckebacker could not have agreed more, but the content of the message was kept secret from the rest of the army, as was whatever was said in most of the other arrow-notes that arrived over the next few days. Only two others have survived, one of which reads: 'We did not start this war. Both at Amakusa and Shimabara, we merely acted in self-defence against your acts of deadly aggression.' The other contained a message so unbelievable that the generals initially refused to pass it on to either their men or Dutch allies.[25]

It was time to bring up the big guns. A shipment of bronze Japanese cannon, two 15-pounders and a 12-pounder, arrived from Hirado. For the duration of 5 March, there was no firing from the landside. The *Rijp* kept up a steady barrage from the sea, while the Dutch and Japanese installed the new guns at the battery. On 6 March, the *Rijp* fell entirely silent, while the land-based guns opened up.

There seems to have been an element of friendly competition among the land-based gunners. The Dutch guns managed thirteen shots against ten from the Japanese. They might have managed more, but for Matsudaira's wish to try an even more devastating form of assault.[26]

At a predetermined point, two emaciated, dirty figures were dragged out into full view of the castle walls by armoured samurai. They were Jerome's mother Martha and sister Regina, brought along the archipelago from Kumamoto. The castle and camp both fell silent. One of the captors yelled up at the castle walls, 'If you want to talk to them, you can!'

But from the castle, there was no response.[27]

The Christians inside the castle were behaving very strangely. Matsudaira fretted that the rebels were signalling to someone outside the castle, and he was determined to confirm that there were no other forces lurking among the forests on the hills. Military reports from the besiegers for the next couple of days note that samurai were sent out to comb the region around the castle. However, the reports came back from his scouts – the entire population of the region was surely concentrated in Hara Castle and its environs. The rest of the peninsula was eerily deserted.

The daily bombardment continued, although many among the besiegers felt that the benefits were diminishing. From the first day, when Matsudaira had observed the rebels through a Dutch telescope, it was known that they were taking steps inside the castle to protect themselves from the bombs. As many rebels as possible were now hiding during the bombardments in trenches, bunkers and makeshift sandbag shelters, while the firing from the landside cannons continued.

More guns were taken off the *Rijp* and rowed ashore to join the bristling landside batteries – the vessel was, after all, only presenting one side to the coast, so its remaining guns were sitting idle. On 9 March, the combined forces of the Dutch and Japanese gunners managed an impressive sixty rounds. On 10 March, forty-two rounds.

On 11 March, the group was fatally split in two. A few gunners returned to the *Rijp* to fire off some more shots from the sea, leaving a less experienced crew behind to continue the landside firing. Tragedy struck when one of the Dutch landside cannon exploded, disembowelling one of its operators, a stonemason called Gillis who really should not have been anywhere near a gun battery in the first place. The explosion blew the unfortunate Gillis clean over the top of the nearest bamboo palisade. 'He died on the spot,' commented Couckebacker, 'without uttering a single word.'[28]

The next day, as the remaining Dutch busied themselves around their guns, Matsudaira sent word that they were free to go. As he waved them off, he told them that the Shōgun was grateful for their assistance:

Captives have reported that the inmates of the Castle have suffered from the Dutch guns; now presuming they are right, this achievement is obtained at the cost of the gunner Gillis's death. I am greatly moved at this. We have been making your comrades join this affair for some time, and one has fallen. How can I look you in the face henceforth? I shall bring to the ears of the Shōgun your deeds; there should be some compensation. Now be pleased to go, the Army is unable to offer you anything, you are manifestly a true person.[29]

Couckebacker was mystified by the Japanese leaders' decision to excuse him, so much so that he rowed ashore the following day, approached the generals in person and offered to stay. When Matsudaira restated his desire that the Dutch should leave, Couckebacker did not linger. Instead he rode home overland, leaving the *Rijp* to sail behind him. All but four or five of the *Rijp*'s cannons were left behind at Hara for the Japanese to use as they saw fit. The Japanese were determined to end the rebellion without further foreign assistance.

CHAPTER NINE

The Traitor's Arrow

....

The hotel looks out over the small docks of Shimabara's outer harbour, a modern addition to the town, a couple of miles south of the castle. Here, guests can sit in a hot pool that looks out over the beachfront, and watch the ferries as they come in from Kumamoto. Even though the hotel is quintessentially Japanese, the guests come from all over. Two heavyset girls push past me in the elevator, their sibilant Mandarin conversation betraying the hiss of a Taiwanese accent. There are Koreans, too, says my maid, and white people – from what I can glean, usually puzzled pensioners partway through a world cruise. Their ferries offload them at Nagasaki onto a tour bus, and they do the Bomb in the morning, up the hill to Unzen for lunch, and down the other side to Shimabara for dinner and a castle.

Dining can be something of a chore in small-town Japan. I blame the television. When crime-fighting Shōgunate officials hit a different samurai village each week, the scriptwriters try to liven things up with a bit of local colour. Oh, they'll say, you must go to Such-and-Such a town. They have a special kind of noodle. There's a unique broth they use. The rice is a slightly different colour! Sometimes it's a treat, but in most cases, there is a reason why a local delicacy remains local.

In my room, I sit on the tatami mat floor and pretend my legs don't hurt, while the maid shoves an unending series of tiny plates onto the low table. There is readily identifiable sashimi, chunks of raw fish, as well as abalone gutted into slices, and daunting snail-like creatures. But she knows why I am here, and she has prepared a special surprise.

She lights a burner underneath a small earthenware pot, and points at the meagre food inside. I see long-stemmed mushrooms, strips of tough bamboo, lumps of mochi paste and a few leaves of seaweed, along with a couple of small shell-fish. The high-powered candle underneath slowly cooks the mixture through, boiling it in its thin broth.

'This,' she says proudly, 'is guzōni. It was invented by Jerome Amakusa at Hara Castle.'

Guzōni is almost tasteless, chewy and bland, but I have never been so happy to be presented with a local dish. As I struggle to swallow the warm lumps of mochi, I feel like I am being taken back in time, to the damp, rainy springtime when the rebels huddled in their huts and eked out their diminishing food supply.

'It's made of all the bits and pieces they could find during that siege,' she continues. 'They ripped up seaweed outside in the shallows, and they found a few shells and wild mushrooms. This is what they ate.'

'That's very interesting,' I say. 'But how did you work out what people ate inside the castle?'

She laughs far too loudly, and looks out over the bay, not meeting my gaze.

'I don't know,' she lies.

Couckebacker stopped off in Nagasaki, where Suetsugu Heizō was swift to claim credit for the change of heart. Suetsugu boasted that he had told the generals that the Dutch would suffer great financial losses if the *Rijp* were not able to sail with the trade winds, and that, pleased with the courage of the Dutch, the generals had kindly granted them the right to leave.

Couckebacker did not fall for it. In his report to his own bosses, he instead suggested that the death of Gillis had been a great loss of face to the Japanese, as they had assured the Dutch that the siege of

Hara Castle would offer no risks. Matsudaira was true to his word, and mentioned Gillis's death in his own despatches to the Shōgun. This in turn had irritated several of the other samurai generals, who were already annoyed that a massive force of samurai was bothering to call on foreign assistance at all. 'We had been partly informed,' wrote Couckebacker,

> that the Lords of Higo [Hosokawa] and Lusoysjo [Nabeshima] . . . had expressed the opinion that the foreigners might have been excused from aiding in this matter, as it would not be furthering their own reputation, when foreigners were summoned for aid and assistance at the moment when there was already such a powerful army in arms.'[1]

The leaders had been annoyed even more by discovering that their rebel enemies were in agreement with this – clearly the taunts contained within the 1 March arrow letter had ruffled a few feathers. None of this might have mattered, thought Couckebacker, but for the additional, unavoidable fact that the Dutch contribution to the siege had not gone as well as the samurai had hoped. Matsudaira, it seems, had looked upon the arrival of the Dutch as some sort of doomsday device, with which he hoped to end the siege before even more samurai reinforcements arrived. Instead, the Dutch had been only marginally helpful. Now that the siege works were so close to the castle itself, the risk of casualties from friendly fire was sure to increase, making the cannons less useful.

Couckebacker was almost correct. The theories he listed all had some contribution to the Japanese decision to let the Dutch go. There was, however, one fact of which he was unaware – the Japanese had decided to try some new means of assault, none of which required the assistance of the Dutch.

One of them, undertaken when the *Rijp*'s sails were barely over the horizon, was a dotty scheme by Hosokawa Tadatoshi and his

Kumamoto contingent. It is perhaps understandable, considering some of the things that the Kumamoto samurai tried, that later, doubtful sources have been prepared to suggest that they had a company of ninja with them. On many occasions in the Japanese chronicles, it is the Kumamoto samurai who try something pro-active. It was, after all, House Hosokawa that had embarked upon wily epistolary espionage before its soldiers were allowed to cross their own borders; House Hosokawa was the division that placed the highest value on hostages, and it was often Hosokawa samurai who would go out into the hills searching for the stragglers and deserters who could provide crucial information under interrogation. With the Dutch gone, the division from Kumamoto commandeered a large amount (some 1,800 litres) of the remaining gunpowder, and stuffed it deep within a tunnel that they had been digging beneath the north-east side of the castle. One of Hosokawa's men, either the bravest or the most stupid (the sources do not elaborate), then lit the fuse, and sent all the powder up in a monstrous flash.

When the smoke cleared, the walls of Hara Castle were still stand-ing, and the besiegers were now a cart full of gunpowder short.

It was time for Matsudaira to pull out his secret weapon, which he had been keeping to himself for several days. With the Dutch gone and the Kumamoto samurai's demolition scheme proving to be a damp squib, Matsudaira revealed to his fellow samurai the contents of an arrow-letter that had been kept top secret.

When it had first arrived, he had refused to believe that it was genuine, but as time had passed, he came to believe that one of Jerome's closest associates was ready to turn on his own people. Matsudaira now believed he had a new weapon that was immensely more powerful than Dutch guns. The letter read:

Yamada Emonsaku addresses you with true reverence and respect. I desire to obtain your forgiveness and restore tran-quillity to the Empire, by delivering up Jerome and his followers to be punished. We find that, in ancient times, famous rulers ruled beneficently, proportioning their rewards to the merit of the receiver, and the punishments to the demerit of the offender . . . This has been the case with hereditary lords; much more will it be the case with villagers who rebel against the government. How will they escape the judgements of Heaven? I have resolved these truths in my mind, and imparted them to the 800 men under my command.

My men, from the first, were not sincere Christians; but when the conspiracy first broke out, they were beset by a great multitude, and compelled to support the cause. These 800 men all have a sincere respect for the armed class. Therefore, speedily attack the castle, and we having received your answer, without fail, as to time, will make a show of resisting you, but will set fire to the house [i.e. the keep] in the castle and escape to your camp. Only I will run to the house of Jerome and make as if all were lost; and having induced him to embark with me in a small boat, will take him alive, bring him to you, and thus manifest to you the sincerity of my intentions . . . Please give me your approval immediately, and I will overthrow the evil rebels, give tranquillity to the Empire, and, I trust, escape with my own life. I am extremely anxious to receive your orders. Yamada Emonsaku thus addresses you with true regard.[2]

At first, the generals had refused to believe that Jerome's right-hand man, the designer of his personal banner, and one of the ringleaders of the rebellion, would write such a thing. Instead, they suspected that the letter was a ruse designed to draw the samurai into coming within range of some sort of booby trap in a particular part of the castle.

Matsudaira was able to put matters to the test after 10 March, when new reinforcements arrived, among them a company of samurai led by Lord Arima Naozumi. Several other letters, one written in both Chinese and Japanese, reached Arima's sector of the battleground, all seeming to confirm that Yamada Emonsaku was ready to switch sides. Arima had once used the name Michael Arima; he was the grandson of André Arima and the son of Protasio Arima, and at one time the husband of Augustin Konishi's niece, but had turned firmly aside from the faith that briefly brought benefits to his family. He had grown up in Hara Castle, and, some twenty years previously, had briefly been its master before being ordered to relocate to a new domain by the Shōgun. Back on his old turf, he was troubled by the sight of his childhood home, now an overgrown ruin, occupied by peasant rebels and under attack from fellow samurai. His spirit was further assailed by more pressing, logistical concerns – he had dutifully arrived to help out in the siege, but had reached Hara so late in the proceedings that there was literally no room for him in the immediate camp of the besiegers. If any fights broke out, Arima and his men would be obliged to stand at the back while the vanguard got all the glory.

However, Arima felt that he had something else he could offer – a personal touch. With Matsudaira's agreement, Arima arranged for archers in several different parts of the siege works to shoot ten copies of an arrow-letter into Hara Castle. It read as follows:

This land is our old home ground. For that reason, we would like to ask you the reasons for your confinement. Is it really all because of religion? Since this land is our old fief, after listening to your demands, I would like to consult with the envoys of the Shōgun and settle the matter fittingly. Henceforth, I would like to discuss face-to-face with you, rather than by correspondence, the prospect of an armistice. Set a date for me to send an envoy into the castle, or even by the wall if you prefer. Initially, to negotiate terms, we will send Tanaka Gyobunosho, with whom we are sure that many of you are familiar.[3]

Although the letter was addressed to Jerome, its message was intended for others. Arima suspected that many of his father's old samurai were among the leaders of the rebels within the castle, and that many of them would remember their former comrades from Sekigahara and Korea, such as the aforementioned Tanaka – presumably one of the retainers who had been permitted to leave the area with Arima when he was reassigned in 1614.

Inside the castle, facing what appears to have been dissent in the ranks, Jerome issued an edict to the other rebels, calling for individual group leaders to maintain authority. The proclamation, known as the *Shirō Hattogaki* ('Laws of Jerome'), is a primary source for the attitude and belief of the rebels' young general. A copy, shot out of the castle by an unknown archer, fell into the hands of House Hosokawa, but it was largely ignored at the time because it used many Latin and Portuguese terms that were meaningless to non-Christians. It said:

Needless to say, all of you are already aware of these things, but I write them down anyway.

- We who are confined within this castle now are all, myself included, sinners whose redemption in another life is in doubt. You never know the great fortune that finds you as one of the chosen few in this castle, through God's will. Let us serve without being negligent.
- Not only good behaviours such as *Oratio* [prayer], *Jejun* [fasting] and *Disciplina* [flagellation], but also construction work in the castle, measures to defend against the *Herege* [heretics] and accomplishments in weapons, are also service to God.
- It is said that our life in this present world is as short as a dream but I think for us within this castle, our doom is even closer. Let us be diligent, atone for past misdeeds, and pray.
- As you know, despite enjoying immeasurable favour from God, whose plan we cannot know, we have ignored the warning from people around us and have kept our

selfishness. To be honest, our lack of patience and modesty caused these latest events. All of you in this castle are friends in this world and also in another. Let us console each other and make praiseworthy the remainder of our lives.

- Carelessness cannot be permitted at this crucial time. Especially as now is the period of *Quaresma* [Lent]. Let us serve by holding our positions night and day. I heard some of you have gone into your huts to rest, but that is impious.

- Those who do not understand what I have said will be abandoned to the law of the *tengu* and will lose their lives. To avoid this, stay at your posts.

- I heard that some of you have gone out of the castle to collect firewood and to get water. If you need to do so, keep to the rules and follow the orders of your chief. Each leader should supervise.

- The leaders should communicate the above points so that everyone will understand. Above all, if you are patient, modest and work hard to do good deeds, God will show you mercy.[4]

There are some strange inconsistencies in the proclamation. Despite the scattered use of Latin, the word *Deus* does not appear. Instead, when Jerome speaks of God, he uses the Japanese term, *kami*. The document is also signed with two names. One of them, Masuda Shirō, is Jerome's. The other is a Christian name – Francisco. It is unclear if the signature is intended as a parenthetical addition (i.e. that Jerome had, for some reason, adopted a new Christian name), or if it is the name of a second individual. There were undoubtedly *padres* within the confines of Hara Castle, but it has always been assumed that they were of native Japanese origin. There is no record in church annals of any foreign missionaries among those at Hara, but could Couckebacker's earlier supposition have been correct, that at least one forgotten European priest was among the rebels at Hara?

If truly the work of the youthful leader, the *Laws of Jerome* throws many of the folktales of child prodigy into sharp relief. The text gives the strong impression of a wise and thoughtful leader, fluent in many theological concepts, ably dealing with what appears to be schisms within the castle between pacifist Christians, radical warrior-Christians, and other denizens ready to give up on their duties or disobey strict regulations. The leader of House Hosokawa, even though he did not understand much of the foreign terminology, later commented that this Jerome was fit to run his own domain.

But if the *Laws of Jerome* dealt with one set of problems within the castle, more were on their way. Lord Arima's chief negotiator, called Gorozaemon in contemporary accounts, seems to have played a role in the next part of the plan. On the same day, 15 March, Jerome's captive younger sister, Marina, and nephew Paulo were permitted to visit him inside the castle. The excuse was that the children would carry a message from the besiegers, reiterating the peacemaking tone of Arima's public arrow-letters. The children were possibly accompanied by armed guards, or had their entry to the castle guaranteed by an exchange of prisoners of similar value to the outside world, because they did not stay in the camp but returned to the siege works after meeting with Jerome. With them, they took a letter, written in the name of Martha and her daughter Regina, and addressed to Jerome and his father Peter:

Shirō is the leader so we understand that he cannot walk around, but we would like to see him somewhere, even if it is just a glimpse through an arrow slit. We will hear your answer soon from [Paulo], but wanted to write ourselves. We have been summoned by the Shōgun's legates, Messrs Matsudaira and Toda, and as [Paulo] is to be sent to the castle, we wrote this letter as well. You have deserted us and become a nuisance to others, which makes us feel wretched. Please set free the *gentios* [heathens] whom you have confined, and then we will be sent to join you in return. If you doubt their word, they say they will set up a meeting with you anywhere you like, all depending on our answer. Anyway, we would love to be reunited with you, so please show sense and agree to an exchange. Awaiting your reply.[5]

Although signed in the names of Martha and Regina, the letter had plainly been written at the instigation of, and with a wording approved by, Jerome's enemies. Determined to put on a good show, the rebels entertained the children with an ostentatious dinner. Back among their captors, Marina and Paulo reported that Jerome had offered them persimmons, Satsuma oranges, sweet buns and a local fruit called *kunebu* – a claim designed to persuade the besiegers that the rebels had plenty of food, and were anything but the starving wretches that the besiegers hoped to see.[6]

However, the besiegers could hardly care less about what impression the rebels hoped to give. The children were sent in as a deliberate tug at the heartstrings, while the true reason behind the trip was likely to have been an attempt to pass a message directly to the traitor-in-waiting, Yamada Emonsaku. Perhaps Yamada received a message from the children's guards; perhaps he had been a hostage exchanged temporarily for the children, and hence able to talk to the besiegers while the children tucked into their fruits and candy. Whatever the means of access, the result was the same – by the evening of 16 March, an excited Arima was able to report to Matsudaira that the original arrow-letter was not a fake. Yamada Emonsaku was indeed trying to contact the besieging generals in secret.

The next day, Yamada was able to engineer another meeting with Arima. This time, under the guise of discussing a ceasefire, the two men met down on Oye beach, in full view of both camps. Yamada

wore his best clothes, 'in honour of the lord to whom three generations of his family had offered loyal service.' Arima had hoped that
Yamada would come with another old veteran, Ashizuka Chūemon,
but Yamada arrived alone, claiming that Ashizuka had been taken ill.

Yamada claimed that he had never wanted to join the rebels. He
said that he was still a loyal retainer of Young Matsukura (Arima's
successor), but that such a majority of his own retainers had flocked
to the rebel cause that he had been unable to order them back. On
several occasions, Yamada claimed, he had planned to escape from
the rebel army, but he had been thwarted every time. It was still
impossible for him to do so, because members of his family were still
inside the castle, and sure to be executed if he ran.[7]

For some of the besieging generals, Yamada's claims still seemed
too good to be true. Could it really be true that the commander of
800 men, a respected pillar of the community, would be swept along
by other people's religious fervour? Matsudaira and his inner circle
decided that they would continue to proceed with caution, as they
had still not entirely ruled out the chance that the entire story was an
elaborate ruse by Jerome to find out the besiegers' own plans.

By late March, it was plain that the siege was approaching its final
days. Several groups of samurai without large enough political clout
were politely told to go home. Others were reassigned to coastguard
duties, in the full expectation that the castle would soon fall, and that
rebels would flee by any means necessary. The government forces
were determined to ensure that nobody at Hara could sneak back to
their former life unpunished. The Amakusa archipelago was almost
entirely deserted – its sole residents were the soldiers and supply
units who kept watch at checkpoints. Nobody was going home.

Within the castle, too, there were those who thought that the
rebels' time was up. On 28 March, Palm Sunday, the six hundredth
shot of the Nabeshima artillery battery hit home with devastating
force. Although the samurai were not aware of its effect at the time,
it smashed through the wall of the main keep, and landed in the

midst of Jerome Amakusa's closest retainers. Five or six of Jerome's lieutenants were killed in the explosion, while their leader, who had purportedly been playing a game of Go at the time, escaped relatively unharmed, but with tattered clothing and a torn left sleeve.

It was a miraculous escape, but not miraculous enough for some of the Christians, who now whispered that Jerome had lost Heaven's protection, and that the close call with the cannonball was a sign that their fortunes were about to change for the worse. In the aftermath of the siege, many weeks later, turncoats cited the damage from Nabeshima cannonball number 600 as the crucial moment when they lost confidence in their leader.[8]

On the north side, the Kumamoto division had hatched another of their unconventional schemes. They returned to the tunnel which they had been digging, on and off, since 10 March, back when the Dutch were still around. The tunnel had been the site of their ill-fated demolition experiment; now it served a more prosaic purpose. Hosokawa hoped that his men would be able to simply dig far enough through the cliffs to reach the interior of the Third Citadel.

At dawn on 28 March, two Hosokawa spies sneaked along the tunnel into the third keep. Both had ropes tied about their waists, so that their colleagues would be able to drag them out of the tunnel. They returned to report that the tunnel had indeed reached the rebel lines – it appeared to have its exit in the side of one of the trenches that the rebels had newly dug in the castle ground to afford protection against artillery. The maze of trenches and piles of earth, and the jumble of bamboo and wooden screens had allowed the tunnel exit to go undetected.[9]

It was a fine plan, but one that was soon guessed by the rebels within, who had no trouble hearing the clangs and scratches of picks and shovels beneath the wall. Veterans of many sieges from the civil war, the rebels had plenty of schemes to make the excavators' lives quite miserable. The rebels lay in wait (some sources suggest they dug a counter-mine of their own), and when the first glimpses of

Hosokawa samurai could be seen they sprang into action. Vats of fetid faeces and urine were poured in through the first holes. For a moment, observers from the far side of the besiegers' camp saw smoke rising behind the walls, and assumed that a battle now raged inside the third keep, but in fact, they were only witnessing the rebels' next defensive move. Within the castle, Jerome's men had lit great bonfires of pine branches, filling the air with pungent, stinging fumes, choking the mineshaft with smoke and threatening the wooden supports with collapse.[10]

Hosokawa's plot was tantalisingly close to success. The diggers and the defenders got close enough to exchange gunfire, but the rain of ordure, flaming wood and musketry was enough to push them back. Immediately afterwards, the rebels blocked the tunnel with a rockfall.[11]

The besiegers were not the only ones to try trickery. Hosokawa Tadatoshi noticed that on some nights the rebels placed a light in a lantern at the topmost point of the main keep. Attributing some sort of religious significance to it, the samurai first paid no attention, but Hosokawa began to suspect that the light was in fact a signal. Once the idea had taken root in his mind, Hosokawa started to imagine signals everywhere. He was particularly suspicious when he saw kites flying inside the castle grounds. It could have been Christian children playing, but Hosokawa was certain that he saw other kites in the hills flying at the same time – as if someone in hiding were answering signals from the rebels in the castle. The kites particularly frustrated Hosokawa, as they appeared at too great a distance for him to send scouts to investigate. The signals became such an irritation to him that he eventually resorted to posting special guards with orders to face away from the castle, and with rather vague instructions to watch for 'anything unusual.'[12]

Other stories of espionage are less convincing. It has become customary among later authors to claim that the siege of Hara Castle was one of the last known historical incidents in which ninja were used in a military context. Such stories take stories of 'spies' and 'sneak attacks' from the historical record, and attempt to embellish them with images born of twentieth-century potboilers – black-clad peasant warriors armed with various tricks and traps. There were certainly lower-class labourers digging tunnels and lashing together palisades, particularly among the Hosokawa forces, who had not come quite so far as some other regiments. Some may have even been co-opted into the samurai numbers for certain special missions. But there is no evidence in the original documents of ninja. The Hosokawa clan's own chronicle reports a night-time sneak attack, perhaps even using the infamous tunnel, during which a samurai led several peasant soldiers deep into enemy territory. He urged them to attack, but instead they trembled behind their shields. Reading between the lines, a group of labourers and their samurai master may have accidentally stumbled in close proximity to a group of rebels. The samurai may have blamed his failure to engage the enemy on the lack of bravery of his non-samurai platoon, but this is hardly evidence of the presence of ninja.

It seems possible that some of the claims for superhuman spies were positive spins put on defectors. In one case, a man came bolt-ing out of the castle, stones pelting down around him from the walls, a flag torn from the walls held tightly in his hand. He was taken to Matsudaira and thoroughly debriefed, reporting on condi-tions in the castle. Popular myth held that the man was a ninja, tasked by Matsudaira himself with the mission of mingling with the rebels and ascertaining the plans. Supposedly, the man was a native of the Shiga region, and consequently was afraid to speak inside the castle lest any of the rebels question his accent. He also claimed to have had trouble himself following the rough rural dialect of the rebels, and was petrified that he might be called upon to perform some sort of religious act, which, too, would have found him out. The story, however, seems suspiciously close to that of a simple defector, assigned a bogus espionage background after the fact.

House Hosokawa's own siege diary noted that a youth from a distant province had fled the castle on 30 March. Interrogated by the samurai, he had claimed not to be a Christian, but a local who had been dragged along with the revolt, and who had no desire to starve or be slain in the name of the Christian Deus and his prophet Jerome. The man gave a detailed report of conditions inside the castle, noting that some of the soldiers were so weak that they performed their 'guard duty' lying down, and that food shortages were so severe that the rebels had taken to dismantling sandbags in the bunkers and boiling the sacks in an attempt to make something edible from the component rice straw.

The defector's story seems plausible, but may have become distorted among the campfires until it became a story of ninja derring-do. There seems to have been little cooperation among the camps, and if Matsudaira and the Hosokawa clan had lucked into some good intelligence from a defector, it is not impossible that the story could have been reversed in the telling, so that the fleeing man was not a disheartened rebel seeking sanctuary, but a tough super-spy making a bold dash back to his own forces.[13]

The samurai regiments continued to concentrate their efforts on siege craft, putting crowds of labourers to work on new mounds, watchtowers and access trenches. On 2 April, Tachibana clan work-men were piling up earth and assembling scaffolding for some sort of tower close to the walls. As soon as they were in range of the castle, rebels began hurling rocks at them. One turned and remonstrated with his attackers, pleading with the rebels that he was only a humble labourer, merely following the orders of his masters. He had no desire to be out here in the wind and the rain cobbling together a watchtower, and neither did any of his associates.

Bizarrely, the workman's complaint caused the barrage of rocks to cease. Even though their activities would certainly be of no benefit to the insurgents, the workmen were left to complete their task without any further harassment. Someone in the castle, it seems, had realised that the workmen were telling the truth, and that many of the men in the camp of the besiegers were not bloodthirsty young samurai at all, but unlucky locals who had been drafted in to do the dirty work. If they were unhappy enough with their lot, the rebels inside the castle might hope to turn them to their own cause.

There were no samurai nearby, so the rebels appear to have been prepared to show their faces at the battlements, watching the labourers with curiosity. As the labourers finished and turned to go back to their tents, one of them shouted up at the walls. 'You there, in the castle! You, living up there in holes and trenches dug in the earth. You've got nothing to eat but soybeans and dried fish. That's the sorry story we hear. Why don't you just give up and come down here?'[14]

A rebel man appeared on the battlements and yelled down a reply: 'We might live in holes, that much is true, but look! Every day we get to eat fresh fish like this!' With that, he held up a fresh mullet.

But despite such banter on the frontlines, the rebels in the castle were still troubled by the change in strategy. Jerome himself called a council and set out the situation:

> Lately the assailants have ceased to attack the castle, and appear to be waiting until provisions in the castle are exhausted. Moreover, the provisions in the castle will not last many days; therefore the overthrow of this place is at hand and we must resolve on some course before our strength is exhausted. What is your advice?[15]

The surviving veterans in the castle hatched a plan of sorts, and chose a fateful day to carry it out. By luck or design, the allotted day for a counter-attack would be 3 April, the eve of the day that Yamada Emonsaku had decided to plan his traitorous surprise.

In a moment of inadvertent historical irony, Yamada's final arrow-letter was fired out of Hara Castle on April Fool's Day. It announced

his intention to set fire to parts of the camp, and to dupe Jerome into
following him onto a boat. It neglected, however, to mention any
rebel plans for a counter-attack.

Yamada had spent the day waiting in the part of Hara Castle
where he might expect a reply to arrive – each of the sub-
commanders were billeted in separate sections of the castle. But
unluckily for Yamada, he appears to have gone to sleep by the time
Matsudaira's reply was shot over the battlements. Instead, the arrow
was picked up by a nightwatchman who was not one of Yamada's
own men, and taken straight to Jerome.[16]

Yamada was dragged before a council of the rebels, where an
angry Jerome was waiting. He had not seen any of Yamada's letters to
the forces outside, but Matsudaira's reply gave enough away to put
Jerome in a murderous mood. Yamada's wife and children were put
to death immediately. The surviving exchange between Yamada and
Jerome seems, if it has any grain of truth in it, to have been delivered
when Yamada himself was being prepared for execution. Even filtered
through a translation, the words retain the desperate sophistry of a
man pleading for his life.

'You are a commander within the inner wall,' Jerome is supposed
to have said, 'and a leader of the [rebels]. For what reason, then, have
you sent a treacherous letter to the assailants?'

Yamada's reply turned the facts of the discovery on their head:

I have never dreamed of doing such a thing. I am indeed
known amongst our troops as the commander of 800 men.
Though I alone might be a traitor, is it probable that all the
800 are such? This is, more likely, a plan of the enemy to raise
discord in the camp, and secure the destruction of 800 men,
and thus render the taking of the castle easier . . . The assailants know where I am posted, and had they shot the letter in
at any other point, it would have failed of its object. Its falling
at my post was well calculated to bring me into suspicion and

subject me to examination. But I have no concern for my life. Having deprived me of my family, despatch me also. The future will prove the truth or falsehood of my words.[17]

Yamada's plea from the execution block was enough to sway at least some of his captors. Unsure of whether they were being strung along by enemy propaganda, and unwilling to believe that all 800 of Yamada's men would have been prepared to betray them, the rebels reached the best compromise they could, and locked Yamada away in a makeshift prison cell.

None of this was known at the time to Matsudaira, nor did he understand the religious significance of the hour – 4 April 1638 was Easter Sunday. At dawn, at the appointed hour for Yamada's scheme, there were the sounds of a scuffle and signs of bonfires inside the castle, but if any samurai attempted to get into the castle, they were unsuccessful. Nor did they receive any assistance from within. Matsudaira's first thought appears to have been that the entire Yamada plot had been a ruse all along. There was a ruse at work, but if there was action within the castle, it was designed to keep the samurai outside from noticing another mission. Although government reports are uncharacteristically cagey about it, it would seem that although nobody got into the castle, a fair number of people may have got *out*, particularly on the night of 4 April.

Tachibana Tadashige, leader of the division camped immediately south of the Kumamoto samurai, thought he heard something scratching in the dark. He peered to the south, to the area of scrubland between his tents and those of Young Matsukura a mere hundred feet away. Tiny red sparks glowed dull in the distance, like fireflies wafting gently on the breeze. Except there should not be any fireflies in April – Tachibana realised that he was staring at the fuses of maybe fifty matchlock muskets, glowing and ready to fire as rebels sneaked up on the camp. He sounded the alarm and the men of the two camps converged on a rebel sneak attack.

Tachibana was only the first to notice. There were groups of other rebels all over the promontory, some with fire arrows ready to unleash chaos into the besiegers' camp. Others were soldiers guarding what could only be described as raiding parties – the strongest and fastest rebels, tasked with stealing anything of value from the samurai camp, with particular emphasis on food.

In the Terazawa camp, nobody heard the rebels until they had smashed through the bamboo fence and were almost upon Lord Terazawa's own tent. One alert soldier raised the alarm, holding off the rebel attack with a single sword, while his fellow retainers scurried to find their own weapons in the dark.

The noise of the fighting in these camps alerted the other leaders. On the southernmost flank, Kuroda Kenmotsu and a platoon of ten watchmen had just enough time to grab their weapons before a hundred attackers 'came on them like a cloud.' Kuroda and his tiny platoon held off the attack during a vital couple of minutes while the rest of Kuroda camp woke. But even as Kuroda's two sons arrived at the scene with a larger force, a lucky musket-shot darted past the faceplate of Kuroda's helmet and into his skull, killing him instantly.[18]

A few hundred rebels died in the skirmish, but they inflicted similar losses on the government forces. Although fighting had been fierce, several rebels had been wounded and left behind by their retreating comrades, providing Matsudaira with fresh victims for interrogation.

In the cold light of dawn, they told Matsudaira that they had been a raiding party in search of food. He asked them if they knew of a Yamada Emonsaku in their camp. The captives replied that there was a man fitting his description, but that he had recently been imprisoned on suspicion of espionage. It was only then that Matsudaira knew for sure that his inside man had been genuine. Now it was too late.

But Matsudaira took heart from other evidence in the aftermath of the raid. The rebels were clearly running low on supplies if they were prepared to mount a desperate mission to steal food from their enemies. The government forces were not above putting every resource to good use – a report survives of the dissection and amateur post-mortem examination of some of the fallen rebels. We know today what the rebels had been eating inside the castle because the samurai hacked open their corpses.

> And when the stomachs of the dead enemy were cut open, it was discovered that they had been eating seaweed, tree leaves, unripe barley, and suchlike. Not one was there whose stomach had rice in it.[19]

Meanwhile, a shipment of new musket balls and ammunition arrived from Ōsaka. The time was right for Matsudaira to put an end to the siege. Accordingly, he called his generals in for another conference, and announced that the grand assault against Hara Castle would commence on 9 April.[20]

CHAPTER TEN

The End of the World

....

Oye beach, where Arima and Yamada had their meeting, has changed beyond recognition in the intervening centuries. Back in the time of Jerome, it was a great swathe of open sand and salt marshes between the high ground of Hara Castle and the shoreline where the besiegers pitched their camps. Their meeting was witnessed by both besiegers and besieged, because the beach itself extended between Hara Castle and the shoreline.

Today, all that has gone. The last remnant of Oye beach is a thin strip of white sand on the outer edge. Modern Hara citizens live on ground that has been snatched from the sea. The river has been locked into its twentieth-century course. A square, artificial harbour has been dredged deep into the shoreline, like an arrow wound. The houses and fields of the modern town of Hara are built right across where the low, tidal marsh once was. Strangely, the old hills remain almost un-occupied – nobody has built on the ruins of Hara Castle itself, but the high ground where Matsudaira's samurai once pitched their tents is also left largely untouched. Even today, it is green and thickly forested.

In 1638, the road to Hara Castle was obvious. Today, even though the castle heights are clearly visible from the station, one must negotiate a maze of houses and side streets to find it. The South Arima Middle School now stands on the spot where Lord Arima and Yamada once tried to negotiate their double-crossing plans. A monument to the rebels sits in the middle of piles of sand at a building site, forgotten by all but the local schoolchildren, who sometimes use it as a goalpost. The last vestiges of Oye beach are now largely forgotten. Anglers with long rods for sea-fishing prefer to perch out on the grey stone of the new sea wall, which juts far past the old coastline.

What's left of Oye beach is strewn with trash, plastic bottles and smashed glass, worn to coral curves by the action of the waves. A long jumble of tetrapods, those massive concrete jacks so favoured by Japanese construction companies, forms an auxiliary sea wall. From the sliver of beach, one can easily see Parley Island in the mist, sitting like an upturned rice bowl out in Shimabara Bay.

It is 28° C when I am there, on an October day only slightly warmer than what the rebels might have faced in April. I diligently try to follow a path marked along the sea wall on my map, but it is soon overgrown with a thatch of grass and bushes. Sharp thorns dig into my sandalled toes, and I retreat, bloodied, to try a different approach.

Eventually, I find the road to the castle, which follows the old path from Jerome's day, leading right up to the Amakusa Keep – so named because from here one can look out across the bay, past Parley Island, to the distant hills of the Amakusa islands in the blue distance. It is a steep climb up to what was once the Oye gate, enough to defeat a modern car driver who is not watching the gears on his vehicle. It is scarcely easier on foot, but I make it. Finally, I see the castle itself, or what is left of it. From what was once the Amakusa Keep, one gets a fine view of the gigantic, steep walls of the main bastion.

Climbing to Amakusa Keep is half the battle. Everybody knew that.

April meant April showers. Soon after Matsudaira's decision, the heavens opened in a downpour that lasted for the rest of the week. When the appointed deadline for the attack arrived, Matsudaira decided to wait two extra days. He had played a waiting game since February, and saw no reason to hurry. The losses from the rebel assault had been regrettable, but could largely be blamed on over-confidence. If the government forces had been mounting proper watches through the night, they would never have been taken by surprise. Matsudaira saw no problem with letting the rebels starve some more until dawn on 11 April, and told his generals to hold fire for the moment.

However, Matsudaira had not counted on the attitude of his soldiers. The late Itakura Shigemasa had not been the only warrior spoiling for a fight, and the Shōgunate force was far from unified. On the northern flank, the samurai from House Hosokawa were more than eager to charge through the Hinoe gate into the third enclosure. On the southern flank, the Kuroda and Terazawa groups were simi-larly keen to attack the Amakusa keep via the Oye gate. In between them, the various other samurai fretted that the soldiers nearest the main entrances would be sure to have an easier time of it. For the ones in the middle – Nabeshima, for example, Ogasawara and even the diplomatic Arima contingent – the coming assault was sure to be a dismal trudge through acres of boggy ground, followed by a death-defying crawl up steep castle walls, quite probably in the dark. And even if the rebels were slowly starving, that would only affect the traditional hand-to-hand fighting likely to be employed at the gates. When it came to dropping a rock on a samurai climbing a wall, star-vation would make no difference – odds still favoured the man or woman who dropped the rock.

Matsudaira's leadership throughout the siege is largely exemplary, but on this occasion, he appears to have misjudged his underlings' desire for glory, for revenge, and for a swift resolution. While he sat in his tent far from the front line and pondered his maps, rivalry among the besiegers reached a critical peak.

The Hosokawa encampment, on the north side, was making great progress – the labourers who had bantered so boisterously with the besieged Christians had almost completed their tasks. They had finished dumping earth to make an artificial mound at around the time of the rebel counter-assault. Working through the night, they commenced construction of a reconnaissance tower on the evening of 6 April. A precarious, rickety lookout post, it was pronounced 'nearly finished' the following day. A Hosokawa retainer risked his life by climbing up to the crow's nest, and peered down at the rebel camp. His fellow samurai provided heavy cannon cover to keep the marksmen from shooting him out of the tower. In breaks in the barrage, he yelled down impromptu advice, as a form of artillery spotter.

His extant report to the clan headquarters showed the customary Hosokawa cunning. The clan was planning ahead, not for the assault on the outer walls, but for the best way to use their resources once inside:

We can see into the third keep without any trouble ... The part that was reinforced with sandbags was not damaged. Moreover, they have dug a ditch behind the wall and the earth was piled up behind the wall, so the men in the trench have suffered no damage. But I can see no men outside of the third wall ... probably they will defend from the second keep.[1]

House Hosokawa was finally reaping the reward of an early arrival. Their camp might be furthest from the main keep, but they now knew that their one problem was likely to be the initial Hinoe gate assault. Once inside, the third keep would be theirs, and they would be able to augment their assault with artillery, the effects of which could be immediately reported to the gunners by the spotters in the new reconnaissance tower.

Whether the Hosokawa shared their intelligence with their fellow samurai or not, the other samurai were determined to make the best of their own situation. The Nabeshima camp sat right in the middle of the promontory, an accident of geography caused it to be closest to a castle ridge that jutted to the west. But for the samurai clustered around the north and south gates, the Nabeshima camp was closest to Hara castle proper. Back in February, when the government forces had last planned an old-fashioned full-frontal assault, the Nabeshima group had counted themselves lucky. They had also benefited from the killing zone generated by the artillery – since they faced the geographical midpoint of the castle, they were most likely to enjoy artillery cover. Now, they were not so sure.

Nabeshima Naosumi, their leader, decided to take matters into his own hands. Matsudaira might have called off the assault, but Lord Nabeshima had hatched a scheme of his own. He said to his lieutenants:

> When we look at the part of the castle opposite us, it appears that the inmates of the castle have ceased to pass by there. This is because of the heavy fire kept on this part from the mounds and the towers. Let us then take the first wall, erect pickets, and keep up a fire. If we do so, the farmers, unable to endure it, will certainly come out and attack our camp; and we, then, will drive them back, and entering along with them, take the castle.[2]

Nabeshima had realised that he missed a golden opportunity on the night of the rebel attack. If he had only been prepared, he could have led his men in a 'counter-attack' and, once in the castle, he could have kept on going. By fighting a defensive action that kept on 'defending' far longer than necessary, he could have been the first in the castle. He would have gained all the glory, like his namesake Ii Naosumi and the Red Devils at the legendary Battle of Sekigahara: he could have 'defended' his way into the history books.

So it was that Nabeshima's men donned their armour and marched out at noon on 10 April, a full eighteen hours before

Matsudaira's revised battle plan was due to commence. Since they were advancing, quite literally, in broad daylight, it was immediately apparent to everyone what they were up to. Observers in both the Arima and Ogasawara camps demanded to know what they were doing, and loudly reminded them that the hour had not yet come. Lying through their teeth, Nabeshima's fully armoured lieutenants replied that they were simply reconnoitring the outskirts of their camp.

If Nabeshima's deception did not fool his fellow samurai, it was certainly not going to fool the rebels, who prepared to repel an attack. However, as rebel marksmen opened up on the Nabeshima group, Nabeshima's own musketeers began a devastating series of salvoes.

Under cover of the relentless musket fire, a platoon of some seven or eight men charged the castle and climbed the wall. It is not clear who their leader was, but by the time the group reached the top of the wall, the highest-ranking survivor was an eighteen-year-old boy.

He yelled back down to the besiegers that the record should show that he, Sakakibara Norinobu, was the first man in the castle. It is not clear if anyone heard him above the noise of the gunfire, but like most samurai he wore a distinctive *sashimono* banner on his back. The Sakakibara colours were a bright yellow, and easily visible in the noon light. Sakakibara's own father identified the family flag, and immediately began clambering up the wall after him. A group of Nabeshima samurai followed suit, and the race was on.

The action by the Nabeshima samurai scandalised the other government forces. But regardless of Matsudaira's order, an attack was under way. Every other division with men close to the castle commenced an assault of their own.

Not to be outdone, the Hosokawa division sprinted for the north side of the castle. As they rounded the headland near the Hinoe gate, they stumbled across a group of some two hundred rebels knee-deep in the water, gathering seaweed. Some of the Hosokawa samurai charged the fishermen, hacking the unarmed foragers down in the shallows. But as the rebels fled back to the castle, other Hosokawa samurai chased after them, towards a gate that remained tantalisingly open.

The Hosokawa division made it into the castle, and swiftly set up makeshift barricades to defend themselves. But their success was short-lived. I have paced over the distance from the sea gate to the central keep – it takes ten minutes, and that is without rocks, arrows and attacks by swordsmen. Hosokawa's men might have made it through one wall, but they did not make it far inside. Instead, they held their position, turning the north gate into their new bastion.

Nabeshima's chancers in the centre had less luck. They might have made it to the lower enclosure, but the castle still held some surprises. They were unable to fan out, as immediately north of their position was the Empty Moat – a large pit that prevented them from rushing up to unite with the Hosokawa division. To the south was a long, thin killing zone that led to the Amakusa Keep. Had Nabeshima's men been able to make it along there, they might have taken the south gate. But there was no way the Nabeshima groups could run a gauntlet of fire, rock, oil, and hot sand from the main keep above them, and they were forced to withdraw.

The only real beneficiaries were the Kuroda samurai, who somehow managed to hang onto the Amakusa Keep. It wasn't worth much, but nevertheless, the Kuroda would have a marginally less arduous climb on the day of the final assault.

Matsudaira's thoughts on the abortive assault are unrecorded. Lord Nabeshima was eventually put under house arrest for disobeying orders, so he did not quite get away with it. But the Japanese records may have attempted to hide something else, in which deception they have largely been successful. It is not disputed among historians that the chaos on 10 April was so complete that some government divisions were injured by friendly fire. But one source, often overlooked by Japanese historians, makes the tantalising claim that, far from merely exchanging angry words, the government forces had actively turned upon each other during the attack.

Nicholas Couckebacker was not present to witness the day's events, but several months later he did describe them in a letter, possibly using sources that were later hushed up or denied a place in the official record:

> The [casualties] in the Imperial army were . . . mostly killed by their own people and guns. The cause of this was that Findadonno [Terazawa?], one day before the day fixed by His Majesty for the attack, went forward with about thirty men to set the nearest houses on fire in the abandoned fortifications. Thereupon followed the Lord of Lusoysjo [Nabeshima] with all his troops to attack the besieged, without the councillors Insindonno [Matsudaira] and Sammondonno [Toda] knowing, and notwithstanding the latter had resolved, early in the morning of that day, to wait for the attack for the following day. There had for some time been some discord between the Lords of Lusoysjo [Nabeshima] and the Lord of Higo [Hosokawa] as to whose troops should form the vanguard. *The whole army became tumultuous and commenced such a furious attack that they did not obey the order to finish with the charge, but commenced to attack each other as if they were enemies.* [my italics][3]

If Couckebacker's claims are true, then it is easy to imagine Matsudaira's deteriorating patience – religious fanatics within the castle, and martial fanatics on the outside, everybody determined to die a glorious death. It was with weary relief that Matsudaira restated his original order. The samurai were to attack at dawn the following day, and take the castle, at long last.

He should not have been surprised that his followers were already planning to disobey him again. Flushed with his success at taking the

Amakusa Keep, the leader of the Kuroda troops made a secret speech to his men:

> Everyone knows the disadvantages under which we have laboured today, and that we could not have done better than we did. Still, it is a matter of grief to me that we were behind the others in storming the walls. The time to begin the attack is fixed at eight o'clock tomorrow morning, but we will begin the attack before daylight, and be the first to mount the inner wall. Let this order be circulated in our camp, and let preparation be made accordingly.[4]

No mention is made of any protest among Kuroda's men. Instead, a series of lieutenants and elder samurai offered their fervent support, determined to prove themselves against what they saw as the sneaky schemes of the Nabeshima and Hosokawa divisions. One old soldier boasted that he would repay his master's years of kindness by leading the charge, and 'leaving his old bones' on the castle wall.

Similar meetings and plots were taking place all over the samurai camp, although only one other is recorded. In the Hosokawa division, the late Itakura Shigemasa's twenty-one-year-old son Shigenori begged to be given a prominent role in the final battle.

'My father . . . was killed by the conspirators,' he said. 'Though I am not ambitious to gain renown by fighting with farmers, I would like to lead my father's troops tomorrow.' His request was granted.[5]

Before the sun was even up on the morning of 11 April, the Kuroda samurai began their attack. Although the Kuroda troops held the Amakusa Keep, they still had a difficult ascent, directly against the forbidding walls of the main keep. For the soldiers that led the charge, it was universally understood that few if any of them were liable to make it off the battlefield alive.

The rebels were waiting, ready to drop more large rocks on the climbing samurai, as well as timbers from the buildings within.

Notably, the record does not mention any musketry from within the castle: the defenders appeared to have run out of ammunition or gunpowder, which helps to explain the desperate supply raid of the previous week. Instead, rebel missiles now took on a tragic, final aspect – Jerome's men and women hurled their own cooking pots at the attackers.

The Kuroda suicide attack took heavy losses, but as wave after wave of yelling samurai rushed the wall, some inevitably made it through. The record shows, somewhat doubtfully, that Kuroda Emonnosuke was the first to reach the top of the wall – it is not impossible, but something of a coincidence that the highest-ranking officer should get the glory. Other Kuroda retainers were close behind him, and fire-arrows arched over his head into the keep.

The tents and makeshift huts of the rebels had had just enough time to dry out after the earlier rains. Now they burst into flames, and the screams of women and children joined the yells of soldiers outside. Not all were unwilling victims – some rushed into the flames rather than face the soldiers. A shocked attacker described what he saw:

> I saw that many wrapped their hands in their sleeves to shove aside the burning embers so they could enter the buildings. They also pushed their children inside and then lay on top of them to perish. Words fail me, that such lowly people could attain such commendable deaths.[6]

All around the castle, the other samurai charged across the marshes and fields, and around the palisades, and began the long climbs up the steep walls – all except the Hosokawa samurai in the north at the Hinoe gate, who obligingly kept their word to Itakura Shigenori. The young samurai, resplendent in red armour and carrying a long spear, presented himself at the haphazardly fortified Hinoe gate, and announced it was time to let him into the castle. The government guardsmen happily smashed down their own palisade, allowing Shigenori and his four retainers through into the castle. There, they immediately ran into a mass of defenders, and battle commenced.[7]

Once Shigenori had led the way, there was no sense in waiting for the appointed hour. The Hosokawa samurai poured in after him. Those left in the northern part of the castle, it seems, largely comprised the less devout rebels – those who did not believe that they were assured of paradise. That, at least, is what implied by one account, which pointedly notes: 'The villagers [around the north gate] fought with desperation, as those whose life was limited to the present moment.'[8]

In the following six hours, thousands of rebels died. Estimates place the number of defenders, slain where they stood or cast, wounded but still breathing, onto the piles of bodies, at some 13,000. Some 23,000 others, chiefly comprising the women and children, were either burned alive, beheaded in the massacre or threw themselves from the battlements and cliffs.[9]

The figures for the wounded on the government side tell the rest of the story. The heaviest losses, some 274 killed and 1824 wounded, were taken by the Hosokawa force that came in behind Shigenori, and then fought its way, step-by-step, across the entire length of the castle. Determined to reach the main keep, despite being as far away from it as it was possible to be without being outside the castle grounds, at least one group from the Hosokawa division veritably sprinted across the castle, ignoring the tents and huts around them, any of which could have harboured enemies ready to resist or block their retreat. But it was now a matter of honour that the Hosokawa samurai reach the keep before the sneaky Kuroda division could benefit from its own early start.

Similar casualties, some 213 killed and 1,657 wounded, were taken by the Kuroda suicide squad that charged the main keep. The other divisions took considerably lower casualties, presumably in falls from the walls as they climbed. For some of the soldiers who were back in the rearguard, the casualty numbers implied that by the time they reached the castle they were able to walk up to the north or south gate and stroll in behind the vanguard, before drawing their swords and joining in the slaughter.

For the soldiers, it was a long day of *ikidameshi* – the testing of swords on the bodies of criminals. Many had not seen action before, and were determined to avenge their fallen comrades. This, in most cases, meant hacking down screaming children, and stabbing women where they lay on the ground, too weak to resist. We must not, either, rule out the likelihood that many of the attackers saw themselves as avenging fallen comrades. Despite Matsudaira's attempt to end the siege with minimal losses to his own side, the four-month affray with 'farmers' in Hara had cost the attackers over 20,000 casualties – 13% of the government forces sent to put down the uprising.[10]

The fall of Hara Castle is sometimes called the last battle of the samurai era. It is only when one reads the reports of the soldiers present that one can understand why many historians are so reluctant to discuss it. The Hosokawa division took several hours to advance from the Third Keep to the Second Keep, a time that was spent largely hacking at the prone forms of starving rebels. They lost a single soldier in their initial advance, but ran into heavy opposition at the wall between the Third and Second Keep – as the lookouts had predicted, the rebels had given up on the outermost wall, and were preparing to make a stand in one of the inner donjons.

Popular myth held that Jerome himself had been planning a divine form of escape. An unlikely story that has somehow survived the carnage tells of an altar built from white stone at the centre of the castle. As the enemy samurai neared, they saw the boy standing on top of the platform, his hands clasped in prayer. As they watched, a dark cloud supposedly hovered near the praying figure. Jerome stepped onto the cloud, ready to make his getaway. A quick-thinking Hosokawa samurai then unleashed a white-feathered arrow, which shot through the magic cloud, dispelling it and leaving Jerome alone and disoriented. He was then stabbed with a lance, and died, pierced through the heart.[11]

Reality, however, was not so tidy or religiously symbolic. In fact, Jerome had not shown himself among the defenders. As the day wore on, the burning ruins of the rebel dwellings collapsed onto castle grounds awash with the blood of thousands. The air was thick with smoke, and the acrid taste of fires partly staunched by human blood. Butchery continued in the castle enclosures, while Hosokawa and Kuroda retainers stood guard over mounting piles of human heads. Hosokawa Tadatoshi wrote to his father's castellan:

Incidentally, we have had many casualties, which is irritating. I did not have time to put my armour on, so I have been running around wearing *calçao* (trousers). If we had followed orders, we would have been late, so I got everyone, even the pages to fight, and many of them were wounded. It is trouble-some because I am lacking competent underlings at the moment . . . I have four or five uninjured ones. I have had the men picking up heads ever since the day after the battle. I still do not know the number. It seems like quite a few have been lost; some were stolen and some destroyed by fire. However, the number that we killed, both men and women, is vast.[12]

Stern, aging samurai were appointed as battlefield accountants, dili-gently cataloguing the heads of men being brought to them, and logging the names of the supposed executioners. As time wore on, and the piles grew, the overseers were prepared to accept noses instead of heads – more portable and convenient. The castle was full of samurai, dragging bodies up to waist height, and then hacking eagerly at the faces. But as the butchery continued, Jerome Amakusa was nowhere to be found.

It was afternoon by the time a Hosokawa retainer named Sasaemon wandered through the ruins of the main keep – the story implies, long after many others had already picked it apart. He had two human heads dangling from his belt, and hoped to find another trophy somewhere nearby. He heard something moving inside one of the burning buildings, and was surprised to find a boy in grubby white robes, badly wounded, struggling to get to his feet. Instead, Sasaemon slashed at the boy with his sword, forcing him back down to the ground. With pieces of the burning roof falling around him, Sasaemon had barely enough time to hew the boy's head roughly from its shoulders, before the beams overhead came crashing down.

Mildly disappointed at such a poor showing of heads, the dejected Sasaemon took his three trophies back towards the west side of the castle, where Hosokawa samurai were flinging them in a massive pile. All the heads were being inspected as they arrived, perhaps in order to avoid an embarrassing incident earlier in the day. A soldier from the Nabeshima division had been caught with the nose of one his fellow soldiers – he had found the body and had hoped to pass off its nose as the relic of an enemy, not a friend. His scandalised superior officer ordered him to kill himself that very afternoon; he was permitted to commit *seppuku*, in an attempt to claw back a little honour.[13]

Perhaps as a result, Sasaemon's trophies were checked by Hosokawa himself as the soldier handed them in. Noting the angelic features on the face of the newest head, Hosokawa asked Sasaemon where he had got it. As Sasaemon explained, his lord nodded with mounting satisfaction. A Hosokawa soldier had just brought home the grand prize.[14]

The head that Sasaemon had taken was only one of several possible candidates, which the samurai leaders had carefully put to one side. Someone would have to identify Jerome for sure, and the list of living witnesses who knew his face was by now getting short. His mother, Martha, was brought up to the castle, and made to walk along a line of heads. Far from being cowed by the sight of Hara Castle in smouldering ruins, she instead courageously turned on her captors, insisting that her son had been sent from Heaven, and that it was likely Heaven had summoned him back again. Her son, she boasted, was no false prophet – surely he had transformed in the final moments of the rebels' last stand, spirited away somewhere beyond the reach of the Shōgun, perhaps to the Catholic Philippines, there to regain his strength, to amass a new army, to return to Japan and destroy his persecutors like the legendary boy-king Sebastian.

It was then that Sasaemon's trophy was held up before her, and her bravado faltered. Martha Masuda was reduced instantly to tears, and cradled the head in her arms.

'Can he really have become so thin?' she sobbed.[15]

CHAPTER ELEVEN

The Secret Places
of the Heart

....

At the base of the main keep, right where Lord Hosokawa once stood examining the pile of heads, there is now a car park. A line of small Buddhist statues gaze benignly down at the empty lot, their features worn away by time. They were put there in 1766 by authorities at a nearby temple – there is supposedly one for each of the villages that lost residents in the rebellion.

I resolve to walk right across the castle promontory, to get a feel for its sheer size. It is immense – large enough to hold the enclosures of Shimabara, Tomioka and Hondo castles combined. It is perhaps three times the size of Dejima, where the Dutch were obliged to make their home for so long.

The modern road follows, approximately, the old path that once ran behind the rebels' auxiliary inner wall. There is an appreciable dip in the ground between where the second and third keep enclosures once were, creating a small valley that plunges down towards the sea. Far in the distance, a farmer is kneeling in one of the fields, plucking at his crops, a small van parked close by. I wonder how many visitors to the castle do not realise that if they stand here, on what appears to be a simple country road, staring up at the ruins in the distance, they are still within the boundaries of the old castle.

Fat crows eye me fearlessly from the trees, until a trio of them sail lazily overhead. It is said that these Hara fields, now home to rows of red peppers, were choked for years with the rotting bodies of the dead. After more than a century, local people began a clearing operation, gathering armfuls of the bones from the fields, and depositing them in a huge stack on its northern edge. In 1766, they covered the macabre remains with earth and erected a small stone on the site. On one side it reads 'Homage to Amida Buddha', and then simply, 'The Tomb of Bones.'

Today it looks like nothing more than a hill, remarkable only because it has not been ploughed into farmland like the acres around it. Close by, at the side of a modern road, is a more obvious grave, the eight-foot-high monolith that marks the last resting place of Itakura Shigemasa, erected by his wealthy descendants more than a century after his death. I gingerly approach the simple stone to get a better look at the long, involved inscription outlining his achievements. The tomb is wreathed in multiple cobwebs. Bulky yellow joro spiders, like armoured samurai at rest, flex their limbs as I draw near. I don't stay long.[1]

A mother's grief was enough for many of the observers, but not all. There was enough dispute over which head was Jerome's for a second opinion to be called for. In the course of the attack, most of the rebels had been slain, but a handful had been found locked in a makeshift prison. They were all retainers of Yamada Emonsaku, the old warrior who had offered to betray Jerome from within the castle, and whose plot had been uncovered with mere hours to go. These men, numbering just over a hundred, are assumed to be the closest retainers of Yamada who were in on the plan, locked away with their master by the rebels, pending some proof that their plot was not a ruse by the enemy to spread dissension.

Yamada himself, starving and weak, was brought from his confinement. The samurai were unsure of how to treat him – now it was confirmed that he had been on their side all along, willing to risk his life in an internal coup, and mourning the family members who had lost their lives over his plan. But Yamada was also a pariah, a warrior who had sworn allegiance to a leader, only to betray him. Some whispered that Yamada would have been better off dying at the fall of the castle. There were even those who still refused to believe Yamada's story, ascribing instead an impossibly intricate scheme to the rebels, that they had drawn lots among themselves to select a warrior with the worst job of all – someone to pretend to be a traitor, so that at least one survivor would live to tell the tale of Hara's fall.[2]

Whatever Yamada's true role in the siege, which nobody could ever be sure of, he wept when he was shown Jerome's severed head. As far as the army was concerned, the identification was positive – their enemy was dead.

With Jerome gone and most of the rebels reportedly killed in the massacre, the days and weeks that followed became a catalogue of grisly bookkeeping. 'Even in the romances of old,' commented one observer, 'there is heard no other example of so many killed in battle.'[3] The hostages from Jerome's own family had outlived their usefulness, and were soon butchered. Jerome's nephew Paulo and younger sister Marina were killed within the week. His father Peter and uncle Sancho appear to have been killed on the day of the castle's fall. His mother Martha, sister Regina and cousin Kozaemon were executed three days later. Nor were these last, petty atrocities limited to those who had been associated directly with Jerome. In a final revelation, it was discovered by House Hosokawa retainers that Martha's mother had been working for them all along as a servant. She, too, was executed, along with Jerome's uncles and cousins. The savagery extended to anyone with the remotest possible connection – Jerome's father's landlord, whose connection was simply to take rental payments on a home and farmland, was deemed enough of a potential sympathiser to warrant execution, along with his entire family.

According to the official record, nobody but Yamada Emonsaku and a handful of his fellow prisoners escaped Hara Castle alive. However, circumstantial evidence in the aftermath suggests that this may not have been the case. The government was keen to draw a line under the Shimabara Rebellion, to proclaim it entirely extinguished, its participants wiped out. This claim was made easier by the firestorm that engulfed the main citadels. Despite exacting accounts of heads taken, and mass graves in Tomioka, Nagasaki and Hara itself, the numbers do not quite match. Estimates of the number of deaths at Hara climb as high as 40,000. But the number of identifiable bodies was substantially less. Couckebacker, for example, recorded in the Hirado diary that '[the rebels] were killed and 17,000 heads put on poles. The others were either burnt to death *or saved themselves by flight.*' [my italics][4]

Two days after the fall of Hara Castle, despite the government's claims that everyone was dead, Matsudaira had platoons of soldiers combing the surrounding countryside for fugitives. In Tomioka, the entire surviving town population was marched outside and made to walk across an image of Christ under the watchful gaze of soldiers. Several days later, some seventy-six Tomioka residents were executed – a sign that some rebels may have made it out from Hara, or perhaps that some never went to Hara at all and somehow evaded the many sweeps along the archipelago in search of stragglers.

Casualties were not restricted to the rebel side: Young Matsukura himself, whose persecutions were believed to have played such a part in stirring the uprising in the first place, was soon ordered to commit ritual suicide, taking the blame for mismanaging the area, but perhaps also dying with several other secrets. It was believed, in inner circles, that the Matsukura family had contributed in other ways to the events in Amakusa, by encouraging and covering up foreign contacts, and even by their abortive plans for foreign expeditions. Even though the Shōgunate had ruled out any more foreign military adventures, it was believed by some that the Matsukura clan had never quite given up on the idea. Some thought that Matsukura had built an arsenal at Kuchinotsu, stocked with guns, powder and supplies for a putative campaign against the Ryūkyū Islands, Taiwan or the Philippines. Although the invasion never took place, its secret stockpiles had been known to the locals, and may have formed a prime contribution to the rebel resources. If that were true, Jerome's rebels had turned Matsukura's own weapons against him.[5]

As for Yamada Emonsaku, once a lay preacher, then a Christian soldier, then an artist, then a rebel, there was no place for him in Shimabara. When Lord Matsudaira returned to the capital after the siege, Yamada went with him. He lived in Matsudaira's mansion thereafter. There is a legend in Japan that, perhaps after many years, the elderly Yamada somehow journeyed back to Nagasaki, where he became a Christian once more. But for this, as for almost every other supposition about Yamada's life, there is no proof.[6]

The Amakusa islands were put under direct government control, and the three neighbouring domains were ordered to cooperate on a small naval patrol to keep out foreigners. A new administrator, Suzuki Shigenari, was sent in to clear up the mess. Suzuki implemented the usual measures, enforcing membership of Buddhist temples, and encouraging immigration from other parts of Japan. The archipelago had been heavily depopulated by the rebellion, and during Suzuki's reign several waves of immigrants arrived from other parts of Japan to take over the land. But life was no easier in post-rebellion Amakusa, which continued to suffer from poor harvests and bad weather. Suzuki soon sent a note to the Shōgunate, reporting that, in his opinion, the tax burden on Amakusa was much too high, and that he did not doubt that it had been a contributing factor to the uprising.

His comments were such an affront to the government that his career was immediately brought to a crashing halt. But Suzuki believed so passionately that the people of Amakusa were being wrongly treated that he committed suicide in protest in 1653. Six years later, the government quietly reduced Amakusa's tax burden by 50%.

The Shōgunate had spoken. Japan was harmonious, Japan was homogeneous – there was no conflict in paradise. The wars were over, the country was at peace, and anyone who disagreed would be imprisoned, tortured or killed. In order to ensure that foreign influences were well and truly purged, Amakusa and Shimabara were integrated into a registry of temple parishioners. The system was pioneered in areas of Christian influence, but expanded within a generation to encompass the entire Japanese state. Every inhabitant of Japan was listed as a member of the congregation of a particular Buddhist temple. That temple would form the centre of their religious existence – the family would worship there when instructed. They would contribute to the temple, when instructed. The temple priest would oversee weddings, bless children, and officiate at funerals. It was all but impossible for an individual to change his or her temple affiliation, except under extreme circumstances.

Parishioners were expected to attend the temple at important anniversaries, festivals, at equinoxes and on the anniversaries of family bereavements. 'Active participation' (including financial contributions, of course) was mandatory, for everyone who was well enough to walk. Failure to participate in the activities of one's local temple would mean a visit from the inquisitor, who was empowered to interrogate the whole family. The temple officials were able to hold the ultimate penalty over a family's head. If they failed to comply with the temple's wishes, they could be struck off the list of registered parishioners. That, in turn, would immediately lead to suspicions of Christian belief, punishable by death.[7]

On New Year's Day each year, stamping on a Christian image was to become something of a party. Giggling children would join the line and eagerly leap onto the simple metal plaque. Their parents would wearily follow, having performed the silly, and to the vast majority meaningless, task once a year for their entire lives.

A generation after the time of Jerome, government officials were still rooting out nests of believers. It is generally agreed that there were 300,000 Christians in Japan around the time of Jerome's birth. By the time of his death, this number had been halved, with many of the reductions made on the spot at the massacre at Hara. But that still left some 150,000 'believers' or former believers, mainly concentrated in south Japan. Some, to be sure, immediately did as they were told, cast aside their religion, and signed up with the Buddhist temples to avoid trouble from the Christian Suppression Office, which was founded in 1640. Others took their religion underground. In 1645, a husband and wife were forced to sign an oath of apostasy, in which they confessed to their crime of Christian belief, and swore never to stray from the Buddhist faith again:

> We have been Christian believers for many years. Yet we have found out that the Christian religion is an evil religion. It regards the next life as the most important. The threat of excommunication is held over those who disobey the padres' orders, whilst they are likewise kept from associating with the rest of humanity in the present world and doomed to be cast into Hell in the next ... In this way the people were led to place their trust in the padres ... Yet all this was done with the design of taking the lands of others ...[8]

Nobody dared comment on the hypocrisy – that the lands of Amakusa residents had been seized by the Shōgunate and parcelled out to newcomers, that the original owners had been starved, burned or murdered in a smouldering castle in Shimabara, or that the very same 'threat of excommunication', albeit from a different faith, was being used by the temple authorities to bully their parishioners. There is another inadvertent irony in the oath: for it denies Christian belief while attempting to enforce the denial with Christian authority.

> We hereby witness this statement in writing before you, worshipful magistrate. Hereafter we shall never revoke our apostasy, not even in the secret places of the heart. Should we even entertain the slightest thought thereof, then let us be

punished by God the Father, God the Son, and God the Holy Ghost, St Mary, and all Angels and Saints. Let us forfeit all God's mercy, and all hope like Judas Iscariot, becoming a laughing-stock to all men, without thereby arousing the slightest pity, and finally die a violent death and suffer the torments of Hell without hope of salvation. This is our Christian Oath.[9]

Knowledge of Latin and Portuguese died along with the Christians at Shimabara. If any Christian books survived the purges of the seventeenth century, there were soon only a handful of government scholars (*Rangakusha*, literally 'Dutch students') who were able to read the strange Roman letters. The output of Alessandro Valignano's Amakusa printing press, which had once promised to introduce Christian ideas to an entire nation, was rendered meaningless and invisible.

Occasional news escaped of further persecutions and clampdowns. Merchants in Macao, for example, told missionaries that 'in the year 1648, six and thirty Christians gained the Crown of Martyrdom. And forty more also the year following.' As the clampdowns became ever stronger, and persecutions wore away at the strongholds of belief, the frequency of the stories dwindled.

The Chinese who were banished out of Japan tell us, that last year [the Japanese authorities] seized on one hundred and thirty Christians at Nagasaki, and put thirty of them to Death for their Religion. Amongst the rest, a Japonian Father of our Society, who had laid for several years concealed in a [Buddhist priest's] house. Moreover, I am informed by the same Hands, that Father Conix, a Japonian of our Society, after infinite Labours and Hardships for many years, was martyred three years before . . . They say that [the] Prince, after he had issued out the late Proclamation, awakened several Times in the

Night, crying out like a Madman 'To Arms! To Arms!' His favourite asking the meaning of it, he answered, because he had seen in his sleep an Army of those Christians he had put to Death, coming to seize his Crown.[10]

But such reportage was of little solace to the missionaries outside Japan. There were attempts to put priests ashore, and to reopen trade, but the Japanese permitted no Europeans in Japan, save the tiny enclave of 'Dutchmen' in Dejima. The Dutch had secured their concession by willingly obeying the new rules on proving one's lack of allegiance to the Christian faith. As Protestants, they set no truck by holy icons, and would happily perform whatever empty ritual the Japanese demanded to secure their cooperation. 'To hinder Catholics from entering into the Country,' wrote one priest, '[the authorities] had commanded that all persons upon their landing should trample upon the Crucifix, which the Hollanders made no scruple of.'[11]

Jerome Amakusa returned, briefly, in 1666 as the antagonist in a puppet show, *Amakusa Shirō Shimabara Monogatari*, but faded from popular culture thereafter.[12] The very characters for writing *Kirishitan* were changed by a vengeful Shōgun in 1680, from the original 'goodness and prosperity', to a series of symbols that could be read as 'cut the limbs until they bleed.' Other persecutors preferred to write *Kirishitan* with characters that read 'a demon's ideology, hungry for the dead.'[13]

Over the ensuing decades, a handful of European missionaries did sneak ashore to minister to their dwindling flock, but they enjoyed little success. There were rewards for turning in a fugitive European, and punishments for sheltering one, and the last recorded, Father Giovanni Battista Sidotti in 1708, lasted all of two days before being arrested by Shōgunate officials. He died seven years later in an Edo jail.

But for the paltry handful of Dutch traders, kept cooped up like zoo animals at Dejima, Japan was closed to the West. A Shōgunate inscription said it all: 'For the future, let none, so long as the Sun illuminates the world, presume to sail to Japan, not even in quality of ambassadors, and this declaration never to be revoked on pain of death.'[14]

Japan remained closed in such a manner for more than two centuries, until modern powers, with modern colonial ambitions, began to bang on the gates of seclusion. After centuries in control, the power of the military aristocracy began to wane. It was eventually brought down by the arrival of foreign powers, when the Shōgun, supposedly appointed as a Great Barbarian-Suppressing General, proved unfit for purpose. Not only did the Shōgun fail to keep out American, British and French warships; he proved unable to assert his authority against foreign merchants and priests. Christians were still forbidden from missionary activity in Japan, but by the latter half of the nineteenth century, the growing community of foreign merchants and industrialists in Nagasaki was allowed to have its own bishop. The rules, however, were strict – he was not supposed to talk to the Japanese, only to meet the religious needs of his fellow foreigners, at the newly completed Ōura Catholic Church in Nagasaki's Glover Hills district.

Shortly after midnight on 17 March 1865, barely a month after the church was completed, Father Bernard Petitjean heard a timid knock on his door. He opened it to find a group of over a dozen Japanese people, peering at him curiously. Petitjean was equally curious himself, as his presence in Nagasaki was barely tolerated by the authorities.

'May I ask,' said a young man after a while, 'if you owe allegiance to the great chief of the kingdom of Rome?'

The baffled Petitjean hemmed and hawed through his beard, and carefully said that Pope Pius IX was probably who they had in mind.

'Have you no children?' asked the same man.

Petitjean was used to strange questions and his missionary gears, although somewhat rusty after months without preaching to unbelievers, began to grind back into action. 'Christians and others are the children that God has given me,' he replied. 'Other children I cannot have. The priest must, like the first apostles in Japan, remain all his life unmarried.'

Just when Petitjean thought that the meeting could not turn any more surreal, the Japanese bowed low to the ground, chattering excitedly. A woman among them attempted to make things clearer. 'The heart of all of us here is the same as yours,' she said, explaining that the delegation had come to visit him from a nearby village. 'At home, everybody is the same as we are. They have the same hearts as we.'[15]

Father Petitjean was speechless. He could not believe what he was hearing, and truly doubted that the people who had knocked on his door knew the implications of what they were suggesting.

One of the women then said something that made Petitjean's heart leap. 'Where,' she asked in Japanese, 'is the statue of Santa Maruya?'

For two centuries, scattered enclaves of *Kirishitan* had continued to worship Deus, despite the Shōgunate's prohibitions. In urban areas and major population centres, it was impossible to be a believer. But out on the periphery, in remote fishing villages and island farmsteads, Christianity clung to life. These 'Hidden Christians' (*Kakure Kirishitan*) adapted Buddhist rosaries for their own purposes. When called upon to tread upon the image of Christ, they duly obeyed to mislead the government inquisitor, and then sneaked off to confess their sin to a sympathetic fellow, who would absolve them. They pretended to worship Kannon, the Buddhist 'Goddess of Mercy', but gave the deity features suspiciously like that of the Virgin Mary. It was the virgin *Maruya* to the hidden Christians – the name gaining a vowel shift to bring it into line with the secret Christian symbol, the *maru*, or circle. When the mere possession of a crucifix was liable to land an entire village in deadly danger, the hidden Christians found new ways to hide their symbols. Huddled around a table in their hiding place, the Kirishitan would form a cross made of coins on the floor – a symbol that could be removed with a sweep of the hand. Christian icons were hidden in phony table bases, or in a false back to a household shrine. The city of Nagasaki, under direct government control, supposedly had no Christian presence at all, although it somehow gained four shrines to Matsu, the Chinese Goddess of the Sea, and several more to Kannon.

With the Jesuit books burned or rendered illegible by the absence of those who could read Roman letters, there was no longer a way to preserve the words of the original missionaries. Transmission of the religion proceeded solely by word of mouth, from generation to generation in isolated communities, and inevitably there were strange drifts in meaning. In some places, Christianity became little more than a cult of ancestor worship, where the ancestors who were revered were secretly remembered as Christian believers.

On the island of Ikitsuki, near Hirado, the Christians revered the water from a spring where two men were martyred in the 1620s. They used the water for secret baptisms, conferring a new 'Arima name' on each baptised believer. The choice of wording is strange; was this once an *anima* name, from the Latin for soul, or an *aruma* name, in an attempt to pronounce the Portuguese *alma*? Or was it intended to refer to *Arima*, the distant domain where Christianity once took root, and where Jerome made his last stand at Hara?[16]

Christians in another remote coastal region cherished their own legends about a man called Bastian, a porter at a temple in Nagasaki, who converted to Christianity, but then found himself without proper guidance when his Spanish mentor died. Instead, Bastian fasted and prayed for guidance, eventually formulating his own off-kilter version of the Christian calendar. In Kurosaki, the hidden Christians celebrated two 'Sundays' each lunar month – the 20th, in memory of the day that Bastian was sentenced to death in 1657, and the 23rd, in memory of the day of his execution.

Despite the aversion of seventeenth-century Christians to cremation, there was little chance that secret believers would be able to avoid the reach of the Buddhist temples. In some areas, grave monuments have been found bearing a simple, empty circle, like the emblem of House Kuroda. Even though the body of a hidden Christian would have to be cremated at a Buddhist temple, it is thought that they would go to their pyre with one last secret – a paper crucifix placed under their clothes by their grieving family.

For most communities of the hidden Christians, each cell was managed by two administrators – a *chōkata*, or calendar-man, who counted the dawns to the next holy day, and a *mizukata*, or baptiser. But in recent years, hidden Christianity was dealt a death blow by modern freedoms. There is no longer any incentive to stay below ground. Christians could worship freely – as the older generation born before the Second World War start to die off, there are many communities that lack a *chōkata* or *mizukata* to replace them.

Some of the Latin survives in gibberish. A researcher on Ikitsuki Island was able to record a modern service, including the following chant:

> *Patiri notiri, ke-sense-rya*
> *Santimosen timo nomentu wa . . .*[17]

Just within reach, just out of sense, we can hear the Latin version of the Lord's Prayer:

> *Pater noster, qui es in caelis* (Our Father, Who art in Heaven)
> *Sanctificetur nomen tuum . . .* (Hallowed be Thy name)

Another source recounts another curious chant from the Gotō Islands:

> *Ame maruya karassa binno*
> *Domisu teriko-bintsu*
> *Tsuwaeshi moedebesu esu . . .*[18]

in which anyone familiar with the Catholic Mass can probably already see elements of:

Ave Maria, gratia plena (Hail Mary, full of grace)
Dominus tecum (The Lord is with thee)
Benedicta tu in mulieribus (Blessed art thou among women . . .)

The Hidden Christians' grasp of Bible stories suffered from a similar semantic drift. The Kirishitan 'Bible', as written down by one group in the nineteenth century, begins with the creation of the world by Deus. The first man is called Adan, created on the seventh day along with the first woman, Ewa.

Lucifer (*Yusuheru*), another of the creations of Deus, demands that Adan and Ewa should worship him, as he is similar to their creator. Deus admonishes all three of them, and tells them not to eat a particular fruit in the land of Koroteru (Portuguese: *hortelo* – 'garden'). However, Ewa is swindled into tasting the forbidden fruit, and as a result, she and Adan are cursed for 400 million years. The children of Ewa are sentenced to live on the Earth and worship unworthy gods, until a future date when Deus will send a messenger to show them the way back to heaven. Lucifer is transformed into a demonic form, and placed in the sky as the God of Thunder.

Much of the rest of the Old Testament is then skipped over, in favour of the story of Jesus. Mary becomes pregnant by swallowing a butterfly, and spurns the advances of a covetous king in the Philippines. Mary gives birth in a stable, and three days later she is allowed into the innkeeper's house for a bath. Reusing the same bathwater, as is usual in Japan, the innkeeper's son, who suffers from a skin disease, is miraculously cured after touching the same waters as the infant messiah.[19]

The kings of Turkey, Mexico and France come to offer their congratulations on the birth of Jesus (in a stable), but they tell their story to King Herodes (*Yorōtetsu*), who orders the massacre of all children – his two henchmen are named as Pontia and Pilate. Fleeing to Egypt across the river Baptism, Jesus and Mary are protected by local farmers, whose crops magically grow as soon as they are sown; farmers who refused to help them are stuck with barren fields.[20] The young Jesus argues over matters of religious doctrine with Buddhist priests, before he is betrayed by Judas (*Judatsu*), executed and then brought back from the dead.[21]

Sacrament, in the belief system of at least one cell of Hidden Christians, is not a thing but a person – a teacher sent by Deus to educate Jesus. Judas is punished for his betrayal by transforming into a *tengu* – a Japanese demon. These creatures will return to tempt believers during seven years of bumper crops – the last chance for heathens to convert to the true faith.

It is impossible to tell how much of the story of Jerome lies buried within the legends of the Hidden Christians. There are Biblical analogies or understandable errors for almost every element, but some are still tantalisingly similar to reportage of the Rebellion. At the end of the world, say some Hidden Christian legends, 'a great fireball will descend. Winds will roar, torrential rains fall and insects plague the earth. All kinds of human negligence will be visible.' These latter days, it was said, would last for seven years – is this an arbitrary number, a vestige of the 'seven lean years' predicted by Joseph in the Book of Genesis, or an echo of the seven-year persecution initiated by Young Matsukura?[22]

Soon after, the world itself shall be consumed in fire, leading to times so desperate that animals and birds will beg to be eaten by Christians, so that at least some small part of them might survive the apocalypse. Finally, Deus will return to the Earth and sit in judgement upon humanity. Those on his right, the Christian believers, will all become 'buddhas', and live eternally. Those on his left, the unbelievers, will be kicked down into hell along with the *tengu*.

In the legends of the Hidden Christians, we can see the preservation of the Christian faith, seemingly by word of mouth, in the utmost secrecy, throughout the period of the Shōgun's persecutions. It is understandable that much of the material has drifted into doggerel, but incredible that so much of the original meaning was able to survive.

It should be noted that the terms used here: 'off-kilter', 'gibberish', 'doggerel', would be insulting to Hidden Christians themselves. From the early excitement of Father Petitjean over the discovery of such deep-rooted belief, the love affair of the Kirishitan and the Vatican has cooled off. The Hidden Christians, understandably, did not take kindly to the suggestion that their heartfelt and long-nurtured beliefs were somehow flawed – a pidgin form of what they were now told were true ceremonies. Nor was the Catholicism into which the Kirishitan were invited to re-convert unchanged from the religion that their ancestors had attempted to preserve. Some hidden Christians 'converted' to the newly arrived Catholic and Protestant churches as represented by missionaries in the nineteenth and twentieth centuries, but many others repudiated the idea that they were noble, passionate, confused barbarians, at the edge of paganism.

European missionaries soon began to tiptoe around some of the more contentious issues of dealing with the Kirishitan. They were, for example, often reluctant to bring up the fact that several native religious elements had crept into Kirishitan practice, with which the Vatican was unprepared to compromise. For a Kirishitan to become a 'true' Catholic, he or she would have to burn their 'pagan' altar of household gods, giving up on what was regarded by the Church as a vulgar vestige of ancestor worship. The converts would also have to reject extramarital sex and keep to a single spouse – also likely to cause trouble in some quarters, just as it had for the first missionaries in the sixteenth and seventeenth centuries, when trying to talk local lords into giving up their concubines. One missionary wrote in 1893:

Those [Hidden Christians] that remain to be converted seem
to be so obstinate in their blindness that it would take a

miracle to open their eyes ... They still have the remem-
brance of their Christian origin, but outwardly they live like
pagans, observing the Buddhist feasts, and conforming to the
requirements of the Buddhist monasteries in which they are
registered.[23]

There was no single Hidden Christian orthodoxy. The varying kinds
of belief deviated in as many ways as one might expect for isolated
communities operating in total secrecy under an oppressive regime.
When the Hidden Christians came out of hiding, it soon transpired
that they had doctrinal conflicts even among themselves. Not even
the term 'Hidden Christian' is universally accepted. They were
termed 'The Separated' (*Les Séparés*), by the French missionaries who
first reported on them, and the term Separated Christians is preferred
today by those who have refused to rejoin the Catholic Church.
Locally, many seem to have preferred 'The Secret Christians' (*Senpuku
Kirishitan*), while others did not use the term *Kirishitan* at all. The
name seems to have largely been associated with those underground
cells whose point of origin began with a Jesuit missionary. Those
whose ancestors were converted by a long-forgotten Dominican
seem to have preferred to call themselves 'the Padres' (*Bateren*).

What little relics remain of the Shimabara Rebellion can be found
in museums all over south Japan. Of its legendary leader, however,
no original trace remains. Jerome's head, along with those of his
mother, his uncle and at least one of his sisters, made a last, grue-
some journey back to Nagasaki, where all were put on display. Just to
make things very clear, the local authorities put the heads up in plain
sight of Dejima, the island where the Dutch were soon to be
marshalled.

Eventually, the trophies were interred along with those of many
other criminals in a nearby burial mound. An inscription on a stone
slab nearby offered praise to Buddha, and invited passers-by to say a
prayer. This simple monument endured for two centuries until 1945,

when it was blown off its foundation by the force of the Nagasaki atom bomb.[24] The stone was retrieved, but dumped into a landfill, and is now lost to its new role, part of the foundations of a 1950s housing complex.

Jerome's body probably lay out in the fields of Hara for years, like those of his followers. Despite the lack of a proper burial, he gained the questionable achievement of two 'graves', one on the Shimabara Peninsula, and another in Nagasaki.

The Shimabara tomb-marker first came to light in 1898, when Shobei, a sickly three-year-old son, troubled the Kano family in nearby West Ariie. According to family legend, a geomancer examined their house, and told them that a vengeful spirit had cursed them. Every day, the Kano children had been rushing to the nearby beach, and stepping on a stone slab that was either in their garden path, or contained within their garden's boundary wall – sources disagree. The stone's text was difficult to make out, but it was clearly a memorial of some description, and it was believed that the Kano children's feet had insulted the spirit world with much the same effect as apostates who wilfully trampled on the image of Christ.

The slab was unearthed and taken to the Kano family shrine, whereupon little Shobei immediately regained his health. It was revered as part of family ceremonies for several generations, until 1964, when someone finally suggested that the worn, barely legible inscription 'Ama . . . Toki . . .' referred to Amakusa Tokisada – Jerome. Soon afterwards, the Kano family donated their pet rock to the ruins of Hara Castle, where it remains to this day, and is officially Jerome's 'grave'.

Jerome has become a modern hero to the Japanese, particularly in the post-war years, where he found new fame as the icon of disaffected youth. Student protestors in the 1960s and 1970s saw themselves as the inheritors of Jerome's banner – young revolutionaries, standing up to the stuffy bureaucracy that tried to tell them what to do. Jerome soon found his way into novels, comics and movies, but not into the annals of the Church he fought so bravely to defend.

For the author Endō Shūsaku (1923–96), baptised as a child into the Catholic religion, the stories of the Christian century became a recurring literary theme. Endō wrestled throughout his life with the faith imposed upon him by his convert mother, and dwelt upon the intense, unwavering belief of the martyrs of Christian legend. In particular, his short story 'Unzen' focussed on a character visiting the infamous hot springs with a tour group, unable to shake off the feeling that if confronted with the threat of boiling torture, he would cast off his own faith in a heartbeat. Endō also wrote extensively about the undercover missionaries sent in to administer to the dwindling flocks of Hidden Christians, particularly the priest Christovao Ferreira, who gave up his faith under torture, and was rewarded with a dead man's name and wife. It is Ferreira who becomes the antagonist of Endō's acclaimed and controversial novel *Silence* (1966), in which he taunts a captured priest with the prospect of a peaceful life as an apostate, or a horrific death as a martyr. For Endō, as for many who read about the history of Christianity in Japan, there is an insurmountable distance between our superficial modern selves and the fervent, heartfelt resilience of the martyrs of the historical record. Endō concluded that Christianity, at least in its European form, was doomed never to take true root in Japan, but did so despite his own evidence of how deeply those roots had once penetrated during the Christian century. Unsurprisingly, the story soon became a favourite of the film director Martin Scorsese, whose 2016 feature adaptation treads similar ground to his own *The Last Temptation of Christ*, confronting the confidence of faith with the crises of the real world.

Although many hundreds of Japanese Christians from the sixteenth and seventeenth centuries have been beatified and canonised by the Catholic Church, neither Jerome himself nor any of his fellow rebels has attained such an honour. The problem lies with the lingering questions about his Rebellion – was he truly a religious crusader or just a figurehead for a peasant uprising? Even as the Shimabara Rebellion gained a degree of fame in the Christian community, there were those who sought to downplay the role of religion in it, although one Catholic historian could not resist a pot-shot at the Protestants on the way:

> Driven to desperation by thirty years of unrelenting persecu-tion, and finally deprived of pastors to exhort them to patience and prudence, is it surprising that the endurance of the Japanese Christians gave way at last? That the revolt was not brought about by Christians, nor in retaliation for persecu-tions, is proved by all reliable writers. The revolt was due to the misgovernment and cruel extortions of two successive rulers of Arima and was not originated by religious motives in the first instance . . . It was Dutch artillery that brought about the [Shōgun's] victory, and on the Dutch lies the ignominy of the final extinction of Christianity in Japan.[25]

Even if Jerome's religious credentials were somehow assured, it seems that is still unlikely to ever make him a martyr. As one modern Jesuit commented, even if Jerome saw himself as a religious leader, his actions do not accord with what the Catholic Church expects of its heroes. A 'devil's advocate', charged with the task of querying Jerome's canonisation, would have ample ammunition to deny him a place as a Christian saint:

> In fact, there were and are a lot of rules and regulations about candidates for beatification . . . he . . . must have died *in odium fidei* [as a result of persecution for his faith] and without offer-ing resistance. In any attempt to make any of the people slain at Shimabara 'official martyrs,' the *advocatus diaboli* would have had a field day on those two points alone.[26]

Christianity remains a minority religion in Japan. Today, less than one per cent of the population of Japan comprises practising Christians – as one modern missionary has observed, there are more Christians in modern Iraq than there are in Japan.[27] But the Shimabara Rebellion and the events that led to it continue to exert a strange pull on the Japanese mind – a path not taken, a faint memory of a very different world, crushed and annihilated in the early days of the Tokugawa Shōgunate, a genocide against fellow Japanese, all to create a Japan that could claim a unity of belief and purpose. A poem of Kitahara Hakushū alludes to the exotic secrecy of the Hidden Christians, retaining, even in modern times, a sense of the strangeness of Christian ritual and presence in a Japanese environment:

> Meanwhile people fall to their knees
> To pray in the dark with blue-eyed priests
> Drunk on the scent of incense
> Stifled in serenity, hearing the song
> God bless the litany eternal
> Christened by our ancestors' blood.[28]

Notes on Names

....

In an attempt to thin down the surfeit of birth-names, family names, clan names, adopted names, baptismal names, *noms de guerre*, posthumous names, honorifics, variant spellings and outright guesses by numerous sources, I have tried to keep nomenclature as simple as possible. I have followed the same policy as Michael Cooper in his *Japanese Mission to Europe*, using Christian names wherever an individual had one, and, where more than one variant exists, using the Anglicised form. Where an individual has a Christian name, I have used it to identify them throughout the text, even when they have apostatised. Thus I have *Jerome Amakusa*, instead of Masuda no Shirō or Hieronimo Amakusa Tokisada, and *Michael Arima*, instead of his variants Don Miguel or Arima Naozumi.

Amakusa

Called Amacusa (*sic*) in the Latin of its Jesuit printing press, and Amaxa in the letters of Nicholas Couckebacker.

Arima

Arima Yoshisada (1521–1577) is the dying 'king' of Kyūshū who converted to Christianity in his last year, taking the name André. Arima Harunobu (1561–1612) is his son, the Protasio of the Christian accounts, called variously Don Protasius or Protase. At his confirmation late in life, Protasio took the new Christian name of Joao/John, and is referred to as Don John in some accounts. Arima Naozumi (1586–1641) is the Christian Lord Michael (Miguel) Arima who renounced his faith at the time of the exile of the priests from Nagasaki, and turned on the Christians in his domain. He was, however, still moved to a new domain, by some accounts at his own request, after he was left exasperated by the number of Christians in his fief. At the time of the Rebellion, he arrived at the head of his army, and played an important role in the attempts to encourage Yamada Emonsaku to betray Jerome.

Arrow Point
Ōyazaki.

Augustin Konishi
Konishi Yukinaga (c.1558–1600) was a famous Christian, baptised in 1583 with the name Augustin. In 1587, he became the ruler of a domain in south Japan that included the notorious Amakusa islands. He appears in some Portuguese sources as Dom Augustin, and in some Japanese sources as Settsu no Kami ('Lord of Settsu'). In 1607, he was the subject of an Italian play by Giuseppe Pavoni, called *Agostino Tzunicamidono Re Giapponese*. A printer's fancy contracts the name to Don Austin in Crasset's *History of the Church of Japan*. His daughter Maria married Dario Sō Yoshitomo, the lord of the strategically crucial island of Tsushima, but she was disowned when Dario renounced his faith after the Battle of Sekigahara.

Francois Caron
A French Huguenot who sought asylum in the Netherlands and subsequently became the 'first Frenchman in Japan'. Caron married a noble-born Japanese woman, and was a fluent speaker of the language. At the time of the Shimabara Rebellion, he was also a published author, whose book on Siam and Japan appeared in multiple European languages over the course of the next few decades. Some sources, including my own *Coxinga*, use the Anglicised version of his name used in the English edition of his own book – Francis Caron. Ironically, Caron wrote much about Japan, but only before and after the Rebellion. His *Puissant Royaume du Japon* was one of the earliest detailed descriptions in a European language, appearing

in 1636. The French edition (Proust in my bibliography) also includes Caron's diaries from Hirado from 1639–41, during which period he served as Couckebacker's replacement. A year after the death of his Japanese wife in 1643, he married the nineteen-year-old Constantia Boudaen during a return visit to the Netherlands. Constantia's legendarily beautiful elder sister, Suzanne, followed the couple back to the east, and married the Swedish captain Frederik Coyett, who would later become the chief of operations for the Dutch East India Company in Dejima, and the leader of Dutch forces in the battle for Taiwan with the 'pirate king' Coxinga.

Itakura Shigemasa

Called Neysiendonno or Naisendonno in Dutch accounts. I have used his given name Shigemasa, rather than his surname Itakura, to avoid confusion with the Matsukura family that is also prominent in this narrative.

Jerome Amakusa

He was born with the names Shirō and/or Tokisada. Shirō simply means 'fourth child', and suggests that there were two siblings born after his elder sister Regina, but that they died young. His father's 'surname', Masuda, was also sometimes assigned to Jerome. His banner at Tomioka Castle, according to one of the survivors' testimonies, bore the slogan 'Japan's general, Ōyano Shirō', naming him for the island in the archipelago where he was probably born. The *Kirishitan Monogatari* calls him Amano Shirō, literally 'Shirō of Heaven'. An inscription on the mass grave at Tomioka Castle calls him Nirada Shirō. Later accounts have often given him a surname based on his *family's* home island of Amakusa. However, few Japanese outside the noble classes had surnames before the nineteenth century, so calling him Amakusa Shirō is something of an anachronism. He was baptised with the Christian name Jerome (*Jeronimo*, according to Duarte Correa), but at least one arrow-letter sent from the besieged castle seems to give his Christian name as Francisco. Portuguese accounts call him *Maxondanoxirô*, likely to have been a garbling of Masuda no Shirō. French accounts call him *Jérome Machoudano Chico* – the *Chico* likely to have been a transcription error from the Portuguese.

Kuchinotsu
Romanised in the publications of the Jesuit press as Cuchinotçu.

Lion Island
Shishijima.

Matsudaira Nobutsuna
Called Sammondonno in Dutch sources, although this seems to confuse him with his lieutenant, Toda Saemon no Kami. See also 'Sakakibara Norinobu'.

Matsukura
I have simplified matters by referring to an Old and Young Matsukura. The older Matsukura's given name was Shigemasa. Crasset calls him Mathucura Bungo. His son was called Shigetsugu, or in some accounts, Katsuie – literally, 'victory for the house' – a heavy name to live up to. Some letters of the rebels refer to Young Matsukura as Nagato no Kimi (Lord of Nagato). Some accounts confuse the elder, Matsukura Shigemasa, with the ill-fated leader of the besiegers at Hara Castle, *Itakura* Shigemasa – for this reason, I have deliberately used Shigemasa to refer to the latter.

Nabeshima
Nabeshima Katsushige was a retainer of the clan of Ryuzōji, and hence is probably the 'Lord of Lusoysjo' mentioned in Dutch accounts.

Nicholas Couckebacker
Called Koeckebacker in some accounts.

Parley Island
Also known as *Yūshima*. *Dankaijima* ('Parley Island') was its local nickname.

Sakakibara Norinobu
Paske-Smith's account, page 96, calls him Saiemon or Saemon. His full name was Sakakibara Saemon-no-suke Norinobu. I keep to Sakakibara here in order to avoid confusing him with the Sasaemon who supposedly took Jerome's head several days later.

Shimabara
Called Ximbara or Ximabara in Portuguese and French accounts. Some Japanese works using the Kunrei romanisation system prefer Simabara.

Suetsugu Heizō II
Strictly speaking, this Suetsugu is the second of four men to use the name. He was also known as Suetsugu or Shigefusa Heizō Shigesada. Dutch accounts call him Phesodonno (i.e. *Heizō-dono*, Lord Heizō). For more details on his name, see Oka, 'A Great Merchant in Nagasaki', pp.38–9. His father Suetsugu Heizō I, was the apostate who tried to orchestrate a Japanese invasion of Taiwan by arranging for an 'embassy' of bewildered Taiwanese natives to request aid against the Dutch – see Clements, *Coxinga and the Fall of the Ming Dynasty*, pp.60–1. Despite the outrageous behaviour of his father towards the Dutch, Suetsugu *fils* switched his allegiance from Portuguese traders to the Protestant Dutch sometime around 1634. He used his political influence to increase the approved price the Dutch could demand for silk, for which he took a massive kickback of free silk supplied in secret by the Dutch themselves.

Watanabe Kozaemon
Tsuruta's family tree supplies him with the Christian name *Mūshini* or *Murashini* in katakana – but it is unclear which Iberian Christian

name might be intended by this transliteration (Mauricio? Martinez?), and so I have referred to him as Kozaemon throughout. Paske-Smith incorrectly refers to him as Jerome's 'uncle', although he was actually Jerome's cousin. The connections between the Watanabe and Masuda families were so interlaced that he was also Jerome's brother-in-law, as the husband of Jerome's sister Regina. Kozaemon's brother Michael Watanabe Satarō was possibly also married to Jerome's other sister Marina.

Notes

....

Introduction

1 This book lacks space for every example of Amakusa statuary, but other images can be found in Tsuruta, *Saikai no Ran* (2005), on pages 11, 21, 29 and 43. The Shimabara statue and its Hara clone are perhaps the most widely known, as they were the work of Kitamura Seibō (1973), a sculptor internationally famous for the massive Peace Statue in Nagasaki Peace Park. The Oniike and Matsushima statues with their distinctive ruffs are the work of Iwasaki Shigetaka (1982 and 1975); the Hondo statue outside the Christian Museum is by Kamei Yū (1975), the one outside the Memorial Hall is by Takahashi Fumio (1966), and the one in Ōyano is by Fujikawa Tadatsune (1991).

1: The Rending of Heaven

1 The term 'Christian century' (1549–1650) was popularised by Charles Boxer's 1951 book of the same name, and is in common use in both Western and Japanese sources. However, it remains controversial – several historians have expressed their disapproval at such a delimiting and condescending title, including Boxer himself, who regarded the title assigned to his own book, by his publishers and over his own objections, as 'silly'. See Alden, *Charles R. Boxer, An Uncommon Life*, p.348.

2 Elison, *Deus Destroyed*, 325.

3 Dougill, *In Search of Japan's Hidden Christians*, 23, observes that Deus is unfortunately similar to the Japanese *dai uso*, or 'great lie,' leading the missionaries to try several other terms as well.

4 Paske-Smith, *Japanese Traditions of Christianity*, 9.

5 Elison, *Deus Destroyed*, 475–6.

6 Moran, *The Japanese and the Jesuits*, 22–3. Of the fate of the unfortunate Miss Trona, nothing is known.

7 Letter of Alessandro Valignano to Everard Mercurian, 6 August 1580, quoted in Moran, *The Japanese and the Jesuits*, 51.

8 Valignano, quoted in Watanabe and Iwata, *The Love of the Samurai*, 23–4.

9 Letter of Alessandro Valignano to Everard Mercurian, 10 December 1579, quoted in Elison, 'Christianity and the Daimyō', 333.

10 Morris, *The Nobility of Failure*, 396. Morris claims that Nicholas Couckebacker's diary of the events observed a rumour in Edo that Jerome himself had made a similar miraculous escape from the fall of Hara, and that there were already tales that he would return, like Sebastian, in Japan's time of need. However, I have not found such a claim in Couckebacker's diary, only the vaguer assertion that a number of Christians at Hara 'saved themselves by flight.' See Geerts, 'The Arima Rebellion', 116.

11 Cooper, *The Japanese Mission to Europe*, 128.

12 Cooper, *The Japanese Mission to Europe*, 183–4.

13 *Laures Rare Book Database*, Sofia University, Tokyo.

14 Moran, *The Japanese and the Jesuits*, 153–7.

15 This information is from the *Laures Rare Book Database* at the Sofia University Library, http://133.12.23.145:8080/AnaServer?Laures10+1 60927+popupwin.anv

16 Elison, *Deus Destroyed*, 316–7. Elison is quoting *Deceit Disclosed*, a deliberate attempt to ridicule the Christian religion in the wake of the Shimabara Rebellion, but one that met with government approval.

2: The Mirror of the Future

1 Ward, *Women Religious Leaders in Japan's Christian Century 1549–1650*, 115–6. The wayward Sebastian Ōtomo Chikaie's faith is somewhat in doubt, since even the Jesuit chronicler Luis Frois describes it as a possible 'trick' by his father to keep him from taking Buddhist orders in fulfilment of an earlier promise. There may have also been other issues at play, not the least the teenage Sebastian's temptation to ally with a rival samurai clan in order to usurp the inheritance of his elder brother. Notably, Frois avoids using his Christian name, suggesting that his sincerity was always in doubt, even among the Jesuits who baptised him. Indeed, by 1586, Sebastian had already cast aside his new faith as readily as he had taken it up, but not before giving the Christians a bad name as hooligans and temple-wreckers.

2 Yuuki, *The Twenty-Six Martyrs of Nagasaki*, 15.

3 Kronk, *Cometography*, 329 lists comet C/1596 N1 as appearing in Asian skies between July and August, mid-way through the *San Felipe*'s journey.

4 José L. Alvarez-Taladriz, quoted in Yuuki, *The Twenty-Six Martyrs of Nagasaki*, 11.

5 Crasset, *The History of the Church of Japan*, 22. Throughout this book, I have modernised Crasset's spelling, but have retained his idiosyncratic eighteenth-century capitalisations, as they are often clues to slight semantic drifts in the intervening centuries.

6 Yuuki, *The Twenty-Six Martyrs of Nagasaki*, 21.

7 Crasset, *The History of the Church of Japan*, 57.

8 Clements, *A Brief History of the Samurai*, 189–90 outlines the religious rivalries beneath the surface of the Korean invasion, as battalions of Christian samurai sought to outdo their Buddhist colleagues.

9 Costa, 'Tokugawa Ieyasu and the Christian Daimyō,' 49.

10 Costa, 'Tokuygawa Ieyasu and the Christian Daimyō', 53.

11 Costa, 'Tokugawa Ieyasu and the Christian Daimyō', 55.

12 Sekigahara took place on 21 October 1600. However, many Japanese sources, even school textbooks, continue to date it in pre-modern orthography as the '15th day of the ninth [lunar] month,' implying to the casual reader it took place in September.

13 Bryant, *Sekigahara 1600*, 64.

14 Crasset, *The History of the Church of Japan*, 88.

15 Crasset, *The History of the Church of Japan*, 92.

16 Crasset, *The History of the Church of Japan*, 98.

17 Crasset, *The History of the Church of Japan*, 96.

18 Crasset, *The History of the Church of Japan*, 103.

19 Crasset, *The History of the Church of Japan*, 376.

20 Crasset, *The History of the Church of Japan*, 376.

21 Elison, 'Christianity and the Daimyō', 367.

22 Crasset, *The History of the Church of Japan*, 377.

23 Okada, *Amakusa Tokisada*, 22. See also variants in Paske-Smith, *Japanese Traditions of Christianity*, 57, Morris, *The Nobility of Failure*, 144, and Boxer, *Japan's Christian Century*, 378. An abridged version of the same poem can be found in my own *Coxinga*, 85. The version in Morris adds a line that the new messiah shall be 'twice times eight' in age, which would have made Jerome fifteen – '16' by the Japanese system, which counts one's birth year as one's first.

3: The Mouths of Hell

1 Crasset, *The History of the Church of Japan*, 275. Crasset's original has *Chicugen* not Chikuzen.

2 Crasset, *The History of the Church of Japan*, 280–83.

3 Moran, *The Japanese and the Jesuits*, 145.

4 Miyazaki, *The Story of Building the Shimabara Castle*, 180. If true, the claim would apply to full-blooded Chinese emigrants and the mixed-race children of liaisons between Chinese or Europeans and local Japanese. Miyazaki cites one famous example, the half-Italian girl Jagatara ('Jakarta') Oharu, who briefly hid close to Hara Castle in Fukae before being rounded up and shipped abroad. Some of her homesick letters to her relatives are preserved in the Hirado Tourist Museum. Refugees in Shimabara would have been half-Japanese, as those were the genetic group banished by the edict. Those with only one foreign grandparent, i.e. '75% Japanese', were permitted to stay. See, for example, Clements, *Coxinga and the Fall of the Ming Dynasty*, 285, note 24.

5 Keith, 'The Logistics of Power,' 87. Note that the modern *koku* is significantly larger than the *koku* of the seventeenth century. In 1891, a *koku* was defined as 278.3 litres, but shortly afterwards, Japan went fully metric.

6 Crasset, *The History of the Church of Japan*, 273–4.

7 Nicholas Couckebacker, letter to Anthony van Diemen, Governor General at Batavia, 18 January 1638, quoted in Geerts, 'The Arima Rebellion and the Conduct of Koeckebacker,' 57.

8 Yanagida, *Shimabara Hantō Mukashibanashi Shū*. The stories are numbered for ease of identification: horse that shits money (41), vengeful magic mice (5), framing the neighbours' daughter (1), serpents in Unzen (13), human sacrifice to river gods (12), animated Buddhist statue (31).

9 Tsuruta, *Amakusa no Rekishi Kyōiku*, 284.

10 Miyazaki, *The Building of Shimabara Castle*, 66. As an indication of the castle's fame, Miyazaki offers the entertaining but unlikely supposition that *castella*, a Nagasaki sponge cake which first gained popularity in the 1620s, was not named for Castile, as is often thought, but for the 'Castle'; Miyazaki, op. cit., 170.

11 Miyazaki, *The Building of Shimabara Castle*, 104. Miyazaki suggests another possibility, that the weakness of the last section may have been caused by the presence of a secret passage beneath it, but Occam's Razor favours the less exciting explanation.

12 Miyazaki, *The Building of Shimabara Castle*. 81. Miyazaki also suggests another explanation for some of the rocks that still littered the region, that it was considered unlucky to try to move a rock that had fallen off its transport – such stones were considered bad omens for the castle, and were left to lie where they had 'decided' to roll.

13 Miyazaki, *The Story of Building the Shimabara Castle*, 122.

14 Letter of Nicholas Couckebacker to Anthony van Diemen, 10 January 1638, quoted in Geerts, 'The Arima Rebellion and the Conduct of Koeckebacker', 57–8.

15 Crasset, *The History of the Church of Japan*, 430. '[A]n accusation was laid against him for ill Management and . . . the [Shōgun] was half resolved to take off his Head, but by the great Interest of Friends, the Storm in a little time blew over, and he was sent Home to repair his Fault by open War against Religion.'

16 Crasset, *The History of the Church of Japan*, 432.

17 Crasset, *The History of the Church of Japan*, 445.

18 Crasset, *The History of the Church of Japan*, 442.

19 Cobbing, *Kyūshū: Gateway to Japan – a Concise History*, 47. These phantom lights seem to have only faded in modern times, defeated by the ambient glow from towns around the Ariake Sea, and the concurrent draining of many of the swamps that may have fuelled them.

20 Crasset, *The History of the Church of Japan*, 488–9. I have changed Crasset's *Nangasaqui* to our *Nagasaki*. Compare to suspiciously similar accounts of the dying days of the grand villain of medieval Japan, Taira no Kiyomori, e.g. in McCullough, *Tale of the Heike*, pp.209–10.

21 Crasset, *The History of the Church of Japan*, 489. I have altered Crasset's *Ungen* to the modern transliteration of *Unzen*.

22 Miyazaki, *The Story of Building Shimabara Castle*, 186.

4: The Latter Days of the Law

1 Kitahara Hakushū, 'Songs of Amakusa', quoted in Hondo Shiritsu Amakusa Kirishitan-kan, *Amakusa Kirishitan-kan Shiryō Mokuroku*, 36. According to Hyam, *Empire and Sexuality*, 140: 'Most of the *karayuki* [Japanese prostitutes abroad in the Victorian era] came from northern Kyūshū, which was among the most impoverished regions of Japan . . . The criminalisation of infanticide by the Meiji regime only increased the number of daughters going into prostitution.'

2 *Menkō Shūroku*, quoted in Kanda, *Shimabara no Ran*, 34.

3 *Kirishitan Monogatari*, quoted in Elison, *Deus Destroyed*, 362.

4 So claims Okada, *Amakusa Tokisada*, 11. Tobacco was a recent arrival in the Far East, only reaching China in 1620; see Lin Renchuan 'Fukien's Private Sea Trade', 205. The fact that a crop existed in Shimabara for tax collectors to claim is further evidence of the depth of penetration of foreign shipping and contacts before the Sakoku Edict.

5 *Gokechū Buntsu no Naibatsusho*, testimony of Ura no Magosuke, salt merchant, dated 21 December 1637 (6th of the 11th lunar month), quoted in Kanda, *Shimabara no Ran*, 35.

6 Crasset, *The History of the Church of Japan*, 526–7.

7 Although it's not as simple as that, since one prisoner testimony obtained by House Arima in the aftermath suggested that Jerome Amakusa had 'red hair', which would suggest that he was a foreigner himself! The claim is mentioned in Yoshimura, *Amakusa Shirō no Shōtai*, 150–2, although the author accords it little credence.

8 Cooper, *The Japanese Mission to Europe*, 187.

9 *Hosokawa-ke Ki*, quoted in Okada, *Amakusa Tokisada*, 85. My date for the citation reads *tsugomori* (the last day) of the tenth lunar month, Year of the Ox, as 15 December 1637. The original text's '16-*cai*' is translated here in English orthodoxy as '15'.

10 Tsuruta, *Amakusa Shimabara no Ran to Sono Zengo*, 288. I have not seen any mention of a Francisco Pordorino (or Poldorino?) in Jesuit records – the name has been transliterated from Japanese sources and I have been unable to confirm it in European ones.

11 Okada, *Amakusa Tokisada*, 86. I have not found a direct reference to this in any other contemporary source, only in an old man's reminiscence as reported in the *Hosokawa-ke Ki* and itself quoted in Okada, which makes me wonder if Okada was not more caught up with the twentieth-century traditions of Jerome than with what was actually said about him in the seventeenth century. See, for example, Watanabe and Iwata, *The Love of the Samurai*, 28: 'In certain popular novels of our own period, [Jerome] is loved, even raped by pederastic men. One of the symbols of the kirishitan movement which struggled against homosexuality is being absorbed into the Japanese homosexual tradition.'

12 Arai Hakuseki, quoted in Okada, *Amakusa Tokisada*, 89. It is too much to hope for that this 'Iquan' was Nicholas Iquan, the same trader and smuggler who was later ennobled by the Southern Ming government in China. 'Iquan' simply means eldest son, and was applied to numerous Chinese residents in Nagasaki. See Clements, *Coxinga*, 10.

13 Okada, *Amakusa Tokisada*, 87 (*kogasa*) and 91 (*hizenkasa*). Okada does not comment on the differing diagnoses. Neither inquisitors nor informants were doctors, and even if the alibi were genuine, neither Martha nor Jibei may have seen Jerome's condition for themselves.

14 Tsuruta, *Amakusa Shimabara no Ran to Sono Zengo*, 291–2. The terrible weather, which reached its peak in 1640, had arguably worse effects in China, where it helped bring down the emperor. See, for example, Clements, *Coxinga and the Fall of the Ming Dynasty*, 1–2.

15 Brook, in *China's Troubled Empire*, 269–70.

16 Okada, *Amakusa Tokisada*, 20. The original Japanese reads, '*Shimotsuki Sorori wa Kozorori / Akisangatsu wa Sanhorori*,' a deeply cryptic tongue-twister. My translation assumes the farmers were making a satirical, punning link between an old harvest song and Armageddon.

17 *Hosokawa-ke Ki (Records of the Hosokawa Clan)*, quoted in Okada, *Amakusa Tokisada*, 4–5. Additional confusion has arisen over place names, since Arima is not one village but three or four in a cluster near Hara Castle, vaguely differentiated by the points of the compass. Arima can also be defined as the former domain of *Lord* Arima, i.e. the entire Shimabara Peninsula. Sources in this case all match if they are taken to refer not to 'South Arima' the village, but the south of the peninsula, i.e. Kuchinotsu.

18 Statement from Watanabe Kozaemon in *Hosokawa-ke Ki*, quoted in Okada, *Amakusa Tokisada*, 6–7. Okada faithfully reproduces the seventeenth-century interrogators' inaccurate transcription of what was presumably once 'Piato, Gaspar' as the meaningless 'Beyato Gasaharu'. The original text gives the date as the tenth day of the tenth [lunar] month.

19 Morris, *The Nobility of Failure*, 149.

20 *Zassō Kiroku (Chronicle of Weeds)*, quoted in Okada, *Amakusa Tokisada*, 6–7.

21 Tsuruta, *Amakusa no Rekishi Monogatari Kyōiku*, 287–8. Note that Tsuruta's '25 October' is actually 11 December by the Gregorian calendar. The original sources read '30 *hyō*' – a *hyō* is a sack of rice, significantly less than a *koku*. Since a *koku* is a subsistence-level quantity of rice, the suggestion that the farmers could not spare one is further evidence that they had truly been taxed into starvation.

22 Tsuruta, *Amakusa no Rekishi Monogatari Kyōiku*, 288, suggests that the arrest and public torture of family members might have been a measure adopted 'when the jails were too full.'

23 Steichen, *Les Daimyô Chrétiens*, 404–5. Steichen gives the date for this incident as 17 December 1637, long after the rebellion was underway. However, if we assume he is repeating a date from Japanese sources of the '17th of the 12th [lunar] month', the event would take place on 2 November 1637.

24 *Kuroda Nagaoki Issei no Ki (Kuroda Nagaoki's Chronicle of the World)*, quoted in Okada, *Amakusa Tokisada*, 9–10.

25 Duarte Correa, quoted in Boxer, *Japan's Christian Century*, 377–8; Okada, *Amakusa Tokisada*, 11. However, he may be reporting a completely different uprising – modern Ōmura is north of Isahaya, and far from the events described. If Correa saw rebellious farmers on the 'road to Shimabara' as he claims, they would have had to be coming from Nagasaki!

26 Ibid. The same event is the source of a passage translated in Morris, *The Nobility of Failure*, 152, although Morris loses the 'only', and emphasises that the father had not expected his daughter to be killed, or indeed tortured. Tsuruta, *Amakusa no Rekishi Monogatari Kyōiku*, 296, suggests that a red-hot brand was applied to some as a form of torture. The brand would sometimes be marked with the word 'KIRISHITAN', marking the victim forever as one of the banned sect.

27 Letter of Nicholas Couckebacker to Anthony van Diemen, 10 January 1638, quoted in Geerts, 'The Arima Rebellion', 59. The same passage is quoted in Okada, *Amakusa Tokisada*, 17, in a translation that pushily substitutes 'rape' for the original's 'infamy.'

28 So at least claimed the hated Yamada Emonsaku at his debriefing in the aftermath. He even boasted that associates of the Gang of Five had been told to 'expect something' on the 15th of the 10th lunar month, implying that the Amakusa revolt was already underway at the time that the official Hayashi Heizaemon or Hayashi Heizō was lynched by an angry mob in Arima. Okada, *Amakusa Tokisada*, 22.

29 Okada, *Amakusa Tokisada*, 25. This report was given by a messenger fleeing Shimabara Castle, and so may be backdating Jerome's leadership of the rebels. It seems, however, that he was certainly considered to be a leader by the time the rebels moved on Shimabara. A very similar text appears in Tsuruta, *Amakusa Shimabara no Ran*, 88, although there are enough minor differences between the two for them to be two accounts that share a single source.

30 Letter of 'Juan Kazusa' distributed on the Shimabara Peninsula, dated 28 November 1637 (13th day of the tenth lunar month), quoted in Kanda, *Shimabara no Ran*, 31–2. The reference to the 'left foot' evokes the biblical Day of Judgement in Matthew 25: 32–33: 'He will separate them one from another, as a shepherd divides his sheep from the goats. And He will set the sheep on his right hand, but the goats on his left.'

31 There may be some truth to this unlikely story, although the 'miracle' should be located at Hara itself, not at Parley Island. Couckebacker, in his letter of 18 January 1638, notes that the insurrection began on an island 'just opposite to the district of Arima, whence the island may be reached on foot at low tide.' Although he appears to have been confused as to precisely which island he means, it would seem that at some point in the Rebellion, Jerome and his followers used their local knowledge to cross a body of water on foot that their out-of-town enemies did not initially realise was fordable. Geerts, 'The Arima Rebellion', 59. It is worth noting that even in 1637, much of the ground before Hara Castle was still inundated at high tide, which may have led to some of the tales of Jerome 'walking on water.' Even 'old' maps of Hara Castle still post-date the Rebellion, and come from the eighteenth century or later, by which time further silting had led to the placement of rice paddies where once there had been a tidal marsh.

32 Paske-Smith, *Japanese Traditions of Christianity*, 55–6.

33 Yanagida, *Shimabara Hantō Mukashibanashi Shū*, 162.

34 Okada, *Amakusa Tokisada*, 144. Hondo Shiritsu Amakusa Kirishitan-kan, *Amakusa Kirishitan-kan Shiryō Mokuroku*, 10, puts Yamada in the Arima seminary as a youth.

35 Tsuruta, *Amakusa Shimabara no Ran*, 294. The secret meeting was claimed by Mokuuemon Sekido in his statement to the authorities. The plans for the Jōdo temple in Ōyano were recorded in the *Shinsen Gokefu*. Of course, the reference to the cock crowing three times is another reference to the Book of Matthew (26:34).

5: The Farmers' Affray

1 Miyazaki, *The Story of Building the Shimabara Castle*, 215. For a discussion of the political and social ramifications of Japan's 1960s castle-rebuilding scheme, see Clements, *A Brief History of the Samurai*, 311–2.

2 Paske-Smith, *Japanese Traditions of Christianity*, 60–1. Okada, *Amakusa Tokisada*, 27, specifies that the reinforcements came from the hamlets of Futsu, Dosaki, Ariie and Arima.

3 Couckebacker, quoted in Okada, *Amakusa Tokisada*, 27–8. Couckebaker wrote these details down some time afterwards, but they would presumably apply from the moment that the rioters reached Shimabara, if not before.

4 Tsuruta, *Amakusa Shimabara no Ran to Sono Zengo*, 294.

5 Tsuruta, *Amakusa Shimabara no Ran to Sono Zengo*, 294. The precise timing and rebel numbers are quoted from a contemporary report by Yashichizaemon Sano.

6 Paske-Smith, *Japanese Traditions of Christianity*, 63.

7 *Gokechubuntsu no Naibatsusho*, events for 16 December 1638 (1st day of the 11th lunar month) quoted in Tsuruta, *Shimabara Amakusa no Ran*, 295.

8 Paske-Smith, *Japanese Traditions of Christianity*, 61.

9 So claims the *Shinsen Gokefu*, quoted in Tsuruta, *Amakusa Shimabara no Ran*, 294. However, the testimony of Sano Yashichizaemon, quoted on the same page, claims that Jerome was already among the rebels attacking Shimabara Castle the previous day.

10 Debriefing of Yamada Emonsaku, quoted in Okada, *Amakusa Tokisada*, 28.

11 Tsuruta, *Amakusa Shimabara no Ran*, 293–4. The testimony of one Sano Yashichizaemon, presumably Sano Sozaemon's son or brother, is the crucial document in proving that a Christian uprising was being plotted ahead of the outbreak of fights and riots over tax collection. Rumours of trouble in Shimabara reached Sano on 5 December, at around the time that the headman of Mogi sent an envoy to greet Jerome at Amakusa. Mogi village sent inspectors to Shimabara to investigate on 7 December, presumably with Sano among them, thereby explaining his presence in Shimabara Castle on 12 December when the rebels attacked the castle.

12 Okada, *Amakusa Tokisada*, 32.

13 Barnes, *Naval Surgeon: Revolt in Japan*, 182 notes that the diarist Samuel Pellman Boyer thought that Mogi was 'the place where the native Christians were finally exterminated some years ago.' This appears to have been a local folktale that was confused by some of the Western travellers who stopped at Mogi, which became a major embarkation port for ships in the nineteenth century. The story seems to confuse the stopping of the tide of the rebellion at Mogi, with the stopping of the rebellion itself, which was arguably accomplished at Hara Castle.

14 Report of Michiie Sakonuemon, 14 December 1637, quoted in Tsuruta, *Amakusa Shimabara no Ran*, 88. I have reduced the assessment of Jerome's age by one year from the original Japanese numbers that begin with one's birth at age 'one'.

15 Report of Michiie Sakonuemon, 14 December 1637, quoted in Kanda, *Shimabara no Ran*, 33.

16 It is literally within walking distance of the castle – one stop on the local railway line.

17 Paske-Smith, *Japanese Traditions of Christianity*, 63–4.

18 Paske-Smith, *Japanese Traditions of Christianity*, 65. The reference to the beetle and the cartwheel seems to be an allusion to the Chinese philosopher Zhuangzi, who once compared futile endeavour to a praying mantis lifting up its forelimbs to stop an oncoming cart.

19 Letter of Kawakitaku Takufu to House Hosokawa, quoted in Okada, *Amakusa Tokisada*, 71–2. I have translated 'is very close [to the unrest]' as 'could be in danger' as that is what was meant by the watchmen when discussing the possible fate of the castellan of Tomioka.

20 Paske-Smith, *Japanese Traditions of Christianity*, 66. The precise date of their arrest is from Tsuruta, *Amakusa Shimabara no Ran*, 295 (as the 30th day of the 10th lunar month). Morris, *The Nobility of Failure*, 156, drawing on Okada, *Amakusa Tokisada*, 77, suggests that events may have been reversed, and that the womenfolk were first betrayed by a local boy, allowing government forces to lie in wait for an unsuspecting Kozaemon.

21 Tsuruta, *Amakusa Shimabara no Ran*, 297, cites several government reports of the actions of the guards on the mainland. Okada, *Amakusa Tokisada*, 81 fills in the gaps with the confession of a refugee after the rebellion was over. Sekido Mokuzaemon claimed not to be a Christian believer, but was prepared to admit that he had been serving on one of the thwarted rescue boats. His account is the sole evidence for the rebels' intentions.

6: White Flags on the Sea

1 The hackberry tree survived until July 1997, when it was cut down by a municipal council concerned over public safety. By that time, it was more than seven metres tall, and leaning precariously out over the river.

2 Okada, *Amakusa Tokisada*, 93–4.

3 Okada, *Amakusa Tokisada*, 71. Tsuruta, *Amakusa Shimabara no Ran*, 297, places the same events on 16 December, at the town of Suji, and notes that although the messengers were from House Hosokawa, their point of origin was Yatsushiro, not Kumamoto as one might otherwise expect.

4 In fact, both of these estimates (the largest difference of all accounts) are from the same source, the *Shimabara Nikki*, which contradicts itself in the space of a page. See Tsuruta, *Amakusa Shimabara no Ran*,

301. Another source listed in Tsuruta, the *Onsho Hosho Utsushi Gonjo Hikae*, reports a second mass sailing on 27 December. It is likely that the fleet made at least two trips across the bay.

5 Paske-Smith, *Japanese Traditions of Christianity*, 72. Paske-Smith offers considerable detail on the battle of Shimago, from an unknown source. Tsuruta's concordance in *Shimabara Amakusa no Ran*, 301–3, is loaded with incidents for 29 December (14th day of the 11th lunar month), and is one of the busiest days in the Rebellion, at least in terms of panicked diary entries from samurai who had only just real-ised the magnitude of the enemy they faced.

6 Paske-Smith, *Japanese Traditions of Christianity*, 73.

7 Letter of Nicholas Couckebacker to Anthony van Diemen, 10 January 1638, quoted in Geerts, 'The Arima Rebellion', 57. 'As yet, only one single boat with two mortally wounded noblemen returned to Hirado on 3 January.' Ishihara Tarozaemon, a local magistrate in Sumoto, wrote a different account in a letter to House Hosokawa dated 4 January 1638. Ishihara claimed that Miyake had fallen in the battle at Shimago, long before the major confrontation of the battle of Hondo. However, Ishihara himself notes that he is working purely on hear-say, as 'the rebels hold the sea and land.' Ishihara and his thirty retainers waited in their stronghold at Sumoto, fully intending to commit seppuku if the rebels approached. However, they were spared, as the rebel advance continued westward towards Tomioka, passing Sumoto by. See Okada, *Amakusa Tokisada*, 102.

8 *Goke Hisho* (*Secret Book of the Great Families*), quoted in Okada, *Amakusa Tokisada*, 101–2.

9 *Shimabara-ki*, quoted in Tsuruta, *Amakusa Shimabara no Ran*, 308, reading 30 December for the 15th day of the 11th lunar month. The eyewitness was one Yoshiuemon, a merchant from Araikiri in Kurume. It seems that Yoshiuemon's brief account is the prime source for almost all descriptions of Jerome in the ensuing centuries.

10 Events of 2 January 1638 (18th of the 11th lunar month) are collated from several contemporary sources in Tsuruta, *Amakusa Shimabara no Ran*, 306–7.

11 Events of 3 January 1638 (19th of the 11th lunar month) collated from testimonials by the defenders themselves in Tsuruta, *Amakusa Shimabara no Ran*, 307–8.

12 Tsuruta, *Amakusa Shimabara no Ran*, 308. There are no entries recorded in Tsuruta for 5 January 1638 (21st of the 11th lunar month).

Paske-Smith, *Japanese Traditions of Christianity*, 75, records that the rebels' final assault occurred on the 5th (21st), although he also claims that Miyake Tobee was among the defenders, which would have been difficult when his head was on a spike outside Tomioka prison.

13 Paske-Smith, *Japanese Traditions of Christianity*, 75.

14 There are several facsimiles of the banner dotted around the Nagasaki region, including a massive one at Shimabara Castle. The original is at the Hondo Christian Museum, although it is only shown to the public on special occasions. For most of the time, it rests in a locked cabinet beneath yet another copy. It is widely believed in Japan that Yamada Emonsaku made the banner, although as Okada admits, *Amakusa Tokisada*, 299, there is no actual proof of his involvement, and the evidence is merely circumstantial.

15 Paske-Smith, *Japanese Traditions of Christianity*, 77.

16 Okada, *Amakusa Tokisada*, 97.

17 Tsuruta, *Shimabara Amakusa no Ran*, 311.

7: The Speed of Thunder

1 There is an Asian tradition of leaving offerings for the departed. On the day that I visited Jerome's grave, someone had left him some modern-day entertainments. It would appear that, in the afterlife, Jerome Amakusa drinks Gekkeikan sake and smokes Kent Ultras.

2 Kanda, *Shimabara no Ran*, 30–1, with the date '17th of the 11th [lunar] month'. See also Okada, *Amakusa Tokisada*, 21.

3 Correa, quoted in Okada, *Amakusa Tokisada*, 19.

4 Okada, *Amakusa Tokisada*, 49.

5 Letter of Watanabe Kozaemon to the headman of Tobase village, dated 29 December 1637, quoted in Okada, *Amakusa Tokisada*, 95. I have altered Kozaemon's *Jinbei* and *Shirō* to *Peter* and *Jerome* throughout. The Jibee referred to in the letter is Peter's landlord and immediate superior, who was executed after the fall of Hara for his presumed involvement in the rebel plot. The reference to Kozaemon's 'parents and children' tells us that his father Sancho Watanabe was at Hara with Jerome. Or does it? We know that Kozaemon had at least two children, but one of them, Paulo, was demonstrably already in custody. Possibly, Kozaemon had not been informed at this time that some members of his family were already captured.

6 Okada, *Amakusa Tokisada*, 96. Once again, I have altered *Jinbei* and *Shirō* to *Peter* and *Jerome*.

7 Tsuruta, *Amakusa Shimabara no Ran*, 321.

8 See Keith, 'The Logistics of Power', 103, for a breakdown of precisely who arrived when.

9 Stout, 'Inscriptions in Shimabara and Amakusa', 186, reports the bunker as the finding of a nineteenth-century archaeological dig.

10 *Kirishitan Monogatari*, quoted in Elison, *Deus Destroyed*, 364. Miyazaki, *The Story of Building the Shimabara Castle*, 26, notes Hara's earlier nickname of *Hama no Shiro* – literally 'The Beach Castle.' A century before that, in 1496, the site was called 'Hara Island'; see Nagasaki-ken Kōtōgakkō Ikukenkyū Kai, *Nagasaki-ken no Rekishi Sanpō*, 130.

11 See, for example, the illustration on the cover of Tsuruta, *Mizuno-ke Shimabara-ki*, which gives an exacting contemporary rendition of the site. Notably, the 'beach' extends right the way from the north side of the castle to the south, as opposed to later accounts that often substitute eighteenth-century rice paddies for the site of the seventeenth-century marsh. Also, the 'palisades' on the north side extend all the way out to the Dutch ships (*sic*) at anchor. Were they simple fences, or did the workmen build jetties out to the *Rijp*? This illustration is also my source for the locations of the two gun emplacements, which are not specified in any other document I have seen.

12 Testimony of Shikata Hanbee, quoted in Kanda, *Shimabara no Ran*, 35.

13 Paske-Smith, *Japanese Traditions of Christianity*, 79. 'The conduct of Itakura [Shigemasa], throughout the whole campaign,' notes Steichen in *Les Daimyô Chrétiens*, 408, 'remains inexplicable: either he had an extraordinary incompetence as a general, or, which is also possible, he was disgusted at marching against insurgent peasants, of which he knew the greater part were Christian.'

14 *Gokechu Buntsu no Naibatsusho* for 20th day of the 12th lunar month (3 February), quoted in Tsuruta, *Amakusa Shimabara no Ran*, 317.

15 *Kirishitan Monogatari*, quoted in Elison, *Deus Destroyed*, 364.

16 Paske-Smith, *Japanese Traditions of Christianity*, 80.

17 *Kirishitan Monogatari*, quoted in Elison, *Deus Destroyed*, 365. The samurai were not, however, entirely idle during the period. On 4 February, Shigemasa ordered Matsukura and Terazawa, the lords of Shimabara and Amakusa respectively, to send inquisitors into any village that remained inhabited. Any family without a cooking pot was to be suspected of having lent theirs to the rebels, and interrogated about their alleged Christian sympathies.

18 Arrow-letter of 6 February 1638 (23rd day of the 12th lunar month, Year of the Ox), quoted in Paske-Smith, *Japanese Traditions of*

Christianity, 81. I have changed Paske-Smith's 'borne to enjoy the highest rank' to its Christian analogue 'raised up on high', which is surely what the rebels meant. Strangely, this arrow letter is not repeated in Tsuruta's concordance, although Morris, *The Nobility of Failure*, 162, alludes to both its existence, and the existence of many like it.

19 Kanda, *Shimabara no Ran*, 36.
20 Okada, *Amakusa Tokisada*, 79.
21 Letter of Toda Ujikane to Itakura Shigemasa, 12 February 1638, quoted in Tsuruta, *Amakusa Shimabara no Ran*, 317.
22 Paske-Smith, *Japanese Traditions of Christianity*, 84. For the original Japanese, and questions over its authenticity, see Okada, *Amakusa Tokisada*, 161, but note that Okada's version (and its translation in Morris, *The Nobility of Failure*, 165) lacks the first three lines.
23 Gravestone of Itakura Shigemasa at Hara Castle, quoted in Stout, 'Inscriptions in Shimabara and Amakusa', 187–8. Note that his age is given as fifty-one, but that it would be fifty under Western reckoning. The memorial, which goes into exhaustive detail about Shigemasa's alleged deeds, and the achievements of his descendants, was completed in 1681, but not actually raised at Hara until 1791. Miyazaki, *The Story of Building the Shimabara Castle*, 193, identifies Itakura's killer as the rebel Harishita Kinsaku.

8: The Waiting Game

1 Barnes, *Naval Surgeon: Revolt in Japan*, 183, recounts a nineteenth-century folktale that Dejima gained its odd shape when the Shogun was asked for his opinion on what it should be. Instead of answering, he flung out his fan contemptuously, and his servants obliged with what they assumed was his suggested shape.
2 *Hosokawa-ke Ki*, quoted in Okada, *Amakusa Tokisada*, 252–3. The original text is corrupt, and even Okada is unsure as to its relevance, although it was an incident often discussed over the campfires in weeks to come. The meaning of *nikesa* is unclear – my interpretation assumes that Toda's pun was on the word *nigesa* – literally 'a readiness to run.'
3 Paske-Smith, *Japanese Traditions of Christianity*, 91. The passage in Paske-Smith is far out of chronological order, but assuming Matsudaira's speech was delivered on his arrival in the third week of February, his predictions were spot on. Starvation would bring the castle down within six weeks.

4 *Kirishitan Monogatari*, quoted in Elison, *Deus Destroyed*, 365. The Shōgun's comment evokes that of Sun Tzu's in *The Art of War*: 'Where terrain is surrounded, make plans' [i.e. wait]. See Clements, *The Art of War: A New Translation*, 88.

5 Ibid.

6 Arrow-letter bearing the date 'The New Year' (i.e. around 14 February 1638), quoted in Tsuruta, *Amakusa Shimabara no Ran*, 193. Rose of Sharon is the literal translation of Jerome's term *mukuge* – there is no direct Biblical allusion in the original Japanese, although it may well have had the same implications for him. The reference to 'flowering fortune', *eiga*, may have been an allusion to the *Eiga Monogatari*, a cycle of stories from the eleventh century. My 'soon payable in kind' fills a lacuna in the original that Tsuruta leaves blank – the original is indistinct in places, and parts are as much Tsuruta's guesswork as mine. Keith, 'The Logistics of Power', 187, repeats an alternate view on what appears to be the same approach, or at least a very similar one. According to the 1680 French chronicler Tavernier, a letter was sent to Matsudaira suggesting that the rebels were ready to lay down their arms, 'but the Messenger that carry'd it was nail'd to a Cross in sight of the whole Army of the Christians.'

7 Letter of Nicholas Couckebacker to Anthony van Diemen, 24 January 1638, quoted in Geerts, 'The Arima Rebellion', 67.

8 Dougill, *In Search of Japan's Hidden Christians*, 123, asserts that the Dutch invented this distinction themselves, and credits the revelation to a maritime museum in Kuchinotsu. The term *komō* seems to be a direct calque of the term *hong-mao*, Red Hair, already in use in Chinese. The term survives today in Singapore, where Europeans are still disparaged as *ang-mo*, which seems to derive from the Hokkien pronunciation of the same term.

9 Letter of Nicholas Couckebacker to Itakura Shigemasa, c/o Murasame Saburō, 17 January 1638, quoted in Geerts, 'The Arima Rebellion', 63. Mulder, *Hollanders in Hirado*, 191, sees things differently, and is prepared to believe that the gifts were sent in thanks for a Japanese decision *not* to use Dutch services, which was later overturned. But Mulder's own evidence does not appear to support this claim.

10 Letter of Nicholas Couckebacker to Anthony van Diemen, 27 January 1638, quoted in Geerts, 'The Arima Rebellion', 71–2.

11 Nicholas Couckebacker, letter to Anthony van Diemen, 17 February 1638, quoted in Geerts, 'The Arima Rebellion', 81. See also, Mulder, *Hollanders in Hirado*, 192.

12 Nicholas Couckebacker, letter to Johan van der Burch, 17 February 1638, quoted in Geerts, 'The Arima Rebellion', 85.

13 *Petten* left port on 19 February 1638, reaching Fort Zeelandia on Taiwan on 3 March, staying there for a week before leaving for Batavia, which it reached on 14 April. In doing so, it overtook the *Otter*, which Couckebacker had sent running from Hirado a week earlier – we may presume that the *Petten* was in more of a hurry because Francois Caron was onboard and under orders to report the events in Japan directly to Couckebacker's masters in Batavia. Couckebacker hoped that the trouble in Shimabara would blow over by the time his letters reached Batavia, which turned out to be true – Hara Castle fell two days before the *Petten* reached its destination. The next Dutch vessel to reach Batavia from Japan was the *Rijp* itself, which sailed south soon after bombarding Hara, with only a brief stop outside Hirado to scrape off barnacles. The ship went on a grand tour of Dutch bases in the area, the Pescadores, Taiwan and finally Batavia itself, presumably to ensure that everyone had their story straight. The actual news of the fall of Hara may not have arrived until early the following year, as the next vessel to make the trip from Japan to Batavia, the *Nieuw Zeelandia*, did not reach its destination until January 1639. See Mulder, *Hollanders in Hirado*, 294–5.

14 Nicholas Couckebacker, letter to Johan van der Burch, 25 March 1638, quoted in Geerts, 'The Arima Rebellion', 97–8. If Couckebacker really intended to say 'red crosses', then he presumably saw the *fleur-de-lys* design of the Cross of Saint James, copied from the Spanish and Portuguese. However, although Dr Geerts's Dutch is sure to be infinitely better than mine, I suspect that the *roode cruyssen* of Couckebacker's original text refers to 'rude crosses'– a reference to the rough manner of their execution, rather than their colour. Certainly, I have never seen specifically red crosses on flags in any Japanese illustrations of the siege.

15 Mulder, *Hollanders in Hirado*, 193.

16 *Shimabara Amakusa Nikki*, quoted in Okada, *Amakusa Tokisada*, 253. The song was first heard the day before Couckebacker's arrival, on 23 February. A similar song is repeated in Perrin, *Giving Up the Gun*, 65–6, quoting the 1909 Cary *History of Japan*:

> While powder and shot remain,
> Continue to chase the besieging army,
> That is blown away before us like the drifting sand.
> Hear the dull thud of the enemy's guns: Don! Don!

> *Our arms give back the reply:*
> *'By the blessing of God the father,*
> *I will cut off your heads!'*

17 Nicholas Couckebacker, letter to Jan van Elserack, 1 March 1638, in
Geerts, 'The Arima Rebellion', 89. As noted in the main text, I suspect
this is an unfortunate transcription error for the common Japanese
name Iemon, and I have altered it to Iemon in all subsequent appearances in this book.

18 Nicholas Couckebacker, letter to Johan van der Burch, 25 March
1638, quoted in Geerts, 'The Arima Rebellion', 93.

19 *Shinsen Gokefu* and *Shimabara-ki* for 25–26 February 1638 (12–13th
days of the 1st lunar month, Year of the Tiger) quoted in Tsuruta,
Amakusa Shimabara no Ran, 319–20.

20 Nicholas Couckebacker, letter to Johan van der Burch, 25 March
1638, quoted in Geerts, 'The Arima Rebellion', 97. Léon Pagés, the
French writer who compared Couckebacker to Pilate, is quoted in
Morris, *The Nobility of Failure*, 399.

21 Nicholas Couckebacker, letter to Jan van Elserack, 1 March 1638,
quoted in Geerts, 'The Arima Rebellion', 89.

22 Nakagawa family manuscript, quoted in Tsuruta, *Amakusa Shimabara
no Ran*, 320.

23 Nicholas Couckebacker, letter to Anthony van Diemen, 9 November
1638, quoted in Geerts, 'The Arima Rebellion', 105. There is an obvious contradiction between Couckebacker's complaints on the day to
his colleagues that his time was being wasted, and his boasts to his
boss several months later that Dutch artillery had contributed significantly to the destruction of Hara Castle. Notably, he praises the
'mortars', i.e. those guns that could fire up at a high angle, and not
the cannons that he had earlier pronounced useless. I have substituted 'grenade' for Geerts' nineteenth-century translation of the
Dutch *granaten*, which he renders as 'garnets'.

24 Nicholas Couckebacker, letter to Jan van der Burch, 25 March 1638,
quoted in Geerts, 'The Arima Rebellion', 95.

25 *Shinsen Gokefu* for 4 March 1638 (19th day of 1st lunar month),
quoted in Tsuruta, *Amakusa Shimabara no Ran*, 321.

26 Mulder, *Hollanders in Hirado*, 195.

27 *Ikeda-ke Shimabara Jin Oboegaki*, quoted in Tsuruta, *Amakusa
Shimabara no Ran*, 321.

28 Nicholas Couckebacker, letter to Johan van der Burch, 25 March
1638, quoted in Geerts, 'The Arima Rebellion', 95. Notably,

Couckebacker tells his friend in Taiwan about the death of Gillis, but he does not mention it in his official report to Batavia in November. Boxer, *Jan Compagnie in Japan*, 28, is my source for Gillis being blown over the fence, although he gives the unfortunate man's name as Gylak. Morris, *The Nobility of Failure*, 167, recounts another incident, in which 'two Dutch sailors lost their lives, one having been shot down from the topmast onto the deck . . . where he crushed a shipmate to death.' However, this is not mentioned in Couckebacker's letters, nor in any Japanese sources that I have seen.

29 Mulder, *Hollanders in Hirado*, 196.

9: The Traitor's Arrow

1 Nicholas Couckebacker, letter to Johan van der Burch, 25 March 1638, quoted in Geerts, 'The Arima Rebellion', 95–6. When the campaign was over, Gillis was posthumously awarded 100 *taels* of silver as part of the spoils; Mulder, *Hollanders in Hirado*, 196.

2 Yamada Emonsaku (attrib.), letter to 'the commanders of the Imperial Army', 4 March 1638 (20th day of 1st lunar month, Year of the Tiger), quoted in Paske-Smith, *Japanese Traditions of Christianity*, 88–9, and, in a slightly different translation, in Morris, *The Nobility of Failure*, 174–5. I have substituted *Jerome* for *Shirō* throughout. The date given in Paske-Smith (and a day later in Morris) is doubtful – it is more probable that Yamada would have written his epistle in *response* to the overtures from Lord Arima a week later, but not impossible that it was Yamada, not Arima, who initiated secret negotiations. A passage in Kanda, *Shimabara no Ran*, 189, reports a moment in which Matsudaira tells Arima, *before* Arima's meeting with Yamada, that Yamada's loyalties lay with the besiegers and not the besieged. For Matsudaira to know this, he would have had to be in communication with Yamada before Arima's arrival.

3 *Arima Gorozaemon Hikki*, quoted in Kanda, *Shimabara no Ran*, 188. The order of events in Gorozaemon's own account differs slightly from those written by others, although it is impossible to determine whether this is because he had privileged information through his central role in the deceptions, or if he was simply building up his own role.

4 *Shirō Hattogaki* of 15 March 1638, quoted in Tsuruta, *Amakusa Shimabara no Ran*, 206–7, and Ōhashi, *Kenshō Shimabara Amakusa Ikki*, 96–105. Both books include photographs of the original document. For Tsuruta, the presence of the name Francisco is a chance to

suggest that it would be more appropriate if Jerome were referred to as Francisco by historians. Nor is the *Shirō Hattogaki* the only place in the surviving documentation where Jerome is called Francisco – the best of several unlikely explanations is Tsuruta's, that Jerome changed his name during the siege. My rendering of *Quaresma* is Portuguese, as the katakana used, *Kuwarezuma*, seems marginally closer here to Portuguese than to the Latin equivalent, *Cuaresmae*. For the history of the document itself, see Kanda, *Shimabara no Ran*, 195. Dougill, *In Search of Japan's Hidden Christians*, 51, observes that the term *tengu*, or crow-demon, had been adopted by the early Jesuit missionaries in Japan as a term for Satan.

5 Letter from Martha and Regina Masuda to Peter Masuda and Jerome Amakusa, 15 March 1638, quoted in Tsuruta, *Amakusa Shimabara no Ran*, 202–3.

6 *Arima Gorozaemon Hikki*, quoted in Tsuruta, *Amakusa Shimabara no Ran*, 322.

7 Kanda, *Shimabara no Ran*, 189.

8 *Amakusa Shimabara Kirishitan Ikki Hatsu no Koto*, quoted in Okada, *Amakusa Tokisada*, 258. Yamada Emonsaku was present at the time, and appears to have been the source of the detailed description of the damage, and, of course, chief among those who began to doubt their leader's divine power.

9 Okada, *Amakusa Tokisada*, 254. Okada is eager to read *shinobi mono* (men of stealth, spies, sappers) as *ninja*, even though the latter term is largely a creation of twentieth- century novels and movies. Both terms, however, are written with the same characters, a fudge that has allowed some apologists to claim an entirely undeserved provenance. Dubious claims about ninja at Hara Castle chiefly originate in the 1965 *Ninja no Seikatsu* (*Life of the Ninja*) by Yamaguchi Masayuki. Loaded with credulous re-readings of historical events, Yamaguchi's book shoehorns ninja into almost every battle he can think of, and seems to be the point of origin, sometimes at one and two iterations removed, for most other subsequent references to ninja at Hara Castle. Yamaguchi, for example, forms the major part of the evidence cited in Turnbull's *Ninja*, 85–88. Turnbull cites Morris's *The Nobility of Failure* to back him up, but the passage in Morris cites Okada's *Amakusa Tokisada*. The trail then goes cold again, since Okada, usually a stickler for references, cites no source of his own. It would seem that most stories about ninja literally sprang out of thin air in the 1960s, in the midst of a movie and

manga fad for tales of black-clad assassins. Notably, the day-by-day concordance of primary sources found in Tsuruta, *Amakusa Shimabara no Ran*, 291–326, makes only a single reference to *shinobi*, and even then it is merely to scouts from Satsuma arriving on Lion Island. See also Clements, *A Brief History of the Samurai*, 348. Remarkably and nobly, Turnbull has since recanted some of his conclusions, although this newly critical approach to his own materials has yet to filter through to many who have relied upon his earlier work; see Turnbull, 'The Ninja: An Invented Tradition?', 11.

10 Okada, *Amakusa Tokisada*, 206.

11 *Ikki Kojō no Kokunichi Nikki*, quoted in Okada, *Amakusa Tokisada*, 206, and Tsuruta, *Amakusa Shimabara no Ran*, 324, reading 25 March 1638 in both cases for the 11th day of the 2nd lunar month. The story is repeated in Morris, *The Nobility of Failure*, 164, but out of chronological order, before the death of Itakura Shigemasa.

12 Letter of Hosokawa Tadatoshi to Hosokawa Tadaoki, dated 30 March 1638 (16th day of the 2nd lunar month), quoted in Okada, *Amakusa Tokisada*, 255–6. Kuroda samurai collecting firewood on 13 March had indeed stumbled across two men praying to a crucifix in the hills, so Hosokawa may have been right to assume that the rebels had allies in the hinterland. However, they did not show themselves, and do not appear to have been much help to the Christians besieged in the castle. The claim that Matsudaira had actively employed ninja (*shinobi no mono*) was supposedly made in the *Shimabara Amakusa Nikki* (ibid.), but I simply do not believe Okada on this occasion.

13 Letter of Hosokawa Tadatoshi to Hosokawa Tadaoki, dated 30 March 1637, quoted in Okada, *Amakusa Tokisada*, 255.

14 *Ikki Kojō no Kokunichi Nikki*, quoted in Okada, *Amakusa Tokisada*, 195, reading 2 April 1638 (Good Friday) for the original's 19th day of the 2nd lunar month, Year of the Tiger. This is also presented out of order in Morris (see note above).

15 Paske-Smith, *Japanese Traditions of Christianity*, 92–3. Paske-Smith places the speech halfway through the 2nd (lunar) month, in late March or early April 1638. The conspirators decide to attack on the 21st day of the 2nd lunar month (i.e. 4 April, Easter Sunday). Notably, in the detailed account of the planning, Yamada's name is not mentioned even though the entire story probably comes from his debriefing, so he was presumably already imprisoned, or was part of the planning but subsequently incarcerated.

16 Paske-Smith, *Japanese Traditions of Christianity*, 89–90.

17 Paske-Smith, *Japanese Traditions of Christianity*, 89–90. It should be noted that, with the exception of unreliable hearsay and occasional observations from a distance like those of Couckebacker and Matsudaira, Yamada's debriefing testimony is the sole source for what was said and done within the castle during the siege. Hence Jerome's strange use here of the term 'conspirators' (I have replaced it with 'rebels') to describe his fellow Christians – the words are taken from a report assembled by the winning side, and are unlikely to be the ones that he actually used.

18 Paske-Smith, *Japanese Traditions of Christianity*, 93–5. Paske-Smith's sources give casualty figures on a camp-by-camp basis. It is easy to glance at his text and assume that there are only a handful of deaths, but his cumulative total of Shōgunate deaths during the one raid is easily over 300. Terazawa Watataka was the son of Terazawa Hirotaka, who had ridden into battle at Sekigahara on the heels of the Red Devils.

19 *Kirishitan Monogatari*, quoted in Elison, *Deus Destroyed*, 366. See also, Tsuruta, *Amakusa Shimabara no Ran*, 325, which puts the attack at the 21st day of the 2nd lunar month.

20 *Shimabara Amakusa Nikki*, quoted in Tsuruta, *Amakusa Shimabara no Ran*, 325.

10: The End of the World

1 *Hosokawa-ke Ki*, quoted in Okada, *Amakusa Tokisada*, 196.

2 Paske-Smith, *Japanese Traditions of Christianity*, 93. The *Kirishitan Monogatari* has a different spin on events, and notes that the night attack was made on 'scouts sent out by Nabeshima' – Elison, *Deus Destroyed*, 366. Perhaps Nabeshima was already trying his luck at provoking an opportunity to make a 'counter-assault', as he would later do on 10 April?

3 Nicholas Couckebacker, letter to Anthony van Diemen, 9 November 1638, quoted in Geerts, 107.

4 Paske-Smith, *Japanese Traditions of Christianity*, 97.

5 Paske-Smith, *Japanese Traditions of Christianity*, 98, calls the youth Mondo and faithfully translates his age as twenty-two, which is what Japanese sources would have claimed – in English terms, he was twenty-one.

6 Hosokawa Tadatoshi, letter to Hosokawa Tadaoki, c.13 April 1638, quoted in Okada, *Amakusa Tokisada*, 281–2. Hosokawa began the assault on the far side of the castle, through the third keep, but his

letter specifically describes the self-immolation of rebel families in the main keep (*honmaru*). Reading between the lines, Hosokawa was interested in the manner of death of *honmaru* residents because some soldiers were making bogus claims for bounties on badly burned heads.

7 Paske-Smith, *Japanese Traditions of Christianity*, 98. Predictably, there are many differing accounts of who was where, and when, during the last day of the attack, and I have only repeated two of them. Veterans of the Nabeshima division made the unlikely claim that one of their own had somehow 'seized Jerome's banner' (implying entry to the main keep) before dawn. Similarly, Hosokawa veterans bragged that it was one of their own who had shot the fire arrow that burned down Jerome's inner sanctum, which was as far from the Hosokawa clan's point of entry as it was possible to be without leaving the castle. See Tsuruta, *Amakusa Shimabara no Ran*, 326.

8 Paske-Smith, *Japanese Traditions of Christianity*, 99.

9 Keith, 'The Logistics of Power', 164. There are many conflicting figures over the casualties. I choose Keith's not only because he reflects the most modern availability of sources and their computerised tabulation, but also because his dissertation is concerned with battlefield accountancy, and hence liable to weigh the sources appropriately.

10 Keith, 'The Logistics of Power,' 164.

11 Morris, *The Nobility of Failure*, 400. In this version, the killer of Jerome was recorded as one Nagaoka Tatewaki.

12 Letter from Hosokawa Tadatoshi to the Rusui Karō, dated 6 May 1638 (23rd day of the 3rd lunar month), quoted in Okada, *Amakusa Tokisada*, 280–1.

13 Okada, *Amakusa Tokisada*, 292. The offending samurai's name was Kamegawa Katsuemon. His crime was logged by Nabeshima Katsushige, although one is tempted to speculate – how many other false claims went unreported? Each false rebel 'death' might suggest another rebel who may have got away.

14 Morris, *The Nobility of Failure*, 172. But even here there is disagreement: Tsuruta, *Amakusa Shimabara no Ran*, 326, states that the credit for spotting Jerome's head belonged not to Lord Hosokawa, but to Nishimura Gohei, a samurai from Hirado. Local legend in Hondo claims that Jerome was wounded in the ruins while coming to the aid of a young girl, possibly his lover, who was cut down along with him. An inscription in an obscure corner of Junkyō Park, in the grounds of

what was once Hondo Castle, even gives the girl's name, Machika, although it offers no explanation how this knowledge might have escaped every other chronicler of the rebellion.

15 Morris, *The Nobility of Failure*, 173.

11: The Secret Places of the Heart

1 For the text of Itakura's tombstone, see Stout, 'Inscriptions in Shimabara and Amakusa', 187–8. Stout's work also appears to have been lifted wholesale to form one of the documents compiled in Paske-Smith. The *joro* spiders are *Nephila clavata*. As an aside, someone had also left a bizarre offering at this grave. It would appear that, in the afterlife, Itakura Shigemasa likes to watch a Hitachi remote-controlled television.

2 Okada, *Amakusa Tokisada*, 302. Stranger things have happened in the Shimabara Rebellion, but even so, the idea that Yamada Emonsaku might have been appointed by Jerome to be a designated Judas seems overwrought and romanticised. Possibly Okada, who made the suggestion in 1960, might have been inspired less by historical evidence than by the publication of *The Last Temptation of Christ*, by Nikos Kazantzakis, in English that same year (it was not translated into Japanese until 1982). For the fate of Yamada post-Shimabara, see Morris, *The Nobility of Failure*, 175.

3 *Kirishitan Monogatari*, quoted in Elison, *Deus Destroyed*, 367.

4 Hirado journal, quoted in Geerts, 'The Arima Rebellion', 116.

5 Miyazaki, *The Story of the Building of Shimabara Castle*, 196.

6 Hondo Shiritsu Amakusa Kirishitan-kan, *Amakusa Kirishitan-kan Shiryō Mokuroku*, 10.

7 Tamamuro, 'Local Society and the Temple-Parishioner Relationship within the Bakufu's Governance Structure', 266–8. Tamamuro's account is a shocking litany of abuses and bureaucratic corruption, which makes a mockery of genuine Buddhist belief. After reading it, one will never look at a Japanese religious festival in quite the same way again.

8 Boxer, *The Christian Century in Japan*, 441.

9 Boxer, *The Christian Century in Japan*, 441.

10 Crasset, *The History of the Church of Japan*, 540.

11 Crasset, *The History of the Church of Japan*, 541.

12 Leiter, *New Kabuki Encyclopedia*, 330. There was another play about the uprising, *Keisei Shimabara Kairo Gassen* (1719), but already the Christian elements were being stripped away in favour of a

straightforward dialectic of rebels versus samurai. Plays about the uprising did not flourish again until after the withdrawal of the prohibitions in 1873. Leiter's list of early twentieth-century plays from this Kirishitan renaissance includes pieces on Jerome, the voyager Hasekura Tsunenaga, and 'Sonin' – presumably a typographical error for Sōrin (Francisco Ōtomo Sōrin).

13 Whelan, *The Beginning of Heaven and Earth*, 11.

14 Crasset, *The History of the Church in Japan*, 529.

15 Hoffman, 'Japan's "Hidden Christians"'; also Harrington, *Japan's Hidden Christians*, 103. The same story, told in Petitjean's own words, can be found in Paske-Smith, *Japanese Traditions of Christianity*, 102. In an unfortunate coda, Petitjean encouraged the Hidden Christians to proclaim their beliefs openly, which led to several of them being executed, and many of the others banished. It was still several decades before Christianity would be permitted openly in Japan.

16 Harrington, *Japan's Hidden Christians*, 49.

17 Harrington, *Japan's Hidden Christians*, 69. I have deliberately used Kunrei romanisation here instead of Hepburn. Japanese phonetics usually deform a 'tu' to a 'tsu', and a 'ti' to a 'chi', which would make the similarities less obvious in Hepburn romanisation.

18 Turnbull, *Kakure Kirishitan of Japan*, 145; Hoffman, 'Japan's "Hidden Christians".'

19 Turnbull, 'Acculturation Among the Kakure Kirishitan,' 69, notes that the story can be found in two apocryphal works, the *Gospel of Nicodemus* and the *Arabic Infancy Gospel*, which appear to have gained a higher canonical value in Japan, where bathing was the centre of communal culture. We might also note the presence of warm, healing waters and a skin disease – possibly inadvertently associated with half-remembered tales of Unzen and Jerome's own supposed affliction?

20 Whelan, *The Beginning of Heaven and Earth*, 53 and 96. The farmers tell the pursuing authorities, truthfully, that Jesus and Mary passed by when they were sowing their crops, i.e. a few minutes earlier. But since the crops have already grown and ripened, the pursuers assume that the trail is several months old, and give up the chase. A similar story was told in Europe during the Middle Ages, but is not part of the Bible proper.

21 Turnbull, 'Acculturation Among the Kakure Kirishitan', 65–6.

22 Whelan, *The Beginning of Heaven and Earth*, 64. In the Hidden Christian version, the seven years of bumper crops come *after* the

seven lean years. Note that although commonly referred to as the 'Bible' of the Hidden Christians, *The Beginning of Heaven and Earth* is actually only a text used by a small group of them. One of Turnbull's late twentieth-century Hidden Christian interview subjects, a man in his nineties, noted that he had never actually heard of the book until Turnbull came to talk to him about it, at which point he had obtained a copy and read it.

23 *Compte Rendu des Travaux de la Société des Missions-Etrangères*, quoted in Harrington, *Japan's Hidden Christians*, 120.

24 The Nagasaki atom bomb also obliterated Urakami cathedral, and killed three quarters of the 12,000 Christians in the city. Dougill, *In Search of Japan's Hidden Christians*, 193 makes the wry but mathematically incorrect assertion that 'In a single flash, the Truman administration had killed more Christians than in the whole history of Japanese persecution.'

25 Sister Mary Bernard, *Japan's Martyr Church*, 88.

26 Letter of Michael Cooper, SJ, to Ivan Morris, 7 May 1974, quoted in Morris, *The Nobility of Failure*, 402.

27 Hoffman, 'Japan's "Hidden Christians"'.

28 Kitahara Hakushu, 'Songs of Amakusa', quoted in Hondo Shiritsu Amakusa Kirishitan-kan, *Amakusa Kirishitan-kan Shiryō Mokuroku*, 36.

29 For these most recent examples and many more, see Rebecca Suter's *Holy Ghosts: The Christian Century in Modern Japanese Fiction*.

Sources and Further Reading

················

In the late nineteenth century, as missionaries became excited about the discovery of the Hidden Christians, there was an immense outpouring of work about the history of Christianity in Japan, with the Shimabara Rebellion usually featuring as its tragic centrepiece. Most notable are Geerts' translations of the Dutch records of the siege, a major source for my eighth chapter, and Paske-Smith's handy collation of several documents circulated in the Yokohama and Nagasaki expat communities, as reported in his *Japanese Traditions of Christianity*.

With what seems to have been a deep sense of disappointment, the river of material ran dry in the early twentieth century as many of the Hidden Christians refused to play along, or were simply subsumed within the newly arrived denominations from the West. Despite the immense amount of material still to be examined, there was also a sense in the academic community that the Shimabara Rebellion was done and dusted – later generations have shunned it as a worthy topic. It also seems unpopular with the two main interest groups that might be expected to study it – many Christians are put off by the ever-present doubts over the rebels' motivation, and military historians are similarly disheartened by the ignominious, one-sided, bloody conclusion.

There was a flowering of interest in the 1960s, in the wake of a series of fictional accounts, but these often served to muddy the waters – many dubious 'facts' about the Rebellion appear to have come into being at this time, as the popular imagination favoured more photogenic or easily digestible accounts of complex events. Jerome was the hero of Ōshima Nagisa's feature film *The Rebel* (1962, *Amakusa Shirō Tokisada*), but a generation later was reframed as the demonic necromancer of Fukasaku Kinji's *Samurai Reincarnation* (1981, *Makai Tenshō*, based on the book of the same name by Yamada Futarō), in which he turns from God, rises from the dead, and leads a zombie army. The generation in between saw a flurry of works about Japan's 'Christian century', most notably Endō Shūsaku's play *The Golden Country* (1966, *Ogon no Kuni*) and his novel *Silence* (1966, *Chinmoku*), both dealing not with Shimabara itself, but with the long, grim aftermath of Christian persecutions and purges. *Silence* was itself made into a feature film by Shinoda Masahiro in 1971.

Amid such interest, two important Japanese non-fiction books were published. Ebisawa and Okada have become the main sources for most later works, including the chapter in Morris's landmark *The Nobility of Failure* – for most Western readers, this latter has been the most accessible source available. For more specialised readers, the best accounts are in Elison's *Deus Destroyed* (for the religious historian) and Keith's 'The Logistics of Power' (for the military historian).

In more recent times, Jerome has remained a figure of elaborate speculation. He became one of the major antagonists in the video game series *Samurai Spirits* (1993 onwards), periodically proclaiming his hatred for the Tokugawa. After a Japanese production of *Jesus Christ Superstar* lifted elements and designs more redolent of Shimabara than Jerusalem it was only a matter of time before Jerome became the hero of his own rock musical, *Shiroh* (2004). In the manga field, the most enduring series has been Akaishi Michiyo's *Amakusa 1637* (2001–2006), in which a time-travelling schoolgirl from our present is mistaken for Jerome and inadvertently swept up in the events of his revolt. The story ends with a return to a radically different present, altered by a scenario in which the Shimabara Rebellion achieved a substantially different outcome, and transformed Japan ever after.

The last and perhaps the most important strain of material has been that of local historians and archaeologists in Japan. Archaeological excavations persist at Hara Castle, and continue to uncover chilling untold tales of the rebels, such as the discovery of numerous skulls with crosses or Christian medallions in their mouths – where a samurai looter might not think of looking. Recent archaeological finds are summarised in Ōhashi, *Kenshō Shimabara Amakusa Ikki*, pp.76–88.

The name Tsuruta is particularly prominent in the region's local historiography, particularly that of the pseudonymous Tsuruta Bunji, who has published a multi-volume history of popular movements in the Amakusa region, including useful tables of people, places and artefacts that played a role in the uprising. Tsuruta Kurazō's massive, multi-part 2005 history of Upper Amakusa includes in its third volume a day-by-day concordance of all known Japanese accounts of the Shimabara Rebellion, allowing the modern historian to triangulate various contending sources with previously impossible accuracy.

Alden, D. et al., *Charles R. Boxer: An Uncommon Life* (Lisbon: Fundação Oriente, 2001).

Barnes, E. and Barnes, James (eds), *Naval Surgeon: Revolt in Japan 1868–1869, The Diary of Dr. Samuel Pellman Boyer* (Bloomington: Indiana University Press, 1963).

Boxer, C., *The Christian Century in Japan 1549–1650* (Manchester: Carcanet Press, 1993).

———, *Jan Compagnie in Japan* (The Hague: Martinus Nijhoff, 1936).

Brook, T., *The Troubled Empire: China in the Yuan and Ming Dynasties* (Cambridge, Massachusetts: Harvard/Belknap, 2010).

Bryant, A., *Sekigahara 1600: The final struggle for power* (Botley: Osprey Publishing, 1995).

Caddell, C., *A History of the Missions in Japan and Paraguay* (New York, Sadler and Company, 1866).

Chang, H., et al. (eds), *The English Factory in Taiwan 1670–1685* (Taipei: National Taiwan University, 1995).

Clements, J., *Coxinga and the Fall of the Ming Dynasty* (Stroud: Sutton Publishing, 2005).

———, *A Brief History of the Samurai* (London: Robinson, 2010).

———, *The Art of War: A New Translation* (London: Constable, 2012).

Cobbing, A., *Kyushu: Gateway to Japan – A Concise History* (Folkestone: Global Oriental, 2009).

Cooper, M., *They Came to Japan: An Anthology of European Reports on Japan, 1543–1640* (Ann Arbor: Center for Japanese Studies, University of Michigan, 1995).

———, *The Japanese Mission to Europe, 1582–1590* (Folkestone: Global Oriental, 2005).

Costa, J., 'Tokugawa Ieyasu and the Christian Daimyō during the Crisis of 1600,' in *Bulletin of Portuguese/Japanese Studies*, Volume VII (2003), 45–71.

Crasset, J., *The History of the Church of Japan, written originally in French by Monsieur l'Abbé de T, and now translated into English by N.N.* (London, 1707). All quotations in this book are from Volume II (Books 11–20).

Dougill, J., *In Search of Japan's Hidden Christians: A Story of Suppression, Secrecy and Survival* (Tokyo: Tuttle, 2012).

Ebisawa, A., *Amakusa Shirō* (Tokyo: Jinbutsu Ōraisha, 1967).

Elison, G., *Deus Destroyed: The Image of Christianity in Early Modern Japan* (Cambridge, MA: Harvard University Press, 1991).

Elisonas, J. (George Elison), 'Christianity and the daimyō' in Hall (ed.), *The Cambridge History of Japan, Volume 4, Early Modern Japan* (Cambridge: Cambridge University Press, 1991), 301–72.

Endō, S., *The Golden Country*, translated by Francis Mathy (Tokyo: Tuttle, 1970).

———, *Foreign Studies*, translated by Mark Williams (London: Peter Owen, 1989).

———, 'Unzen' in *Stained Glass Elegies*, translated by Van C. Gessel (New York: New Directions, 1990), 96–107.

———, *Silence*, translated by William Johnston with a foreword by Martin Scorsese (London: Peter Owen, 2007).

Geerts, A., 'The Arima Rebellion and the Conduct of Koeckebacker', in *Transactions of the Asiatic Society of Japan*, Volume XI (1883), 55–116.

Goodman, G., *Japan and the Dutch* (Richmond: Curzon, 2000).

Harrington, A., *Japan's Hidden Christians* (Chicago: Loyola University Press, 1993).

Hawley, S., *The Imjin War: Japan's Sixteenth Century Invasion of Korea and Attempt to Conquer China*, (Seoul/Berkeley: Royal Asiatic Society/ University of California, 2005).

Hoffman, M., 'Japan's "Hidden Christians"', in the *Japan Times*, 23 December 2007.

Hondo Shiritsu Amakusa Kirishitan-kan [Hondo Municipal Amakusa Christian Museum], *Amakusa Kirishitan-kan Shiryō Mokuroku [Catalogue of Data for Amakusa Christian Museum]* (Hondo: Amakusa Kirishitan-kan, 2002).

Hyam, R., *Empire and Sexuality: The British Experience* (Manchester: Manchester University Press, 1992).

Kanda, C., *Shimabara no Ran: Kirishitan Shinkō to Busō Hōki [The Shimabara Rebellion: Christian Belief and Armed Uprising]*, (Tokyo: Chūōkoron Shinsha, 2005).

Kawano, T. (ed.), *Nagasaki* (Tokyo: Japan Tourist Board/Rurubu, 2007).

Keith, M., 'The Logistics of Power: Tokugawa Responses to the Shimabara Rebellion and power projection in 17th-century Japan' (Ph.D. thesis, Ohio State University, 2006).

Kondō, T., 'Shirō no Romance', in *Hara-jō* (handout on Hara Castle) (Hondo: Amakusa Kirishitan-kan, undated).

Kronk, G., *Cometography – A Catalogue of Comets, Volume 1: Ancient–1799* (Cambridge: Cambridge University Press, 1999).

Lago, M., 'Nagasaki Martyrs to Draw Record Crowd,' in *Zenit* magazine, 12 December 2007, http://www.zenit.org/article-21265?l=english

Laures, J., et al., *Laures Rare Book Database* (Tokyo: Sofia University Library, ongoing), http://133.12.23.145:8080/html/index.html

Leiter, S., *New Kabuki Encyclopedia: A Revised Adaptation of Kabuki Jiten* (Westport, CT: Greenwood Press, 1997).

Lin, R., 'Fukien's Private Sea Trade in the 16th and 17th Centuries,' in E.B. Vermeer (ed.), *Development and Decline of Fukien Province in the 17th and 18th Centuries* (Leiden: E.J. Brill, 1990).

[Sister Mary Bernard], *Japan's Martyr Church* (Exeter: Catholic Records Press, undated – c.1926).

Matsuda, K., et al., *Nihon kankei Iezusu-kai genbunsho: Kyoto Gaikokugo Daigaku Fuzoku Toshokan shozo [Jesuit letters from Japan in the XVIth and XVIIth centuries in the Library of the Kyoto University of Foreign Studies]* (Kyoto: Dohosha Shuppan, 1987).

McCullough, H., *Tale of the Heike* (Stanford: Stanford University Press, 1988).

Miyamoto, K., *Vikings of the Far East* (New York: Vantage, 1975).

Miyazaki, S., *The Story of Building the Shimabara Castle*, (Nagasaki: Dejima Bunko, 2003).

Moran, J., *The Japanese and the Jesuits: Alessandro Valignano in sixteenth-century Japan* (London: Routledge, 1993).

Morris, I., *The Nobility of Failure: Tragic Heroes in the History of Japan* (New York: Ballantine, 1975).

Mulder, W., *Hollanders in Hirado 1597–1641* (Haarlem: Fibula, undated).

Nagasaki-ken Kōtōgakkō Ikukenkyū Kai, Chireki Kōmin Bukai Rekishi Bunkakai [Nagasaki Prefectural Society for Educational Research,

Local History Division], *Nagasaki-ken no Rekishi Sanpō [Historical Walks in Nagasaki Prefecture]* (Tokyo: Yamakawa Press, 2005).

Nei, K., *Shugendō to Kirishitan [Sorcery and the Christians]* (Tokyo: Tōkyōto Shuppan, 1988).

Nosco, P., 'Secrecy and the Transmission of Tradition: Issues in the Study of the "Underground" Christians', in *Japanese Journal of Religious Studies*, Volume XX (1993), 3–29.

Ōhashi, Y., *Kenshō Shimabara Amakusa Ikki [Verifying the Shimabara-Amakura Uprising]* (Tokyo: Yoshikawa Hirobumi-kan, 2008).

Oka, M., 'A great merchant in Nagasaki in the 17th century: Suetsugu Heizo II and the system of Respondencia', in *Bulletin of Portuguese/ Japanese Studies*, Volume II (2001), 37–56.

Okada, A., *Amakusa Tokisada* (Tokyo: Yoshikawa Hirobumi-kan, 1960).

Ōyama, K. (ed.), *Meijō o Yuku: Shimabara-jō Hara-jō [Visiting Famous Castles: Shimabara and Hara]*, issue 37, 21 September (Tokyo: Shōgakukan, 2004).

Paske-Smith, M., *Japanese Traditions of Christianity, Being some old translations from the Japanese, with British Consular Reports of the Persecutions of 1868–1872* (Kōbe: J.L. Thompson et al., 1930).

Perrin, N., *Giving Up the Gun: Japan's Reversion to the Sword, 1543–1879* (Boston: David R. Godine, 1979).

Proust, J. and Marianne (eds), *Le Puissant Royaume du Japon: La description de François Caron (1636)* (Paris: Éditions Chandeigne, 2003).

Shiba, R., *Shimabara, Amakusa no Shodō [Wanderings in Shimabara and Amakusa]* (Tokyo: Asahi Bunko, 1987).

Steichen, M., *Les Daimyô Chrétiens: Ou Un Siècle de L'Histoire Religieuse et Politique du Japon, 1549–1650* (Hong Kong: La Société des Missions Étrangères, 1905).

Stout, H., 'Inscriptions in Shimabara and Amakusa', in *Transactions of the Asia Society of Japan*, Volume VII (1879), 185–194.

Suter, R., *Holy Ghosts: The Christian Century in Modern Japanese Fiction.* (Honolulu: University of Hawai'i Press, 2015).

Tamamuro, F., 'Local Society and the Temple-Parishioner Relationship within the Bakufu's Governance Structure', in the *Japanese Journal of Religious Studies*, Volume XXVIII (2001), 262–92.

Tsuruta, B., *Amakusa no Rekishi Monogatari Kyōiku [Educational Stories of Amakusa History]* (Hondo: Amakusa Bunka Shuppansha, 1986).

_____, *Saikai no Ran: Amakusa Minshū Undō Shikenkyū [Turmoil in the*

Western Sea: Historical Research in Popular Movements in Amakusa (Hondo: Amakusa Bunka Shuppansha, 2005).

———, *Saikai no Ran: Amakusa Minshū Undō Shizuroku [Turmoil in the Western Sea: Historical Records of Popular Movements in Amakusa]* (Hondo: Amakusa Bunka Shuppansha, 2006).

Tsuruta, K., *Amakusa Shimabara no Ran to Sono Zengo [Before and After the Rebellion in Shimabara and Amakusa]* (Amakusa: Municipality of Upper Amakusa, 2005).

——— (ed.), *Mizuno-ke Shimabara-ki [House Mizuno Chronicle of Shimabara]* (Ōyano: Yamazaki Shinichi, 1999).

Turnbull, S., *Ninja: The True Story of Japan's Secret Warrior Cult* (Poole: Firebird Books, 1991).

———, 'Acculturation among the *Kakure Kirishitan*: Some Conclusions from the *Tenchi Hajimari no Koto*,' in John Breen and Mark Williams (eds), *Japan and Christianity: Impacts and Responses* (Basingstoke: Palgrave Macmillan, 1996), 63–74.

———, *The Kakure Kirishitan of Japan: A Study of their Development, Beliefs and Rituals to the Present Day* (Richmond: Japan Library, 1998).

——— (ed.), *Japan's Hidden Christians 1549–1999, Volume 1: Open Christianity in Japan 1549–1639* (Richmond: Japan Library, 2000).

——— (ed.), 'The Ninja: An Invented Tradition?' in *Journal of Global Initiatives: Policy, Pedagogy, Perspective*, Volume 9, No.1 (2014), 9–26.

Üçerler, A., 'Alessandro Valignano: man, missionary, and writer,' in *Renaissance Studies* 17 (3) 2003, 337–366.

Uchida, T., *An Epic of Christianity in Shimabara* (Unzen: Unzen Information Bureau, 1928).

Ward, H., *Women Religious Leaders in Japan's Christian Century, 1549–1650* (Farnham: Ashgate, 2009).

Watanabe, T. and Junichi Iwata, *The Love of the Samurai: A Thousand Years of Japanese Homosexuality* (London: Gay Men's Press, 1989).

Whelan, C., 'Written and Unwritten Texts of the *Kakure Kirishitan*,' in John Breen and Mark Williams (eds), *Japan and Christianity: Impacts and Responses* (Basingstoke: Palgrave Macmillan, 1996), 122–37.

———, *The Beginning of Heaven and Earth: The Sacred Book of Japan's Hidden Christians* (Honolulu: University of Hawai'i Press, 1996).

Yamamoto, H., *Edojō no Kyūtei Seiji: Kumamoto-ban Hosokawa Tadaoki Hosokawa Tadatoshi Oyako no Seifuku Shojō [The Imperial Politics of Edo Castle: Military Dispatches of the Heads of House Hosokawa, Hosokawa Tadaoki and His Son Hosokawa Tadatoshi]* (Tokyo: Kodansha, 2004).

Yanagida, K. (ed.), *Shimabara Hantō Mukashibanashi Shū [Legends of the Shimabara Peninsula]* (Tokyo: Sanseidō, 1943).

Yoshimura, T., *Amakusa Shirō no Shōtai: Shimabara no Ran Yominaosu [The Identity of Amakusa Shirō: Rereading the Shimabara Rebellion]* (Tokyo: Yōsensha, 2015).

Yuuki, D., *The Twenty-Six Martyrs of Nagasaki* (Tokyo: Enderle Book Co., 1998).

Index